The Techniques of
Glass Engraving

Jonathan Mattham and Peter Dreiser

B. T. BATSFORD LTD, LONDON

This book is dedicated to Fritz Glössner,
a selfless and devoted teacher

Frontispiece
A traditional wheel engraver using a nineteenth-century
Bohemian brass treadle lathe, about 1900 (*Science Museum,*
London)

First published 1982
© Jonathan Matcham & Peter Dreiser 1982

ISBN 0 7134 2536 9

Filmset by Keyspools Ltd, Golborne, Lancs.
Printed in Great Britain by Butler & Tanner, Frome, Somerset
for the publishers, B. T. Batsford Ltd,
4 Fitzhardinge Street, London W1H 0AH

Contents

FOREWORD

The critic does not necessarily have to be an artist; but it is a useful tool in his critical kit if he is familiar with the materials and implements, and the technical processes, which the artist employs for his effects. This is especially the case where the means of producing an effect involve technical procedures which are not immediately recognizable in the finished product. There is little difficulty in appreciating the means by which a pencil drawing was created, but more in understanding an etching or an aquatint. In some of the mechanical arts the artist's method of producing an effect is often even more inaccessible to the onlooker. Glass decoration by means of engraving is certainly a case in point. Engraving with a diamond may have delusive similarities to techniques of drawing with a pencil or etching with a needle, but its effects are reversed, the line or dot appearing as light on a dark ground. The habit of thinking in reverse, as it were, is reasonably easily achieved, and the analogy of the hardstone- or tungsten-point with the pencil or the needle is reasonably close. When it comes to wheel engraving, however, the means used to produce it tend to be shrouded in obscurity. The uninitiated hardly bother to ask themselves how it is done; the better informed have a rough idea of the principles involved, but usually little real idea of the complexity of the process, or its *finesse*.

On the other side of the coin, the aspiring artist has little to help him. The budding point engraver, it is true, can learn much from the publications of the Guild of Glass Engravers and the encouragement of his many fellow-executants in that field. With the wheel engraver it is otherwise. Wheel engraving has normally been a craft learned by apprenticeship within the glass industry. Outside it, not only are courses and instructors hard to find, but written help is almost non-existent. The only manual is H. Strehblow's *Der Schmuck des Glases* (The Decoration of Glass); that came out as long ago as 1920; and is in many respects outmoded. There is all the more cause to welcome Peter Dreiser's and Jonathan Matcham's book, which sets out in great detail the workshop procedures required for the production of engraved (and etched) glass. Here the insight of the artist is combined with the expertise and experience of a craftsman who is not afraid to reveal to the world all the secrets of his craft. This book must inevitably become a landmark in the technical history of glass decoration.

R. J. Charleston
Formerly Keeper of the
Department of Ceramics & Glass,
Victoria & Albert Museum

ACKNOWLEDGEMENTS

The authors would like to thank the following institutions and individuals for their kind permission to reproduce illustrations: The British Museum, The Victoria and Albert Museum, South Kensington Science Museum, Royal College of Art, Imperial College of Engineering, Steuben Glass, Museum of Decorative Art, Prague, Municipal Museum, The Hague, Rheinbach School of Glass, Mr. George Miller, for the access to H. Strehblow's *Der Schmuck des Glases*; R. Wilkinson & Sons, for permission to photograph glass cutting in action; Clark Eaton (James Clark & Eaton Ltd), for their valuable assistance and for the illustrations of the brilliant glass cutter at work; Messrs G. Merker, for photographs of modern equipment, and Mrs Marigold Hutton, for photographs of work by her late husband John Hutton.

Thanks are likewise due to K. Northwood for permission to reproduce the quotation from his father's book, 'John Northwood' (Pub. Mark and Moody), and to the Lord Chamberlain for permission to illustrate the Royal Coat of Arms. The authors also extend their gratitude to Mr R. J. Charleston for supplying illustrations of early equipment from his archives, and for kindly agreeing to write a foreword to the book; to Dr Dominique Collon (Western Asiatic department, British Museum) for allowing them to handle and examine a selection of Babylonian Seals; to Mr J. Hutton of Berkhamstead, for access to his glass collection; to Alena Adlerova, Museum of Applied Art, Prague; Ivan Kolman (Liberec), Colin King, R. Hugo of Dent Glass, and all who have helped to provide practical information: Martin Hunt (R.C.A.), Brian Gardner, Diana Radford, Jo Birrell and William Randell.

For reasons of space we have been obliged to leave out from a massive overspill of information a great deal of engraved glass. The choice has been mainly directed towards representing practical categories of work, and many fine examples of English, Scandinavian and Continental glass have had to be omitted. This is greatly regretted.

We owe much to our wives; to Tina Dreiser for the endless task of typing the manuscript, and to both for their forebearance with what may have been seen as a prolonged attack of vitreous tunnel vision; and we are particularly indebted to Pauline Stride for her kindness, patience and professional expertise in vetting the manuscript.

Artist-engravers who have kindly supplied photographs of their work are separately credited in the captions, and we are grateful to the following photographers: Jindrich Brok, Gabriel Urbanek, Jiri Erml, Majka Pavlikova, Adolf Vrhel, G.V. Herbert, P.J. Gates, J. Heyhurst, G. Perks, E. Leigh, W. Hatton and the Royal College. With the exception of pages 128, 129, 130 and 141 all other photographs and drawings are by Peter Dreiser.

PREFACE

During the past five years there has been a resurgence of interest in glass decoration which can be said to be a uniquely British phenomenon. The professional engraver has always been with us but, separated from this main stream, a small number of artist-engravers has been quietly producing important work for over 30 years; this has resulted in glass of great individuality, ranging from presentation pieces to church windows and altar pieces. And it is the example, indeed the active encouragement of these craftsmen, that has stimulated many amateurs, and artists in other media, to explore the craft. Further, as the wider public has been made more aware of engraved glass by exhibitions such as those organised by the Guild of Glass Engravers, the demand for information on every aspect of the craft has vastly increased.

As will be seen, the range of methods by which glass may be decorated is formidable-and this excludes enamelling, an artform in itself. All methods will be dealt with in this book, but it is the first of these, copper wheel engraving, to which most attention will be given. Without reflecting on any other method, it is the incising or carving of glass by the wheel which has contributed most to the art of glass engraving; stemming as it does from earlier rock crystal and hardstone cutting by means of closely related mechanical techniques, wheel engraving is a skill which stretches for thousands of years. It is in this area, it is felt, that information is most lacking; of the small amount that has been written, there is little that describes the practical problems of the wheel engraver on the master-to-apprentice level. One notable exception is the paper, 'The Art of Glass Engraving', by Helen Monro MA, which was read to the Royal Society of Arts in 1960. Helen Monro, herself a wheel engraver trained in Europe, gave a high quality lecture full of 'teaching' information rarely to be found.

This book will plot a similar but much more detailed course, reflecting the personal opinion and experience of a professional wheel engraver of wide knowledge. It cannot cover every detail or solve every problem – only a teacher giving personal supervision can do this – but it is meant to be detailed enough to enable the student engraver, craft teacher or beginner to set up and master this hitherto rather guarded skill.

It is not intended that this book should give a complete digest of glass history, but the past must be discussed or speculated upon when it has some bearing on the present, in order to measure the new ability against the old, or to determine the direction which glass decoration is taking.

Vexed questions on the criteria of 'art forms' or 'social utility' will be mostly set aside, though the elements of design must be a constant preoccupation in any craft. It is enough for the moment that the glass engraving skills be developed, as fully as possible, for it is from the high level of competence – the plateau of action as it were – that the commanding heights of real aesthetic invention may be reached.

INTRODUCTION

This book may be regarded as being divided into two parts. Chapter 1 to 12 cover the whole range of decorative engraving, including cutting, which is produced at the lathe. The first seven chapters deal with the essential techniques of copper wheel engraving. It starts with the formation of simple shapes which the beginner must learn to master, and progresses in order of difficulty to full-scale intaglio (incised) projects which the engraver is likely to encounter. Each project is discussed so as to allow the beginner to understand and follow a similar project. Chapters 8 to 12 then introduce more advanced and specialised engraving, including sculptural relief (raised) work, cut glass and brilliant cutting.

The second part of the book, Chapters 13 to 17, covers techniques which are quite different from wheel engraving, but which may occasionally be used in combination with it: diamond point engraving, flexible drive engraving, glass etching and sand blasting. In general, diamond point and flexible drive engraving are used with more frequency than wheel engraving, while etching and sand blasting are not so widely practised owing to the greater difficulty in controlling the medium and the high cost of safe equipment.

The reason why rather more emphasis has been given to the technique of copper wheel in the first half of the book is that, of all the forms of glass engraving, it is the wheel which offers the best all-round training for the beginner in terms of patience, sculptural control and versatility. It is the traditional method by which glass has been decorated for many centuries, and its mastery will not only provide a confident and professional base from which to handle other forms of decoration, but will also afford valuable insight into the skills developed by the past masters of the craft.

The Professional Heritage

Until the first World War it was virtually impossible to learn any traditional skill without being legally indentured – apprenticed – to it for from five to seven years. At the end of that time the apprentice would need to have reached a high degree of proficiency before being approved as a professional journeyman – that is, being allowed to practise his craft from place to place. For centuries this had been the accepted means of training and control, not only in limiting the numbers serving the skill, but also in setting the level of excellence which the governing guild sought to impose as a protection against deteriorating standards. This system at its best was the highest form of disciplined training and the resulting standard of work was superbly professional; at its worst it made ruthless use of the artisan and imposed such restraint on the developing artist that all freedom of expression was inhibited. However, emancipation is not all good. There appears to be a tendency for the newcomer to examine the motives and the content of a piece of work long before the means of creativity – the skill – has been mastered.

But without systems of training, how does the beginner begin? Obviously the best approach would be by way of an accredited glass school where art and skill, glass forming, engraving, cutting, indeed every aspect of glass would be integrated. The need for such glass schools to reinforce and supplement the education and design ability of glass workers, separate from industry, was recognised quite early on. One of the first in Europe started off as a Sunday School specifically to supplement the educational needs of the glass workers of Kamenický Šenov (Steinschönau) district in Northern Bohemia. In 1856 it was inaugurated as an independent state-run glass school.

In England both John Northwood and Frederick Carder equally encouraged the skills and knowledge of the Stourbridge Glassworkers. In about 1880 John Northwood actually ran a life class in the works, while Carder, before he joined Corning Glass in America, started the Wordsley School of Art in 1899, though he had fostered the arts for years earlier. But in Britain there appears nothing comparable to the development, organisation and disciplines of the European glass schools which now take the institutionalised place of the old guilds for tuition and selection.

Until Britain has firmly based institutions of this kind, the only way to learn is by working at one's own bench, and by gradually accumulating practical information on every allied subject such as gem cutting, seal engraving or jade carving. By quiet application, the pace of development can be set by the engraver to his or her available time and energy. Two hours of dedicated concentration is worth six hours of desultory time-serving to an indifferent curriculum. And this is the path by which the most gifted amateur artist-craftsman glass engravers have reached their professionalism during the last 40 years in Great Britain.

There is, of course, another heritage, namely that of the archaeologist, the scholar, curator and collector, who between them have built up an immense body of knowledge of glass of the past, and the treasures of our museums. The museums are the life blood of our present culture, no matter how anaemic that may at times appear to be, and the engraver can find much of his inspiration for design, virtually at random, in any section of the fine arts: jewellery, enamelling, medieval painting and tapestry, even wrought iron, besides examples of his own craft, which will prove to be a constant source of replenishment.

Collections of decorative glass are spread throughout the world. They are not always displayed well enough to enable the engraver to examine the quality and technique of individual pieces, but it is still a great privilege to see them. If it is not always possible for the artist to visit centres such as the British Museum and the Victoria and Albert Museum in London, the Corning Museum in the United States or the European collections (given in the appendix), most national museums do produce specialist

English wine carafe, possibly made at Stourbridge during the second half of the nineteenth century

illustrated catalogues, and also photographs of individual pieces, which can be obtained by post, so that he or she need not be too isolated from information.

The best introduction to present-day engraved glass is by way of the Guild of Glass Engravers, now a thriving group of professional and amateur engravers whose work (selected and unselected) may be seen at their annual exhibitions, the most notable of which was 'Glass Engraving Resurgent' held at the Ashmoleum Museum, Oxford, in 1979 and the Guild Church of St Lawrence Jewry-by Guildhall, London, in 1980. (The Guild's address is 19 Portland Place, London W.1.) Though most of the credit for the formation of the Guild must go to Elly Eliades and Elaine Freed. The Guild's Founder President, Vice President and Chairman were Laurence Whistler, the late John Hutton, and David Peace, respectively, all internationally known glass engravers who added their considerable influence to the project.

As regards background reading, there is a vast amount of informed literature and illustrated books on decorative and engraved glass for the engraver to consult, a few of which are selected for the bibliography to this book. Although it is difficult to select a shorlist from the many excellent scholarly works available, the following titles, which are of permanent value, are suggested for the serious student:

'The Hull', elliptical bowl designed by Zevi Blum, engraved by Roland Erlacher, about 1975. Steuben Glass, New York

W A Thorpe, *A History of English and Irish Glass*, Holland Press, London, 1969

Eve Polak, *Glass: its Makers and its Public*, Weidenfeld & Nicolson, London, 1975

Gustav Weiss, *The Book of Glass*, Barrie & Jenkins, London, 1971 Verlag Ullstein GmbH, Berlin, 1966.

R J Charleston, *Wheel Engraving and Cutting. Some early equipment: I. Engraving 1964, II. Water power and cutting 1965*, Journal of Glass Studies, Corning Museum of Glass

The first two books deal with the social and aesthetic history of glass, including engraved glass; the third is an invaluable detailed world history of glass, which contains lists of the most important engravers from 1550 to 1900. The last of these, as the title suggests, is a thoroughly documented study of early engraving and cutting equipment.

The Nature of Glass

As this book is concerned exclusively with the engraving of glass, some thought must be given to the development and quality of this extraordinary and beautiful material.

It makes its first appearance in Mesopotamia and

Egypt about 3000 BC as a siliceous glaze on steatite beads and small stones most probably in imitation of precious stones, which implies that the late Bronze age worker was familiar with the fluxing power of alkalis on siliceous materials.

Hundreds of separated craftsmen must have long speculated on the quality of obsidian (a natural volcanic glass), or the outcrops of glassy slag on kilns or furnace pots before the nature of glazes or glass was creatively interpreted. But once understood, it was only a matter of time before the optimum proportions of the ingredients – silica, alkali flux and limestone (fortuitously included in the first instance) – would have been determined.

These materials have always been abundant in one form or another: silica (silicon dioxide) as sand, quartz pebbles and flint; alkali as potassium carbonate (potash) and sodium carbonate (soda ash) which was obtained from wood or plant ash; and calcium carbonate, the stabiliser, as common limestone. Workers tended to use the alkali (or indeed any other material) which was nearest to hand, whether it came from the lixiviated (i.e. leached) ash of wood, kelp, bracken or fern, and it is for this reason the northern European glass communities exploited the potash-forming hardwoods of their extensive forests while the craftsmen of Southern Europe and the Eastern Mediterranean depended heavily on the soda-yielding marine plant, glasswort, variously known as Barilla and Roquetta.

Although the chemistry of glass is very complex, the principle is easy to understand. Silica is a hard glassy substance which, as natural quartz, has a sharp melting point of about 1610°C (2930°F). It can now be formed into many complicated shapes for chemical and laboratory purposes. It is mechanically weaker than ordinary glass but has the remarkable quality that it can be heated to red heat and quenched in water without fracturing. When silica, together with a little limestone, is heated to a high temperature with an increasing amount of alkali, the melting point of the fused mixture is gradually reduced; in fact it becomes no longer a melting point but a prolonged deformation temperature zone which, with the correct proportion of silica, alkali and limestone, reaches the plastic condition which the glass worker chooses for his forming and blowing. However, if the shaped glass is allowed to cool too rapidly great internal stresses are set up which render it very unstable. This is avoided by annealing, that is, gradually cooling the hot glass in a special oven (the lehr) which brings it to that miraculously stable condition that has fascinated mankind for thousands of years.

Naturally, the materials used in the past were invariably combined with traces of other elements which affected the quality and colour of the glass. Copper and iron oxides are the most common of these elements, and they account for the characteristic greenish coloration of early glass. This basic coloration could only be changed by increasing the intensity of the colour through the addition of oxides to the mix. Cobalt gives a strong blue, copper a blue-green, and manganese a purplish colour; alternatively, it could be disguised (de-colourised) by the addition of another roughly complementary colour – usually manganese purple, which converted the green tint to various shades of grey.

Although such formulations – art rather than chemistry – had made possible glass of great beauty, as well as of utility, for over 2000 years, there had always been a desire to 'alchemise' a glass which might equal the purity and optical quality of natural quartz crystal. Consequently, there was a constant search for purer ingredients: whiter quartz sand, calcined flint (also silica) and higher quality alkali. By 1500 the Venetians were forming thin, exquisitely controlled shapes from an improved, almost colourless, soda-lime glass, cristallo, with an aesthetic mastery which has never been surpassed. It was about this time that the diamond point was found to be effective as a means of surface decoration.

However, sometime previous to 1674 – the date of his patent – George Ravenscroft discovered that by incorporating relatively large quantities of lead oxide with the melt, a whiter, softer, much more brilliant glass was obtained. At first the balance of alkali with the lead oxide was wrong, which resulted in a gradual devitrification (reversion to the crystalline silica state – crizzling) an irreversible condition which in some early examples is sadly continuing. But in a short time a stable, highly refractive, colourless glass was manufactured which was ideal for engraving and cutting of every kind. All the same, full lead glass in its malleable state is highly viscous, and hence the blown forms generally lack the delicacy of the quicker cooling, harder, soda-lime cristallo glass.

Coincidentally with the English development of lead glass (commonly but misleadingly known as flint glass), an improved, hard, potash-lime glass had been developed in Bohemia which could be made thicker without losing its brilliance and which had the appearance of rock crystal. The Bohemian craftsmen found it very suitable for engraving and cutting, and it gave a great spur to their already established engraving reputation.

This then is where the choice for the craftsman still remains. An endless list of other kinds of glass have been developed more recently, such as toughened glass or borosilicate glass (Pyrex), which can be worked by other methods, but for the engraver the choice lies between these two basic types of glass, soda lime and lead. The quality of both varies enormously and in all offers a range from flint-hard coloured bottle glass – which should not be held in contempt – to the almost neutered brilliance of soft, full lead crystal.

One particular potential disaster area for the engraver may now be better understood by virtue of this discussion; that is the danger of engraving on an imperfectly annealed glass. Older glass workers formed their shape entirely by hand. The pieces were continually heat soaked and any excess of a rim would be sheared away and the glass finished off before being placed in the annealing oven. This seldom occurs in commercial establishments, where the glass is mainly formed and annealed *before* the excess is removed, which is dealt with as a separate mechanical process. The rim of the glass is automatically turned against a diamond or tungsten carbide point and then subjected to a thin gas jet which follows the point, with the result that the differential heating and cooling of the revolving glass causes the unwanted rim to break neatly away. The sharp edge is

An example showing how the rim of a glass may be ringed off at the stress line as a result of insufficient annealing

subsequently ground and then melted with fine gas jets to a smooth fire-polished rim. But in doing so invisible stresses are set up further down the glass which are always a danger to the engraver, who may find that after some work in that area a split circlet of glass may detach itself from the rest of the glass. This stress ring may be easily detected by the use of polaroid spectacles and a separate piece of polaroid film in the following manner.

1 View the goblet against a good light source.
2 Interpose a small piece of polaroid film between the glass and the light source.
3 Turn the film round in the same plane as the spectacles. If there is any stress of the kind under discussion, a position will be arrived at when a distinct dark band parallel to the rim will be visible.

These stress marks may be wide or narrow, but in any event care should be taken, or parallel cut lines should be avoided, at that position.

Any problem which may occur with the shape or with a particular quality of a glass will be dealt with at the appropriate moment in the text. One last point: in the absence of interesting modern glass the engraver might be strongly tempted to use an antique piece. Unless this be a question of restoration, where there is no intention to deceive, this should be resisted. Even humble pieces should be respected.

The dark line between the two light fields shows the stress line when seen through polaroid films

Measurement Conversions

Throughout this book all measurements are given in millimetres followed by inches in brackets. The conversions are approximate, and the reader is advised to check the availability of particular tool measurements with manufacturers' lists. In Britain and Europe, tool measurements are listed in millimetres; in the United States they are listed in inches.

As far as engraving wheel sizes are concerned, it is obvious that wear will take place from the moment one is used. The wheel chosen for a particular task should be reasonably close to the size given but a little latitude is acceptable.

Electrical precautions

With any electrical installation professional advice should be sought. As some equipment may be near water or in a damp atmosphere, motors and switches should be set in a safe place; with large equipment a fail-safe switch should be incorporated. Advice is readily available from the manufacturers on any specialised equipment, which should be followed closely. In all, the equipment discussed in this book is rather more reliable than the average domestic appliance, and no difficulty should be encountered in the use of it. However, the authors cannot, of course, be held responsible for any damage which may arise from the use of it or in the installation.

1 Copper Wheel Engraving

ENGRAVING METHODS

At the outset, the newcomer may be puzzled by the various descriptions which are applied to examples of engraved glass, all of which could more simply come under the heading of copper wheel engraving. However, the engraved art forms can differ so much from each other that it is as well to keep to the accepted categories, namely intaglio engraving, relief engraving, cameo glass and cut glass.

Intaglio engraving; footed vase (glass engraved in the rock crystal manner). Thomas Webb, 1900 (*above*)

Intaglio engraving; detail of covered vase, from about 1700 (*left*). *Gottfried Spiller, Potsdam.*

Intaglio engraving

Engraving of any kind which is cut or incised can properly be described as intaglio, but for the engraver it refers particularly to a design which has been modelled negatively into a glass, so as to give the illusion of standing out, naturally, in positive relief.

Some confusion may arise from this term, for there is a bold type of decorative engraving produced by small stone wheels (part way toward glass cutting) that was developed at Stourbridge during the late nineteenth century which is also well known as *intaglio*. It is quite separate in form and technique, and when referred to in the text will be distinguished from the foregoing by being set in italics.

Relief Engraving

This is the very opposite of intaglio engraving. The elements of the design are cut and modelled so as to stand proud of the glass surface. To achieve this relief, the original surface surrounding the design is taken away or ground back to a lower level.

Mattschnitt (matt cutting). It is a mixture of light engraving and variable matting, the decorative shapes of which just break the surface of the glass.

Cameo glass; vase from Stourbridge, 1884, Thomas Webb (*Victoria and Albert Museum*)

High relief; detail of a Silesian goblet, about 1700

Cameo Glass

The term applies to glass which has been encased (flashed) with one or more additional layers of coloured glass, into which a figure or design has been relief engraved, thereby exposing the under layer or layers as a contrasting background. It applies equally to similarly engraved multi-layered semi-precious stones, from which cameo glass probably drew its inspiration.

Cut Glass

Regular, deeply cut and polished geometric patterns, sometimes amending the blown form, is commonly known as cut glass. It is characterised by the highly reflecting and refracting facets formed by the intersecting cuts. It is occasionally used in combination with copper wheel engraving but should not be confused with it. Though it depends on the wheel, it is an altogether different technique.

There is one category of surface decoration for which there is no English equivalent to the German word:

Cut glass; English decanter, about 1820

Mattschnitt; Bohemian beaker, eighteenth century

THE BEGINNING OF WHEEL ENGRAVING

While it may be convenient to accept the turn of the seventeenth century as the starting point for wheel engraving on glass, this craft, in common with all other civilizing skills such as jewellery making or weaving, where the hand still remains the dominant tool, is rooted in the ancient East and has a very long and continuous history. Precious and semi-precious hardstones and natural quartz crystal had been engraved, by what have been very similar means, for many centuries earlier, long before the mid-European masters brought their superb skills to the more tractable crystal glass.

Looking back 5000 years, it could be claimed that the Babylonian cylinder seal is perhaps the earliest known artifact to have been engraved by the wheel. These intaglio seals, many of them masterpieces of skill and design, were cut in a wide variety of hardstone and produced in such large quantities as to suggest well-disciplined and organised artisan workshops. They had great social value as the personal imprint signatures or symbols of officials and important families for edicts and contractual agreements, and the practice of using them to sign inscribed clay tablets spread throughout Mesopotamia, Egypt and the Indus basin.

When the seal was pressed and rolled into the clay

1 Babylonian seal and impression showing elementary rotary engraving, about 3200 BC (*British Museum*)
2 Babylonian seal impression showing more organised engraving

3 A reproduction of a Babylonian seal formed from a flintstone pebble and engraved on a traditional lathe using diamond burrs and diamond paste

tablet, a repeating relief impression was formed which was easily recognisable, and, since each seal had been uniquely engraved, was virtually impossible to forge. The early Greek stamp seals, perhaps formed in the same way, are equally astonishing but, unfortunately there is no hard evidence as to how these entrancing objects were actually engraved.

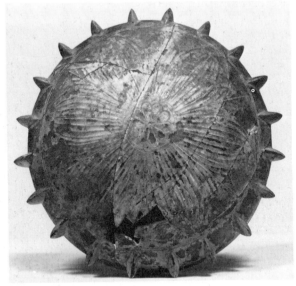

Engraved bowl from Canosa, Apulia, Italy, late third century BC (*British Museum*)

It may be said that this form of engraving is nearer to the work of a lapidary than that of a glass engraver, but this is more a category of specialisation than of skill or mechanics, for the same basic skeletal wheel cuts of 'olives' and 'printies' linked together for patterns or stylised figures (intaglio glass copper wheel engraving in miniature), can plainly be seen. In fact, a skilled engraver did – and still can, move from seal to glass engraving without change of lathe or method and can handle each with equal facility.

As far as glass is concerned, the imprint of the grinding wheel can be seen as early as the eighth century BC. Certainly by the first century AD wheel engraved glass was well advanced but, although one can readily guess at the mechanics or the abrasives which may have been used, a maddening silence surrounds these early skills, a silence which continued until the sixteenth century. What is the reason for this?

Before the invention of printing, the spread of knowledge of any specialised craft was a slow and closed affair. It was passed on either by word of mouth, from master to apprentice or from one travelling worker to another, or it was recorded by some interested (often ecclesiastical) scribe. Even when the printed word and woodblock illustration burst upon Europe in the late fifteenth century, as far as the practical details of crafts were concerned the new information was only moderately instructional. Rarely were the actual methods of craftsmen accurately detailed in such a way as to be a clear and

Perseus and Andromeda; Bohemian panel engraved by Caspar Lehmann, about 1600, the father of modern wheel engraving (*Victoria and Albert Museum*)

certain guide for the future worker.

Even when craftsmen did have access to the written word, they were secretive and self protective, fearful that their new-found knowledge and skills might pass into competitive hands. Often, too, they would be enjoined to secrecy under threat of punishment by their controlling guild or family workshop. And this is no surprise. It is still a common experience to watch a craftsman's eyes go opaque when interrogated about his special and, for him supposedly, unique skill.

Of course there were reasons other than the secretive behaviour of craftsmen which contributed to the lack of progress or expansion of various crafts. Economic pressures, the loss of patronage or the ravages of war would cause glass centres to decline, and when this occurred community workshops would be dispersed, or the workers would move to other occupations. Thus a gradual deterioration would set in only to end with the complete loss of the carefully nurtured practical knowledge, local method and equipment – and this apart from the irreparable loss of a unique aesthetic environment.

However, engraving by means of the lathe, for one particularised skill or another, survived all the calamities

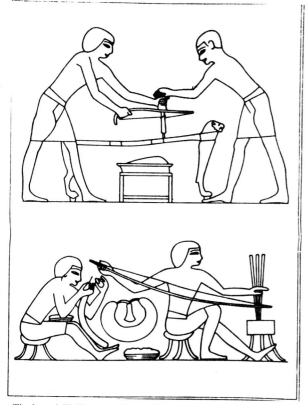

The bow drill, illustrated in a wall painting at Thebes, about **1450** BC

of history and once again came to fruition in the very special environment of Bohemia and Silesia in the seventeenth century when crystal engraving and cutting were greatly in demand. At this time the accelerating thrust of technology in all things – materials, machinery and power – made many revolutionary improvements possible from which glass was to benefit in crystal-clear transparency and general workability, and it could be produced in such increasing quantities as to sound the death knell of natural quartz crystal carving and engraving. It could be said that the wheel had been waiting for this moment when engravers could indulge in every skilful decorative fantasy on the softer, clearer crystal glass.

While we can only speculate on the methods and equipment which were used by these very early craftsmen, we do not have to give a second thought to their patience, skill, ingenuity and mastery over what must have been elementary apparatus. It is all there to be seen in the artifacts. These workers are more than our equals. The ancient hand-held, bow-driven drill, large and small, horizontal and vertical, would certainly have been adapted to every artisan purpose possible. But as far as the physical process of engraving is concerned, the intriguing question is: How was the drilling point or grinding disc actually manoeuvred to the material? They would have known how to grade abrasives or make polishing pastes, but which did they use? How, indeed, did they cut a seal or Portland Vase or cage cup? The

practising engraver can only guess that, for much of the work, the material was held in the hand, or firmly attached to something held in the hand, and offered to a firmly anchored, horizontally mounted, primitive lathe operating on the principle of the modern lathe which, in essence, has remained unchanged since the sixteenth century and, with little doubt, for millenia before that.

Use of the pole lathe; lens grinding, illustrated in Diderot's *Encyclopédie*, 1767

The Working Principle of the Lathe

The main function and working parts of a glass engraving lathe cannot be better introduced than by examining the illustration from *Oculus Artificialis*. It consists of a treadle drive, a driven shaft within simple bearings, one end of which (the throat) projects and has been taper bored, and a series of interchangeable spindles to which small copper wheels are attached. To engrave, the tapered shank of the selected spindle is keyed into the hollow throat of the lathe when, by charging the revolving copper

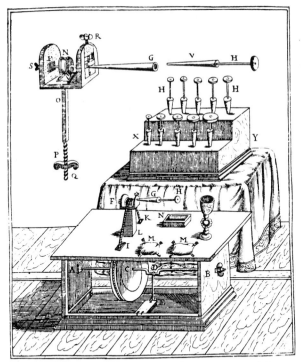

Glass engraving equipment from J. Zahn, *Oculus Artificialis*
1702

Cælator gemmarum. Steinschneyder

INscribo Regum preciosis nomina gemmis,
   Atq super lapides cælo sigilla Ducum.
Nunc & inæquales Beryllos, inde Smaragdos,
Nunc quoq Saphyrum, nunc Adamanta cælo.

Nunc quoq Sardonicen polio, rubrumq Pyropum
   Chrisolythos etiam nunc ego limo rudes.
Deniq principibus quæcunq potentibus vsquam
   Conuenit, illa mea gemma paratur ope.
Hic mihi quo digiti decorentur Iaspis Eoa,
   Hic mihi Chrystallus, leuis & ardet Onyx.
        D 3   Statua

Woodcut representing a hardstone engraver at work, by Jost
Amman, 1568 (*British Museum*)

wheel with abrasive paste, the profile edge becomes a
small but very manoeuvrable cutting or grinding head.

The elementary but obviously adequate bearings are
shown to be of the simplest kind – probably a solid brass
thrust-bearing at the rear and a split lead bearing at the
front. This construction hints at an even simpler design,
since the bearings may just as easily have been made of
hard wood, say, lignum vitae. The accompanying basic
equipment – the abrasive container, spindle rack, elbow
pads and controlling treadle – readily conjures up an
image of the engraver at his bench at that time.

The only detail that has strangely been omitted from
this illustration, but can be seen elsewhere, is the narrow
strip of metal ordinarily suspended over the cutting
wheel, the point of which grips a small leather tongue. The
leather, which just touches the wheel, serves to hold and
smooth out the abrasive paste as it is fed to the cutting
edge.

Early Engraving Lathes

Perhaps the earliest dated illustration of an engraver
seated at his lathe is that of the woodcut, 'Jost Amman,
the gem cutter', published in *Stände und Handwerker*,
Frankfurt, 1568. The size and height of this seal cutting
lathe, and the position of the forearms resting on the
bench, indicate that little pressure was being exerted, or
was necessary, for the specialised work in hand. An almost
parallel illustration of a glass engraver at work, dated
1857, i.e. nearly 300 years later, shows a modification in
the design – though there is little alteration in the
mechanics – to meet another purpose. The lathe is more
robust, has a longer throat to accommodate the larger

material (to allow greater movement round the spindle
end) and is set higher so that the elbows can be firmly
anchored to the bench in order to support the greater
weight.

The earliest existing lathe, dated 1697, is housed in the
Liberec Museum, Bohemia, Czechoslovakia; a comparison between this forerunner and the machines of two
hundred years later shows that little has changed, and
even up to this moment nothing startling has taken place.
Old or new, the difficulties to be overcome, mainly manual
and aesthetic, remain the same. Improved mechanics are,
of course, very convenient, but apart from the sub-
stitution of electrical for manual drive, they are not all
that vital beyond the requirements set by traditional
patterns.

All the examples of glass engraving prepared for this

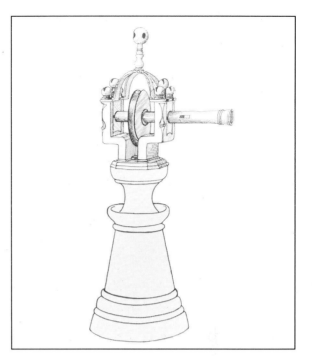

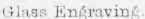

Glass Engraving.

Copper wheel engraver at work. From Pellatt's *Curiosities of Glassmaking*, 1849 (*courtesy of R.J. Charleston*)

The earliest dated lathe, 1697 now in the Liberec Museum, Bohemia, Czechoslovakia (*above right*)

Typical nineteenth century lathe and assembly (*courtesy of Mr. W. Randell*)

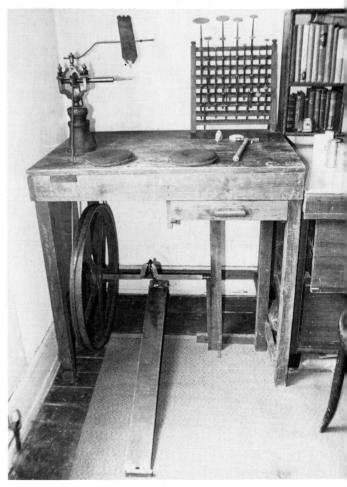

book have been engraved on a traditional treadle lathe made about 1880. This machine has been modified for an electric drive of seven stepped speeds. However, one must hasten to say that there is nothing at all wrong with the earlier two-step treadle lathe. Indeed, in many respects it was a superior machine in that the pressure of the cut via the feet was completely coordinated and a 'feel' could be maintained at critical speeds which was not possible any other way. However, the worker's whole body is used in the treadling movement, and fatigue seriously offsets any such advantage. No one these days would use the old method out of choice, but neither should an engaver pass over one of these invaluable lathes if he has the good fortune to come upon one.

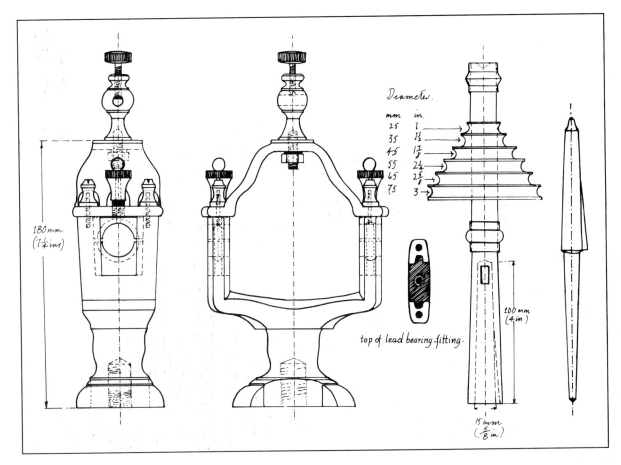

Diameter.

mm	in.
25	1
35	1½
45	1⅞
55	2¼
65	2⅝
75	3

top of lead bearing fitting.

180 mm (7¼ ins)

100 mm (4 in)

15 mm (⅝ in)

Machine drawing of a nineteenth century lathe showing the original drive shaft with a six-step round belt pulley conversion from the old two-step. A matching spindle is included

THE TRADITIONAL NINETEENTH-CENTURY LATHE

The machine drawing gives details of a nineteenth-century, mid-European lathe which has been converted from a two-step pulley treadle lathe to a six-step electric drive. It is drawn in scale which, together with the exploded photographed components of the author's own lathe, supplies all the information necessary for an engraver to make up his own machine. The frame need not be of cast brass; it may just as well be built with billets of steel brazed or bolted together but, beyond that improvisation, all the other details should be fairly strictly followed.

The Shaft

The mandrel must be accurately turned, and the end internal taper to the throat must be drilled out with the appropriate tapered reamer, precisely centred. It is provided with a small keyway. The angle of the internal taper should approximate that of the drawing, but it is not critical, for it is common to cast the spindles in situ so as to ensure a snug fit.

The Shaft Bearings

The bearings consist of two hardened steel rings shrunk or brazed on to the mandrel shaft. It can be seen that the front end bearings section is a deep half-round of the shape to withstand side shock, and that at the back end there is a V-bearing to ensure accurate running.

The Bearing Blocks

The blocks in which the ring bearings run are made of a lead-tin alloy, in the approximate proportion 2:1. They are cast or machined in two halves which stop short of meeting around the shaft by about 3mm (⅛ in) to allow for wear adjustment.

The Bearing Housing

The housing is provided with a channel (keywayed) in which to locate the split bearing blocks but the recess is tapered (wedge shaped) towards the bottom, which allows the housing to take a tight hold on the matching bearing blocks as they are pressed home. This accounts for the numbering on the bearings and housing, which must always marry up together. Any simplification or short cut to the foregoing is fraught with trouble.

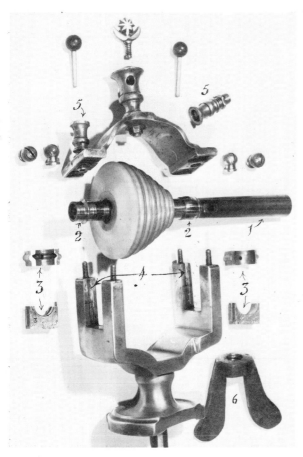

Dismantled lathe showing the main features (*above*):
1 Hollow tapered drive mandrel
2 mandrel bearings
3 Upper and lower white metal (lead-tin) bearing blocks
4 Bearing block housing
5 Adjustable bolts for bearing, containing lubrication channels
6 Bench fixing wing nut

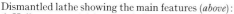

Casting a lead base to a spindle (*right*):
1 The new spindle core (note the serrations to ensure a firm grip of the cast lead)
2 Hollow tapered drive mandrel
3 Centering the casting collar in position
4 Centering the base nipple set in position to prevent the escape of molten metal and to allow a small projection of the spindle shaft
5 The lead cast sleeve
6 The ejector hole
7 Ejector
8 Bottom view of the casting collar
9 Cross section of the casting collar
10 Cross section of the nipple

Running and Maintenance

The other details of the lathe are self evident: the adjusting bolts are centred over each bearing, and when these are screwed downwards, pressure is put on the top half of the bearing, thereby taking up any slack which may be due to wear. Oiling is simple and direct. The

The assembled lathe

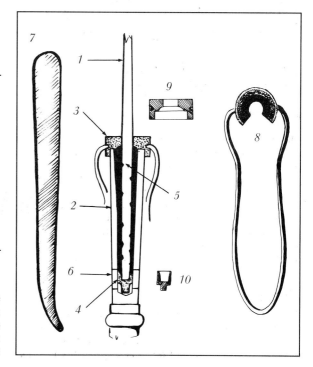

adjustment bolt is drilled right through, as is the upper bearing, which permits the oil to trickle down to the running shaft. And, of course, it trickles out again, hence a turned hollow on the brass base (or the hardwood plinth) of the lathe is provided in order to catch the excess oil.

The whole machine is well thought out, sturdy and functional, and almost maintenance free – made to last longer than one worker's lifetime. Indeed, a lathe had to be strong and simple so that it could be easily dismantled and quickly carried away from one place to another, and so that, if the bearings broke up, it was within the engraver's capacity to melt down and recast them. (Brief details of how to cast and spindles are illustrated.)

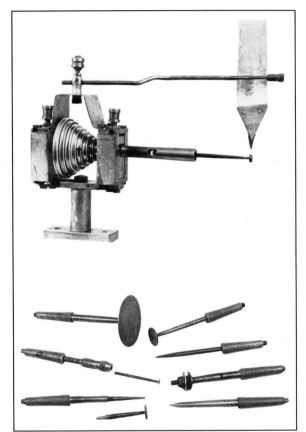

Home made lathe and equipment, based on the traditional lathe using minimal material

MODERN LATHES

It would be as short-sighted to remain with the essential nineteenth-century lathe as it would have to have hung on to the treadle, and as could be expected the modern equivalent is a much more robust and mechanically efficient machine. The illustration of a widely used and reliable lathe made by Spatzier (marketed by Merker) of West Germany which can handle both light and heavy engraving shows little or no change in the system, but in every other respect it is vastly better engineered. Briefly, the main advantages are as follows:

1 The modern machines are very much stronger. The particular model featured serves a dual purpose, that is, its action is delicate enough to handle any copper wheel engraving, and rigid enough to take stone wheels of up to 150mm (6 or 7 in) in diameter (mounted on solid steel spindles) for *intaglio* engraving.

2 They have improved wheel speeds. To handle the extended scale of engraving which is possible on these lathes, a wider range of stepped speeds is provided, namely from 300 to 3500 revolutions per minute. The maximum needed for orthodox copper wheel engraving is about 2000 rpm.

3 They have a superior mainshaft and bearing system. A more robust hardened steel shaft runs between phosphor bronze bearings which are continuously lubricated by a floating ring within the bearing, which continuously replenishes the oil from a sump as it is turned by the revolving shaft. The bearings are horizontally slit on one side only to allow a vertical adjustment for wear. Critical side play is taken up by lock-nuts which bring the shaft up to a thrust bearing.

To the engraver familiar with the traditional lathe, the modern machine may seem rigid, or rather, feel hard or resistant against the glass. This difference may be due to the shock-absorbent quality of the lead bearings. However, this should not prove any obstacle in choosing one, if it could be afforded, for the increased range of work that could be handled – carving, high relief or intaglio – without fear of mechanical strain, would be an enormous

Early example of a modern lathe, about 1920, showing cast iron frame, flat belt pulley and thrust bearing. After H. Strehblow

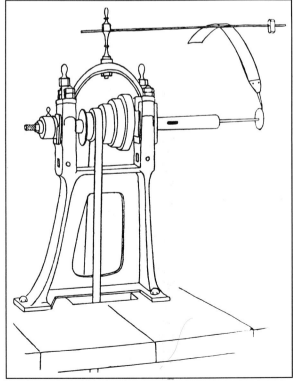

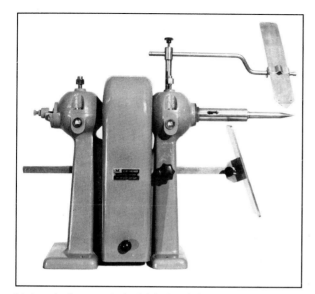

Modern dual purpose lathe (with chamfering plate) made by Spatzier

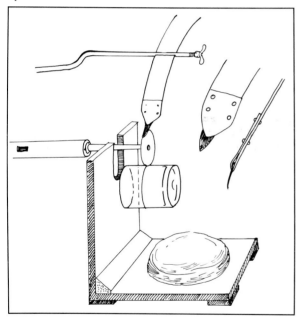

A traditional chamfering device

advantage. To sum up then, the modern lathe is the most efficient tool but the older form is the most sensitive. Neither is cheap; indeed the older type, which is still reproduced, is much dearer than the newer models, but it is a lot extra to pay for being a purist. The most sensible choice would be a modern machine.

The Drive

A stepped pulley of six or more ratios, with the reciprocal drive via a $\frac{1}{2}$ hp (horsepower) motor ($\frac{1}{3}$ hp for the lighter machine), is the common and still the most reliable system of speed control. It is obviously not the ultimate in drives. Electric motors are now available, either separate or integrated with the lathe, which will give a continuous controllable speed range, without loss of power (torque), from zero to well past the maximum required. All such equipment is initially exorbitantly expensive, and in the long run inconvenient and very costly in lost time when they break down. For the individual artist-craftsman, the simpler the control the better.

A few words of warning. The bearings of belt-driven lathes, old or new, are designed for vertical drives from below or above the lathe, preferably below. Illustrations sometimes show converted lathes being driven horizontally from behind the lathe, perhaps because the alternative may have meant slicing away the cast base where it fouled the running belt. This horizontal drive is not to be recommended, for there is no way of taking up sideways wear of the bearings.

The Spindle

The spindle, the business end of the lathe, has remained unchanged. The only modern advantage is that it is nicely manufactured and can be obtained in a wide variety of tapered, screwed and chucked ends for specialised work.

Basic Lathe Equipment

All ancillary equipment may be obtained from the suppliers of the lathe and, as it is specifically designed for that particular machine, it would clearly be a comforting advantage to purchase everything outright: lathe, bench, motor, spindles and all tools. But it would be good sense to limit the investment to the basic need, and then add to this as experience suggests.

lathe: ten-step, round belt pulley, speed 300 – 3500 rpm

25 spindles: 5 @ **2.5**mm ($\frac{7}{64}$ in) end of taper size
          10 @ **5**mm ($\frac{7}{32}$ in) end of taper size
          5 @ **7**mm ($\frac{1}{4}$ in) end of taper size
          3 screw-ended: fine, medium, large
          1 adaptor for collets, **2.35**–6mm ($\frac{7}{64} - \frac{1}{4}$ in)
          screw-ended with flange and nut

1 spindle ejector
1 spindle corrector (bending iron)

A more powerful half-hp standard motor is required for this heavier, dual-purpose lathe. If it is to be obtained locally the size (diameter) of the motor shaft must be notified to the lathe manufacturer so that the counter pulley can be supplied with the correct bore.

2 The Workshop

SETTING UP A WORKSHOP

The Bench Operating Position

Before a new bench is built, or an old one modified, some thought should be given to the engraving position which the operator must endure for hour after hour. A small impediment to comfort, hardly noticeable to start with, can become a raging irritation after prolonged sessions at the lathe. For example, a bench tie bar which appears to be a reasonable foot rest may make it difficult to shift the leg position without rubbing ankle and calf. Therefore, if possible, it is better to fit the equipment to the worker than the other way about.

While individual variety in size and in habits of posture make it impossible to say which position is best, it is very sensible to determine in advance the most comfortable height of the stool which will allow a relaxed, but reasonably anchored, position of the legs under the bench,

and the related height of the bench top upon which the arms must rest to handle the glass. Elbows should be cushioned in pads which give a secure triangulation with the cupped hands, say, holding a goblet bowl to the bottom of the spindle end. Properly positioned the arms should be capable of moving backwards and forwards, comfortably apart, giving plenty of manipulative freedom to the hands. The head and vision should be inclined downwards to the cut at an angle of about 30°. As a rough guide the navel would be just at, or below, the bench edge.

The Bench

The lathe itself is quite heavy, hence the bearing surface should be very strong and flat, not much less than 25mm (1 in) thick. It could consist of a simple platform of high quality blockboard fitted up to, and anchored to, the wall, but if free standing the bench must be well constructed with solid timber legs 100 × 50mm (4 × 2 in), and well braced so that when it is anchored to the floor there is no side shake. For the reasons already given, there should be no obstruction of any kind to the worker's feet and legs, So all bracings should be at the back and sides. While sized or matt varnished whitewood makes a very good surface for most purposes, for glass it may in time become dangerously shiny or slippery, a condition best avoided by covering it with matt, neutral-coloured vinyl or linoleum. It should be flat and fine enough to keep the glass sufficiently level and soft to prevent damage. Lead crystal

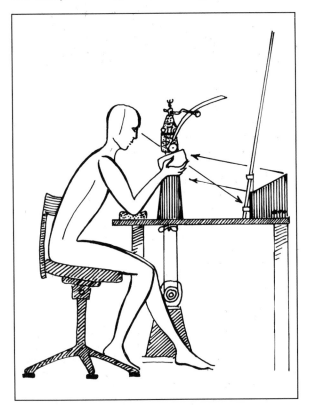

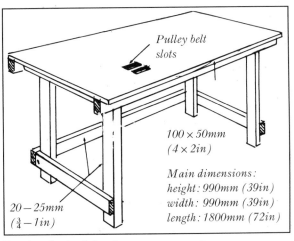

Pulley belt slots

100 × 50mm (4 × 2in)

Main dimensions:
height: 990mm (39in)
width: 990mm (39in)
length: 1800mm (72in)

20 – 25mm ($\frac{3}{4}$ – 1in)

Drawing of a simple bench

(*Left*) Position of the engraver at work

A student at work in a glass school, positioned against open daylight

is easily marked. Avoid all hard plastics such as Formica. Naturally, circumstances will dictate the dimensions, but the working surface should be as long as one can conveniently allow, and in depth should be not less than 850mm (34 in), preferably 900mm (36 in).

Lighting

Good daylight is essential, and some window must be found against which to position the lathe and bench. In conditions of extreme heat or brightness, the light may be controlled by placing tracing paper or a semitransparent blind over the window. In any event, all glass should be kept out of direct sunlight, for a goblet or particularly a crystal paperweight may act as a burning glass – with disastrous consequences.

Before anchoring the lathe, it is as well to consider the special lighting requirements for work at the wheel. This is best understood by reference to the accompanying drawing, which shows the most effective system by which both daylight and artificial light may be controlled. In brief, the eye needs the maximum illumination at the point of work itself, so that the work is shown up in contrast against a dark background. This is done by reflecting the light from the sky via an adjustable mirror set a little above the bench, and by providing a matt black square in line with the angle of view. The interposing glass screen acts as a splash-guard. By these simple means the engraving can readily be followed, even if partially obscured by paste or water. In lieu of daylight, a tungsten light (the common light bulb) positioned over the mirror is equally effective. Unnecessary extraneous light may be shaded off.

Supplementary artificial light in the workshop is, of course, very necessary and, in this respect, tungsten lighting is better than fluorescent which, although whiter, has a high peak in ultra violet light which may seriously worry some sensitive eyes. Thus, while fluorescent lighting may be excellent at ceiling height for shadowless

general bench illumination, it is suspect at low level for concentrated engraving. The average anglepoise light which may be directed or shaded is ideal.

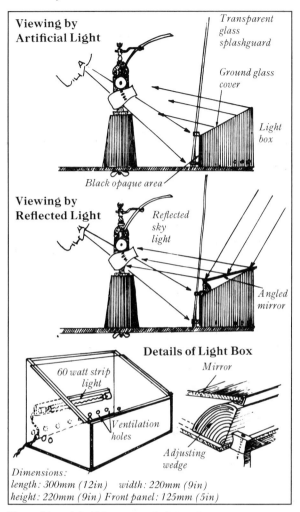

The position of the light source relative to the eye

Anchoring the Lathe

Once the best position has been found, and after the slots in the bench have been located and provided for the running belt, finally bolt the lathe down, 280mm (11 in) from the front bench edge to the centre of the lathe. This would be the average distance. For a large person it could be 300mm (12 in), for a small operator 260mm (10 in), but this should be the outside limit of adjustment necessary. The spindle end should be set to the right.

The Spindle Rack

The rack on which the spindles are ranged in order, at the ready for the engraver, is an obvious piece of workshop equipment. It may be fixed to the wall or set on the bench according to available space or individual preference. As the spindle is inserted and taken out by the right hand, it is economical in energy to have the rack on the right side

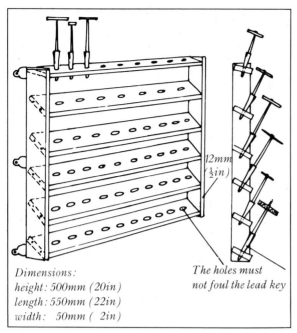

Dimensions:
height: 500mm (20in)
length: 550mm (22in)
width: 50mm (2in)

12mm
($\frac{1}{2}$in)

The holes must
not foul the lead key

Details of a wall mounted spindle rack

of the lathe. However, if the window position does not allow this, the rack will have to go in the next place on the left. Details of construction are given which should be no trouble to a handyman, and the design can be varied at will. If a standing rack is decided upon, it should be secured to the bench.

Setting Up the Motor

The standard 1425 rpm electric motor is quiet and efficient and there is no reason why it should not be

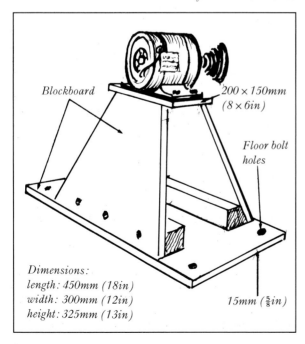

Blockboard

200 × 150mm
(8 × 6in)

Floor bolt
holes

Dimensions:
length: 450mm (18in)
width: 300mm (12in)
height: 325mm (13in)

15mm ($\frac{5}{8}$in)

bought from the nearest reliable source. A power of $\frac{1}{4}$ hp is adequate for the lighter lathes but $\frac{1}{3}$ hp would give a little more latitude; a modern lathe will require $\frac{1}{2}$ hp. The installation is really a job for the expert for, apart from the link-up to the mains, some safety cut-out should be provided in case of overload. The motor should run anticlockwise and its on/off switch should be set close to hand for the frequent speed changes, but not in a position which could allow it to be accidentally knocked.

The motor is best set up on a plinth about 300mm (12 in) from the floor which will bring the stepped drive and belt within manageable distance of the lathe. It must be firmly bolted to the plinth, and the plinth to the floor, with the shaft and counterdrive directly under and parallel to the lathe. The position may easily be determined by a plumb line dropped from above. The plinth may be an angle-iron bracket, a strong wooden plinth or, more simply, a concrete block cast within a stout wooden box, when the anchorages to the floor and motor can be secured by screws into the covering.

It is difficult to offer advice on the pulley system beyond the obvious; that it must fit the motor shaft and be in reciprocal relationship with the lathe pulley to give stepped speeds from about 300 to 3000 rpm, say 300 (slow), 600, 1000 (medium), 2000 and 3000 (fast), or as near as practicable to these. (The actual speeds of the author's own lathe are stepped at 365, 610, 950, 1425, 2137, 3325).

Much depends on the space available on, above and below the lathe shaft itself. Naturally, if the pulley is already attached, the task is much easier but either way the problem should be presented to an engineer, for off-the-shelf pulley systems are unlikely to solve the problems. Pulley belt channels may be round, flat or V-shaped, but for glass engraving the round belt is the best device. It grips adequately and is easy to change. A new lathe, of course, offers no difficulty, for the counter pulley supplied by the manufacturer is designed to give the correct range of speeds.

The Water Feed and Drip Tray

There should be no difficulty in providing a water drip feed to the wheel and a tray in which to catch the waste. Such a system is suggested in the illustration. A trouble free method is to provide a plastic vessel with a securely fitted valve which can regulate the water flow. A simple cut-off clasp on the plastic feed pipe to a syphon is cheaper but less effective.

The drip tray should be large enough for the average piece of work, approximately 500 × 375mm (20 × 15 in) with the corners cut away so as not to foul the elbows.

The Bench Pad

As the main action of wheel engraving depends on the manipulation of the hands and forearms working from the fixed fulcrum of the elbows, some protection for these vulnerable parts is very necessary. This may be solved in a variety of ways but the usual protection consists of a round pad, about 150 or 200mm (6 or 8 in) in diameter,

Details of a plinth on which to anchor the lathe motor

filled with sand, to permit a comfortable depression for a resting elbow. Sand is heavy enough to resist slipping

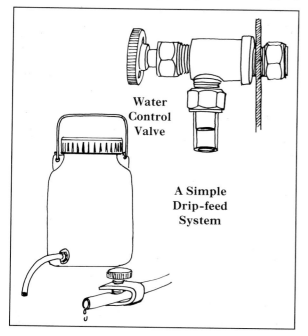

Water Control Valve

A Simple Drip-feed System

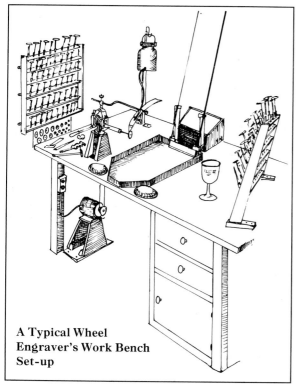

A Typical Wheel Engraver's Work Bench Set-up

under pressure, but if it is used the canvas or soft leather covering must be well sealed to prevent odd grains of sand from escaping. Bird seed or bran may be a softer and safer alternative, in which case some slip-resistant material could be attached to the bottom of the pad.

PREPARING THE SPINDLE

The machine drawing gives a clear picture of the construction and function of this unit. It is a slender, tapered, mild steel shank set into a lead base of the identical shape to the internal taper of the throat of the lathe.

The beginner might at first consider the lead based spindle an odd engineering solution to what, on the face of it, is a precision grinding problem, but the lathe must be seen rather as a sculpting tool, and the grinding process as a means to an artistic end. A few hours' work on well set up equipment will quickly endear the operator to the traditional mechanics which are beautifully fitted to the task: quick interchangeability of spindles, (many are required for the full range of engraving), simple controls for the readjustment or replacement of discs, and the firm seating or grip of the lead shank to the steel seating (keyway) giving a strong, vibrationless 'feel' from the power through the machine to the hands.

Not all spindles are set in lead. For some type of work, which will be discussed later, solid steel spindles are used, but for glass engraving the traditional design has proved to be the best solution.

Inserting, ejecting and Examining the Spindle

The spindle is inserted, or rather, thrown into the lathe head by a quick flick of the wrist so that the lead key firmly fits into its corresponding recessed keyway, in one single movement. What will in time become second nature needs practice and care at first, for if the spindle is inserted recklessly the key projection will be damaged. Therefore it must never be banged into position. If there is any impediment to the seating, even the slightest, the temptation to force it home must be resisted. It is as well, as a matter of habit, to wipe the shaft free of grit before every insertion, as grit is a common cause of trouble.

The removal of the spindle is almost self evident. A slot of about 20×5mm ($\frac{3}{4} \times \frac{7}{32}$ in) in the neck of the mandrel exposes the end of the inserted spindle which, in its design, provides a small projection to take the many blows of the ejection tool. This is best understood from the illustration. Hold the spindle in the left hand, insert the ejection tool into the slot with the right hand, and with a sharp leverage towards the machine and onto the base projection, release the spindle from its firm attachment (see illustration). The hands are in the opposite position from that to be expected, but experience shows that the firm away-thrust of the tool is better done with the right hand rather than the left.

It sometimes occurs that the steel shank is not perfectly secured in its lead base, perhaps due to some slight shrinkage following the casting. To take up this shake, which may be infinitesimal (a thousandth or so of an inch), two or three sharp blows, dead centre, is given to the spindle end as it sits in the lathe. The steel shank within the lead investment is so designed that any slight slackness will be taken up by a firmer bite into the surrounding metal. This precaution should be taken with every new spindle. If perfect it should emit a sharp metallic sound when it is tapped vertically by its blunt

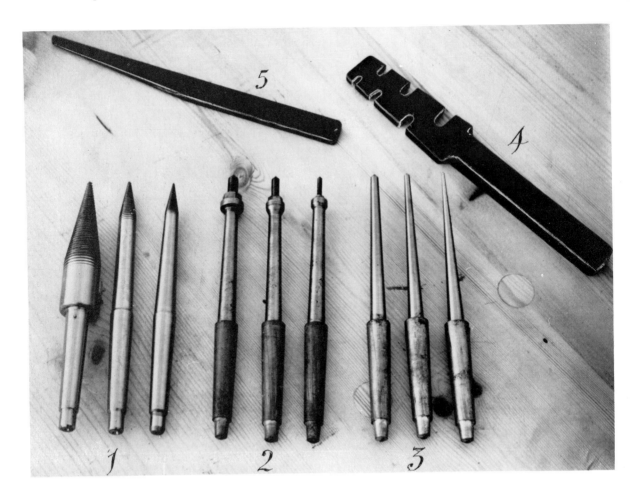

A selection of spindles:
1 Solid steel shanked spindles, screw tapered ends for heavy work
2 Lead shanked spindles with flange and nut for soft polishing felt or cork wheels
3 Orthodox spindles (large, medium and fine) for copper wheels
4 Bending iron
5 Ejector tool

Insertion of the spindle after lining up the key with the keyway of the mandrel

Ejection of the spindle showing the position of the hands to give the maximum leverage as the tool is pushed towards the machine

Showing the final section of the spindle being trued up. Note the position of the hands and the supporting thumb which gives better control to the bending action

end onto an anvil or metal billet. A sound which resembles that of a cracked cup indicates a defect.

Correcting the Spindle with the Bending Iron

Although the spindle may be, mechanically speaking, in first-class condition, it has still to be examined for concentricity. The spindle must run dead centre, and should be corrected if it does not, before the wheel is attached, for the slightest movement away from the axis will be magnified at the wheel. This defect can be corrected in the following manner.

With the spindle securely in position and the lathe switched to middle speed, a piece of chalk is firmly held in the hand – elbows anchored to the bench pads – and steadily offered to the underside of the revolving spindle, proceeding from the thick to the thin end of the tapered steel shaft. The chalk should just catch and mark the steel. Obviously, if the chalk marks the steel continuously around this section it means that the spindle is accurately centred for that particular position. Continue testing in this manner along the length of the spindle, towards the end.

However, if at any position along the spindle the chalk catches one side only, it is clearly running fractionally out of true. This is immediately corrected by the simple expedient of bending it straight. Find the correct slot in the spindle adjusting tool (the bending iron), that is, the slot which fits the diameter at the mark, grip this tool firmly (with arms and tool beneath the spindle), locate it to the uppermost chalk mark, and apply firm pressure to the stationary spindle away from the chalk mark towards the body of the lathe.

It will take a little experience to determine how much pressure should be exerted and it is, of course, much better to repeat the performance than finish up worse than at the start, but the adjustment must be persevered with until a continuous chalk mark is obtained on the running spindle before moving along the spindle to the next distortion.

All this may seem a tedious business but it is essential and is completed very quickly by a skilled engraver. In any event, it is something which is checked once only in the life of a spindle which should never be so seriously out of true as to require on average adjustment at more than one position and at worst at three positions

Flattening an eneven copper disc

Riveting the wheel to the spindle showing the position of the arms

THE COPPER WHEEL

The spindles come from the manufacturers without the cutting discs, consequently they have to be fitted up in profile, size or thickness, according to the cutting technique needed. It is more convenient to buy them pre-cut and holed to a prescribed size and thickness than to make them, though most engravers would have the equipment to do so.

Apart from the very thin discs (from 2mm, $\frac{3}{32}$ in downwards), which require a rebate of the spindle to support the rivet, most are simply riveted to the end of the tapered spindle, which may need to be modified to obtain a better seating. The steps in the preparation of this single spindle, which is to be the model for all others, will be described sequentially.

Flattening and Riveting the Wheel to the Spindle

For the first practice cut, use a flat copper wheel of about 15×4mm ($\frac{9}{16} \times \frac{3}{16}$ in); at this thickness it may be riveted directly to the end of the spindle. The centre hole of this disc, which should initially be too small for the spindle end, must be reamed larger until it reasonably fits the

tapered end, allowing about 2mm ($\frac{3}{32}$ in) to protrude.

With the spindle running at middle speed and the wheel held upright, but just slipping on the section to which it will be finally riveted, a few sharp taps with the hammer dead centre to the spindle end will tighten up the disc, causing it to pull away from the grip. For the final riveting, the thumb and fingers should support the back of the revolving wheel while the spindle end is repeatedly struck with the pin end of the hammer, first on the outer edge, then towards the centre and back again, until a nicely domed rivet is formed.

Any hammer blow should be struck clearly along the axis of the spindle. This is best done by pivoting the elbow on the bench and swinging the hammer in a constant arc so that each centre blow is identical.

Correcting the Wheel

Though the wheel may now be firmly riveted to a true spindle, it may not be square to its axis. The copper wheel must be flat before the engraver should ever consider using it. As with the correction of the spindle, chalk is used to discover how far it might be out of true by carefully just catching the face of the wheel, working from the centre

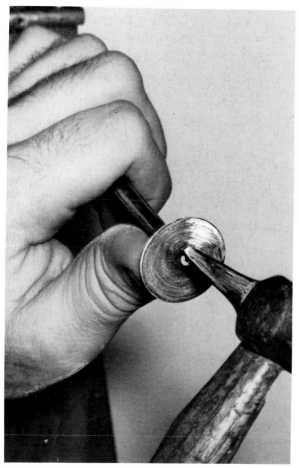

outwards. If the chalk mark is continuous, then obviously the wheel must be upright, but if one segment only is marked then it is out of true and must be corrected. This is simply done by putting the spindle at rest and, with the chalk mark vertical at the top, tapping the rivet edge nearest to the mark. The thumb should act as a buffer and a support to the back of the wheel in case the wheel itself is inadvertently struck. This procedure should be repeated until a continuous chalk mark is obtained. Two or more chalk marks in the initial test would indicate that the wheel is not sufficiently flat, and should never have been chosen in the first place.

Trueing and Forming the Profile Edge

The wheel should now revolve vertically and horizontally but it may still have the final defect of being slightly off centre, either because the reaming of the centre hole was done carelessly or because the original bore was never accurate. This is easily seen by a slight eccentricity in its revolving edge. As the profile is being formed (in this example it is semicircular) both the edge trimming and shaping can be done in one operation. With the machine set at high speed, apply a chisel-edged knife to the bottom of the wheel (about five o'clock position as seen from the front), and using the knife as a lathe turning tool, remove small parings of metal from the high spots.

There may at first be a tendency for the knife to chatter on the edge of the copper wheel, but the critical cutting angle is soon found and adjusted to. It is quicker and easier to trim the edges first until a right-angled mitre is formed, then to modify this shape to the one required, the first of which is dealt with in the next chapter.

A final precaution is to remove any imperfections or self-adhering specks of metal by turning the wheel against

Illustrating the position of the hand in trueing the wheel (making it upright). Note the chalk mark at the top of the wheel

Trimming and forming the profile with a knife

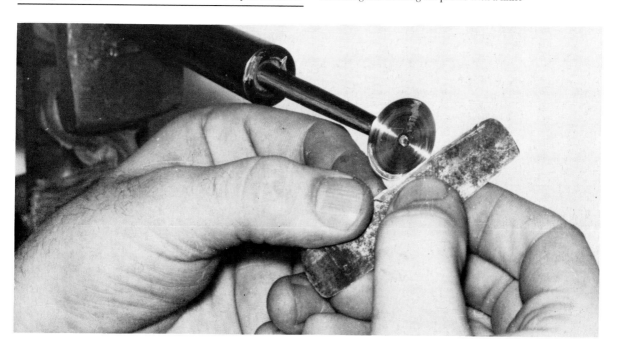

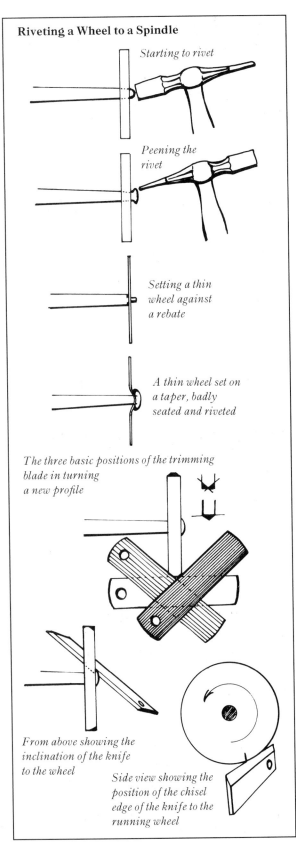

Riveting a Wheel to a Spindle

Starting to rivet

Peening the rivet

Setting a thin wheel against a rebate

A thin wheel set on a taper, badly seated and riveted

The three basic positions of the trimming blade in turning a new profile

From above showing the inclination of the knife to the wheel

Side view showing the position of the chisel edge of the knife to the running wheel

a piece of pumice stone which in a few seconds will give a clean smooth edge. Thick wheels may first need the attention of a fine file, but in every case when a profile has been attended to or there has been a change in abrasives it should be an automatic habit to clean up the edge with pumice stone. Each profile shape is dealt with progressively.

ABRASIVES

Grinding and Polishing Abrasives

A fairly wide variety of natural materials would have been available to the early glass and hardstone or jade carvers: quartz, garnet and black corundum (emery) for grinding, and pumice, tin or iron oxides, and a range of siliceous earths such as rotten-stone (decomposed limestone) for polishing. It is tempting for the artisan to guess that some secretive seal cutters may have used diamonds, but there is little evidence for this. With regard to Babylonian seals, it has been suggested that pumice may have been used as a grinding medium, but this would be so preposterously slow, as against other materials, that it can hardly have been so – even for those patient craftsmen.

The technology by which all these substances were crushed, sieved or floated for particle size grading is fascinating to speculate about, but almost all have given way to modern synthetic materials such as silicon carbide (carborundum), and pure aluminium oxide (corundum), both of which are very hard and obtainable in very accurate gradings.

For most of the wheel engraving presently to be described, the grinding material will be carborundum **320** mesh (grit). If there is a departure from this, the reasons for it will be given. It has been claimed by some experts that aluminium oxide (corundum) is a better alternative to silicon carbide (carborundum) as its sharper crystal structure gives more resistance to wear, but this has not been noticeable in practice. Diamond cutting materials will be discussed at a later stage.

Making Abrasive Paste

One level tablespoonful of carborundum powder is made up into a paste with a mixture of equal parts of paraffin (kerosene) and light machine oil (about half a teaspoonful of each) to the consistency of cream. Add the paraffin to the powder first in order to wet it thoroughly, and then follow with the oil, which should give a good working viscosity (body) to the mix. Allow it to stand until a small pool of oil separates out in the middle of the mixing dish. Any small stable dish will suffice but it would be best to choose a metal one that won't break; truant abrasive paste is a menace. The traditional binder was Colza (rape seed) oil.

Diagram describing the method of riveting and the angles of the knife when forming a profile

3 The Basic Cuts, Elementary Matting and Polishing

THE PRINTY

Everything is now ready for the first cut which, from the illustration, is seen to be a simple circular, concave lens – the printy. It is the first ballet step, as it were, to be mastered in a whole series before creative control can become possible.

'Printy' is one of those peculiar trade words which persists long after the origin has become obscure, though it has been suggested that it might refer to the shape of the imprint of a thumb. There are other competing terms, sometimes embracing both circular and olive-shaped cuts, such as 'prints' or 'punties', which may have greater validity, but to avoid any confusion the term 'printy' or 'printies' will be used throughout the text for circular lens-shaped cuts, large or small.

The Printy Wheel

The size of the first wheel has been set at 15×4mm ($\frac{9}{16} \times \frac{3}{16}$ in) but before the profile is finally determined it would be helpful to understand the simple geometry that is involved. If a truly circular printy is to be engraved, the shape of the profile must be an arc of the cutting wheel. This may be comprehended better if a solid sphere were to be used as the printy-forming tool instead of a disc. However, this can only be true for flat glass. In practice, most engraving takes place on curved surfaces upon which the same profile could form squat or elongated printies according to the angle or position of the cuts. Hence some common-sense adjustment must be made. From this and the illustrations, the following principles can be deduced.

1 The profile should be fitted to its purpose, approximat-

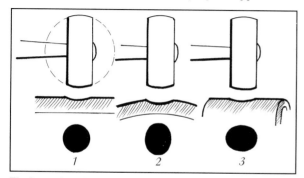

The formation of a printy (*from left to right*); cut on a flat surface; along the axis of a cylindrical glass; transverse to the axis

ing to the shallow arc of the wheel.

2 The size of the printy will be limited by the width of the wheel.

3 The larger or shallower the printy to be formed the larger and broader must be the cutting wheel.

4 Printies of equal area, but of greater depth, must be formed from smaller wheels of equal width.

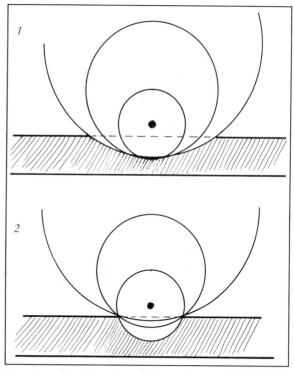

The cuts produced by various sized wheels. (*top*) For the same depth; (*bottom*) for the same width

Choice of Glass

With any of the basic cuts, up to the beginning of intaglio engraving, the choice of glass is unimportant; indeed it is invaluable to get the feel of every quality. If lead crystal blanks are easily available then there is every reason to use them, but as the first half a dozen glasses are bound to be experimental 'wasters', ordinary cheap commercial soda-lime glass will suffice.

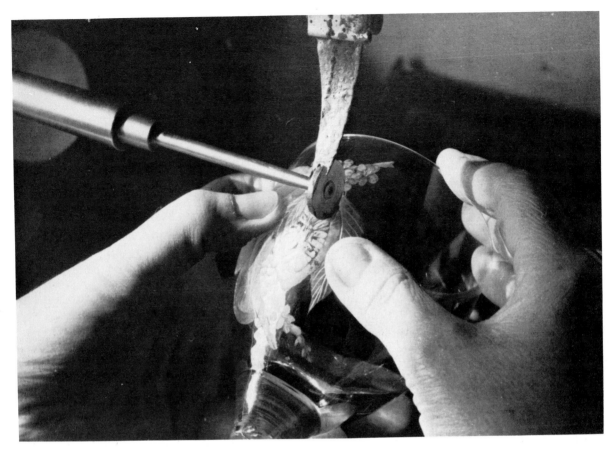

The position of the hands and fingers: note the position of the leather tongue riding on the wheel

The Use of the Leather Tongue

The value of this rather crude but effective piece of equipment can now be appreciated. The detachable leather tongue, which is ordinarily gripped between two pieces of hard 'spring' brass at the very end of the splash-guard, is positioned just forward of the top of the revolving wheel so that the abrasive can remain as long as possible on the cutting edge. A new leather tongue should be conditioned in the oil, for the obvious reason that new absorbent leather would inhibit its action.

The abrasive is selected from the edge of the paste pool in the dish and either fed to the wheel by a finger or offered to the wheel from the edge of the dish. The finger is the most efficient method, though it is a matter of choice and habit. As the wheel must be replenished every few seconds, or as soon as the bite of the carborundum weakens, the dip and wipe towards the bottom of the wheel becomes an automatic movement with scarcely an interruption to the concentration. At first too much or too little abrasive will be picked up – mostly too much – when the hands and glass will be plastered with oil but, with practice, enough will be picked up on the tip of the index finger to be wiped almost free by the edge of the wheel. It is a rule that each grade or type of abrasive must have its own container and separate leather tongue.

Engraving the Printy

The details of this first cut, and of all subsequent basic engraved shapes, upon which the whole expertise of wheel engraving is founded, will be set down sequentially as workshop instructions. For the abrasive paste use the standard mixture of carborundum 320 grit and oil.

1 Clean the bench. Clean the hands and glass. Use a different wiper for each purpose. Keep both wipers conveniently to hand, but habitually separated from each other. It would be quite reckless to get the cleaning rag which had been used for a newly filed wheel mixed up with the one used for the glass.

2 Set the speed at 800 – 1000 rpm (approximately middle speed). Position the leather tongue and charge the wheel with abrasive. Wipe the finger.

3 Take hold of the glass in an upright position with the fingers and thumbs. Position the thumbs forward and relatively close together. The glass must not be smothered, but firmly and flexibly held, with palms well away.

4 Make contact with the wheel so that the cut is effected just above and between the thumbs. Gently press. Too much pressure will squeeze the abrasive out of the cut. Let the abrasive on the profile do its work and gradually bite into the surface. As soon as the wheel makes contact, the ground glass/oil mix will settle around the edge of the cut and obscure the immediate result. The

cut is felt rather than seen.

5 After about five seconds wipe away any free oil and inspect the result. The printy should be circular, but at first is more likely to be elliptical. This is of no consequence for the moment; the feel and the efficiency of the cutting action is the most important consideration.

6 Keep repeating the cut until the process of recharging with abrasive, which is soon exhausted, becomes much more familiar, even though the printies at this stage may be quite rough.

7 Cut a small printy as well as possible. Wipe it clean and inspect it. Try to locate a second cut exactly into the centre of the first one so as to enlarge it and improve the shape. This may now be better controlled by very slightly rolling the cut, just fractionally around the periphery of the printy. This will improve the shape and give a finer quality to the ground surface. At the same time it will preserve the profile of the wheel.

8 Repeat until the action is under some control and it is possible to produce a number of roughly identical printies of about 4mm ($\frac{3}{16}$ in) in size.

Correcting the Worn Profile

At all times the quality of the printy should be critically examined. The slightest change in the shape of the lens to a more squarish circle is a clear warning that the profile has been worn to a flatter arc. This will usually happen at some moment during practice. As the skill improves the profile will be preserved for a much longer cutting time. When wheel wear does occur it is very simply corrected in the following way:

1 Push the leather tongue away from the wheel, set aside all abrasives and clear the engraving area.

2 Run the machine at fast speed and remove any grit adhering to the profile with pumice stone.

3 Correct the profile with a flat, medium to fine file.

4 Run the wheel into a pumice stone to clean up the profile.

5 Clean away all metal filing from the surrounding area with the appropriate wiper.

By now the apprentice engraver should be fairly well conditioned to the habits which make for clean handiwork, separating one action from another, and keeping metal work separate from glass; foreign particles of metal on wheel or tongue or hands can be a great nuisance, and can damage the glass.

Making Patterns with Printies

Chains

Chains of printies can be produced vertically or horizontally, in straight lines or curved. Engrave each subsequent printy in the chain as evenly as possible so that each one just touches the next, neither more nor less.

Rosettes

Roundels and rosettes are more difficult, for unless the printies are accurately positioned, the effect will be quite unpleasant. It takes time to judge the distance between one printy and the starting point for the next. If too close, one circle will bite into another and, if too far away, the printy will be too large by the time they do manage to touch.

A six-petalled rosette is a regular geometric figure, so all the cuts should fit snugly together. Proceed in the order:

A chain of printies with rosettes and roundels

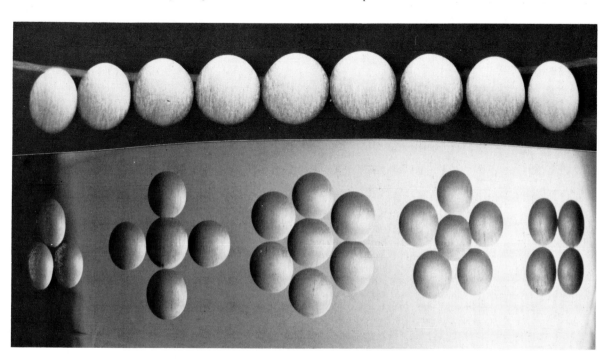

centre, top, bottom. Then fill in the gaps.

The way to achieve a five-petalled rosette shape is either to bite into the centre printy or to start with a smaller centre. Proceed in the order: centre, twelve o'clock, twelve minutes to, and twelve minutes past the hour. Then – with trepidation – fill in the remainder. All such work should be engraved freehand.

Practising and Experimenting

It should be said that it is easier to engrave small printies with a small wheel than a large one. Larger and thicker wheels have their own problems; they are less likely to remain in the shallower arc of the cut, but by the time they are to be used for this purpose it will be an extension of skills already well controlled. After one or two tumblers are covered with every experimental cut and combination of the printy, a keen pleasure in some of that control will have been gained. None of it is easy. Even the most skilled operator may occasionally be stampeded by a careless or ill-formed printy which will call for all his ingenuity to put right.

All this may appear rather daunting, but it is a basic

Detail of a Silesian carafe, 1740, containing large matt and small polished printies; note that when they are overcut – run into each other – they become hexagonal or honeycombed

discipline well worth the mastering. These cutting exercises closely follow the traditional practical methods of the Bohemian glass schools, which the serious apprentice should not avoid. Some artists may not warm to, or be patient with, such exercises. They may think their design capacity is powerful enough to enable them to stop short of some wheel cutting expertise. If this be so, it would be better to find some freer approach to glass than the wheel.

THE OLIVE

The Olive Wheel

The shape of this cut is exactly as one would expect from the word, a neat olive, an elliptical lens, as it were, with the width and depth to complement the printy. However, in order to match up the character of the two shapes, a larger wheel is needed for the olive, 25mm (1 in), of the same width as the printy, 4mm ($\frac{3}{16}$ in), but with a much

Islamic glass, eighth to tenth century AD, showing the powerful use of printies (*British Museum*)

more arched profile. Therefore a new spindle must be set up, following the procedures of riveting and trueing as described in Chapter 2.

Of course, as one's engraving widens in scope many more individual tools will be added to the range and fortunately, once made, have virtually permanent value. As they wear down they can be used for the cut previously undertaken by a smaller wheel. Thus each will take a progressive step down in the spindle rack until it is so small as to call for a new wheel to be freshly fixed to – what by then will have become – an old and familiar spindle.

Engraving vertical Olives

1 Use the standard abrasive paste used for the printy. Set the machine to middle speed, approximately 800 rpm. The increased peripheral speed of the larger olive wheel, at these small diameters, is not all that significant, but it could be run a little slower than the printy wheel.
2 Offer the glass vertically to the wheel and gently allow the tool to make its natural impresseion. If necessary amend the shape of the profile until a good olive has been obtained. (The more arched the curve of the profile, the longer and deeper the olive.)
3 Carefully locate the wheel into one of the practice olives and gradually enlarge it to almost the maximum width of the wheel, 4mm ($\frac{3}{16}$ in). This is best done by imperceptibly rolling the wheel about the edge of the olive.
4 Continue until a fair number of consecutive, identically sized olives have been secured.

Engraving Horizontal Olives

Repeat the foregoing steps but this time take the wheel horizontally across the glass. Engraving olives in this direction is a little more troublesome, for the cut is tangential to the circle of the glass; consequently the natural shape will be shorter – more squat. Therefore the wheel will have to be dragged out, fore and aft of its natural cutting position, in order to give an olive of the same size as that cut vertically.

At first this elongated olive may be marred by ridges or 'creases' across the cut caused by the wheel as it is dragged one way and then the other from its initial cut. As the wheel moves it has a tendency to reseat itself in the new position and the changed arcs of cut throw up the creases. However, a few gentle strokes should soon smooth out the imperfections.

Making Patterns with Olives and Printies

Chains

Judge the cuts so that one just touches the edge of the other. Cut both vertical and horizontal chains of equal size; olives singly or olives and printies combined alternately.

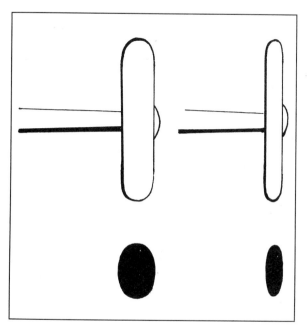

Diagram of the olive-forming wheel profile and cut

Left:
Detail of a very rare sampler, probably of Newcastle origin, 1809, signed by the engraver, J. Richardson. It was used as a pattern book for clients who wished to select a particular motif for their domestic glass. The goblet is divided into four panels which contain every combination of basic wheel engraved forms which entered into the decoration of that time. Olives in various forms, matt and polished, are illustrated

Rosettes

Cut the centre printy first. Follow with four even olives at right angles to each other. Fill in the remaining olives as evenly as possible to complete a neat rosette, with each component smoothly engraved.

Experimenting with combinations

The combinations illustrated by no means exhaust the patterns which may be engraved; the student may find some relief from what he may think cruel drudgery by making experiemnts of his own. And there are no rules that these cuts should always just touch, though this style should be mastered. They may be separated equidistant from each other – though this is not so simple either. However, by the time another two glass tumblers have been covered with these experimental patterns a certain satisfaction may have been gained from the knowledge that the wheel is beginning to produce what is asked of it.

Olives and printies in decorative combination

Roman bowl decorated with large olives, about third century AD (*British Museum*)

LINE WORK

The Line Wheel

Set up a new spindle with a copper wheel measuring 35×1.5 mm ($1\frac{3}{8} \times \frac{1}{16}$ in). It must be remembered that a thin wheel should be riveted against a rebate turned from the end of the spindle, allowing enough substance, in this case about 4mm ($\frac{3}{16}$ in), to ensure a sturdy rivet anchorage. Rivet with great care to avoid distortion. Turn and true up the profile to a very acute mitre (V shape) but with the cutting edge very slightly rounded. Handle the finished spindle with respect, for the thin wheel may easily be buckled. Tougher (beer can) alloy is useful.

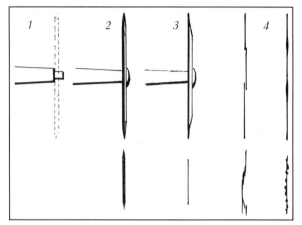

Abrasive

Use a 400 mesh (grit) carborundum/oil paste (2 parts oil, 1 part paraffin) which is rather finer than that used earlier. It ensures a smooth, fine line from the very incisive profile.

Speed

Set the speed to slow, on account of the greater peripheral speed and rapidity of cut from the sharp cutting edge of the relatively large wheel.

Engraving Straight Lines

1 To get the feel of the tool, cut a series of single thin lines, long and short, in one comfortable movement of the glass. Continue the exercise by engraving several lines in parallel and equidistant – as far as is possible at this

Diagram of the line wheel (*from left to right*): the spindle mounting; the line wheel and its corresponding cut; an alternative profile shape; some early imperfect lines

An exercise glass employing straight lines and four-pointed stars

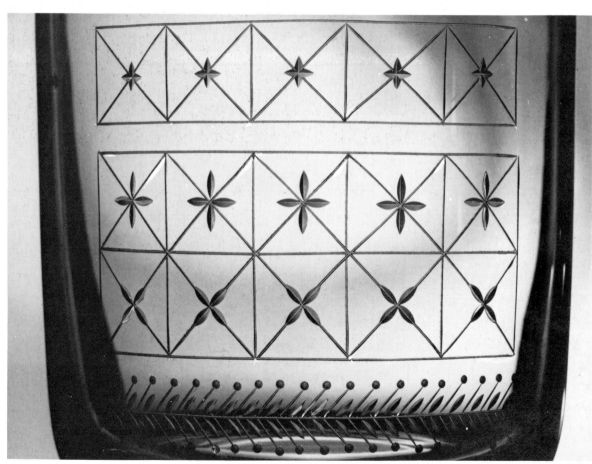

Souvenir glass about 1900, Cologne; a vigorously naïve use of the line wheel

Engraving Curved Lines

1 Mark out and cut an undulating line of about 25mm (1 in). Follow this with a second interlacing line.

2 Cut parallel, curved, wavy lines.

3 Invent and engrave straight and curved lined patterns incorporating the star.

Exercise glass: curved lines and six-pointed stars in a repeated pattern

stage. As the bite of the profile is quite fierce, the tool should be allowed to do its work without undue pressure; remember that line wheels are thin and vulnerable.

2 Keeping the glass stationary to the wheel, engrave a regular four and eight-pointed star made up of very short intersecting lines. There is no difficulty in controlling the length and quality of one-stroke lines, for the profile rapidly settles itself into the surface of the glass when the length of line is determined by the pressure, but some difficulty must be expected in accurately fixing the centre of the six intersecting lines. Continue producing the stars until several of approximately equal size and quality have been obtained.

3 With white or black gouache, thin enough to flow from a pen, mark out a series of evenly spaced intersecting zigzags, at about 15mm ($\frac{5}{8}$ in) intervals. Cut as accurately as possible to this pattern. Make sure the thin lines just meet and do not extend too far.

4 Fill in the spaces with parallel lines.

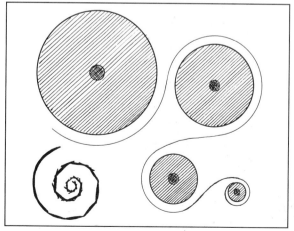

The principle upon which a curved line is based: the wheel should be approximately the same size as the circle it cuts. The closed small spiral is made up from series of segments which are subsequently smoothed out

As a guiding principle, a wheel cannot correctly cut the arc of a circle smaller than its own diameter. In practice, the best results are obtained when the cutting wheel is a little smaller than the circle it is attempting to cut, but the engraver will soon experience the practical limitations.

Line Exercises

When the engraver feels that he has mastered tight curves, the next task in order of difficulty would be complete circles (the virtuoso performance of a regular continuous spiral is something for the future). A further difficulty to be overcome in cutting a long line, straight or curved, is getting back into it again after the cut has been interrupted by a change of hand position in recharging the wheel. It will take a deal of exercise before the wheel can be entered into an unfinished cut without visible trace of a 'knot'.

A glass designed entirely on mitre linework; 'Pluma' by Peter Dreiser (*Victoria and Albert Museum*) (*above*)

Example of a commercial J. & L. Lobmeyer plate demonstrating the difficulties encountered in engraving a close spiral; Bohemia, about 1920 (*above right*)
Edwardian English engraved plate showing superb control over the linework and close spirals; about 1900 (*right*)

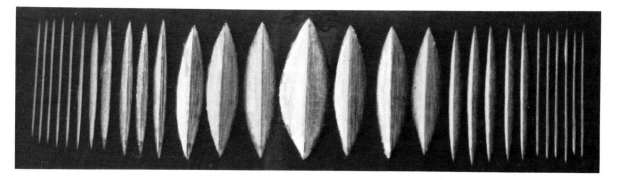

THE MITRE WHEEL

If the profile of a line wheel is accurately trimmed back to a sharp angle of about 30°, the engraved line formed from it will have the inverse shape: a channel having two equal facets. Obviously the shape and quality of the cut will vary according to the size and width of the copper wheel and the angle of the mitre. Thus an olive or printy forming wheel amended this way will produce what may be described as a split-mitred-olive or printy, but the single cut is more in the nature of a small leaf.

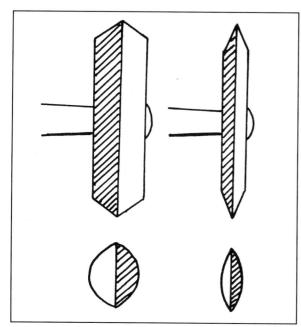

The profile of the mitre wheel and its cut

The mitre wheel (as distinct from sharp line wheels) is rarely used for normal copper wheel engraving and the cut (as a motif) does not become effective until it is quite large, for example in *intaglio* engraving where sharp, hard and wear-resistant stones can be used, for it is the difficulty of keeping the mitre very sharp which is the main obstacle to its use. Once the apex of the profile has become blunted – and this happens very quickly – the resulting cut becomes unpleasantly amorphous. However, where a motif depends for its effect on a sharp,

Cuts from four different widths of mitre wheels showing the point at which the cut made by the thinnest mitre becomes indistinguishable from a line cut

faceted cut – for example the centre leaf of a fleur de lis or in a sharply incised monogram – the mitre wheel is invaluable.

As they are infrequently used, mitres may be prepared from existing line, printy or olive wheels as the need arises, the only requirement being flat, even angles leading to a precise point. For the purpose of gaining some experience with this type of engraving, two wheels should be prepared: one for narrow mitred lines, the other for small leaf motifs.

Mitre line work

Wheel: 50 × 2mm (2 × $\frac{3}{32}$ in), 45° mitre angle.

Abrasive: 400 carborundum/oil mix.

Speed: rather slow.

Straight lines

There is little difference between handling a mitre and a line wheel beyond the constant preoccupation with its sharpness.

1 Engrave a series of parallel lines.
2 Re-enter a cut line in order to lengthen it. This is slightly easier with a mitre wheel than line wheel because it more readily seats itself in the sharp channel of the cut.

Curved lines

1 Engrave a series of shallow curved lines.
2 Engrave a series of arched curved lines. No difficulty should be experienced with gentle curves but the more arched the curve the more unequal are the facets of the cut likely to be. This is due to the need to lean the wheel over slightly in order to negotiate the curve.

Flared curves

Valuable use of the mitre line wheel, particularly where lettering is concerned, is obtained by increasing its width at the centre of a curve as, for example, in an S curve. If sharp, the wheel (depending on its width and angle) will give an almost calligraphic brilliance to a line which no other tool can equal. In order to control the shape of the

Illustrating the shape of the facets cut by a mitre wheel on acute curves; Rheinbach School, 1950

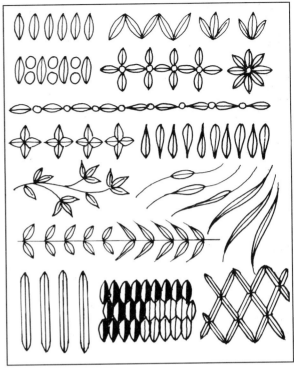

Some simple combinations of the mitre cut

double curve it is best to deal with it in the following manner.

1 Engrave the first half of the curve from the centre to the end, gradually diminishing the depth of the wheel.

2 Reverse the glass and repeat the action with the second half when a balanced S curve should be obtained. If difficulty is found in controlling the shape, cut in a fine pilot line first.

3 Where the two halves meet, enter the mitre wheel and gradually increase the strength and width of the line by slowly stroking the wheel in both directions until the line has an uninterrupted, brilliant flared appearance; that is, having a broad centre nicely diminishing towards fine pointed ends.

4 Repeat this exercise in the other direction: a reversed S.

The Mitred Leaf or Wedge Cut

Wheel: 20 × 3mm ($\frac{3}{4}$ × $\frac{1}{8}$ in).

Abrasive: 400 carborundum/oil mix.

Speed: medium slow (rather faster than the line wheel).

1 Make a single, stationary cut vertical to the glass. A little movement fore and aft of this mitre cut is permissible but it should not be moved or rocked as with the printy. A straightforward, equal-facetted leaf shape should result. This can be dragged out to a more elongated leaf shape.

2 Cut a series of single mitre cuts close to one another.

3 Cut a simple, four-pointed star. Maintain equal length to each component.

4 Form a chain of alternate mitre cuts and printies.

Combination of Line and Leaf Cuts

1 Cut a single, straight mitre line and set the leaves in neat parallel pairs against it.

2 Invent various motifs of the same kind as suggested in the illustrations.

The mitre cut should prove no more difficult than engraving the printies and olives; indeed, it might be found a little easier for the reason that the wheel is self seating. Every variation of angle and width of wheel should be experimented with in order to appreciate the practical limitations. It will be found that as the angle increases, the balance of the facets will be more difficult to keep even. Beyond about 120° the wheel may be difficult to control.

Developing Expertise

In these latter exercises the engraving is now starting to move over the surface of the glass, the hands freely changing position as they reach the limit of control or change of course. It is the beginning of flexibility.

Some fine examples of early glass exist which demonstrate the powerful decorative effect that can be obtained from the elementary cuts of the printy, olive and line wheels. But their simplicity may at times so beautifully complement the shape of the glass as to become part of the sculptural form, and in these instances the word 'decoration' can hardly apply. The engraver has much to learn from such work.

MATTING

Many fine effects may be obtained by grinding selected areas of glass to a white satin surface known as matting. An examination of a few pieces of matted glass, either etched or wheel produced, will show that the quality can vary enormously from an unpleasant, greasy, coarse grain to a fine, white matt. Every quality of finish will sooner or later have its use, but for small glass an even, white, luminous matt is the most attractive.

The Rounded Strap Wheel

Perhaps the best introductory task is to matt in an area of about 20 × 20mm ($\frac{3}{4}$ × $\frac{3}{4}$ in) and for this a new wheel is required, 40 × 3mm ($1\frac{5}{8}$ × $\frac{1}{8}$ in), having a square profile with the sharp edges just blunted (see illustration). (This tool is also known as the panel wheel.) In this instance (for matting), a 'rounded strap' is required.

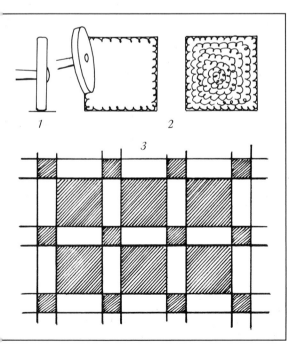

1 The rounded strap profile
2 The method of filling in an area
3 The exercise linework pattern to be matted

Abrasive

For the abrasive use two level teaspoonsful of carborundum 320 mixed with about a teaspoonful of water. Oil may be used but a water mix gives a better, whiter matt.

Mix the abrasive with water into a good slurry and allow it to stand for a short time. When it has become thoroughly wetted and of an even consistency, a small pool of excess water should settle out. As with the oil/carborundum mix, the wheel should be charged with the paste from the edge of the puddle.

In general, the finer the abrasive the finer the matt, but there are increasing difficulties beyond 400 grit. Certainly, at 600 grit it is very difficult to maintain a smooth, even surface.

Speed

The speed should be extremely slow. Matting requires a slow, soft, abrasive and brushing movement over the glass surface and it is in the control of this action that the manually operated lathe can be superior to its modern counterpart where the slow speeds are fixed and limited. However the modern lathe does this job adequately.

The Matting Process

Experiment with the matting wheel on an open area of glass to get the feel of the cut. Keep the profile as square to the glass surface as possible using the slightest pressure; just abrade the surface. The tool should never be stationary, but must be continuously moved over the surface with a slight rotary motion, matting the area as methodically as possible.

When a small, reasonably matted area has been achieved – irrespective of the condition of edges – prepare for more disciplined matting:

1 Mark out the glass in a simple pattern of squares, 20 × 20mm ($\frac{3}{4}$ × $\frac{3}{4}$ in) separated by 6mm ($\frac{1}{4}$ in) spaces.

2 With the same line wheel used in the previous exercise, engrave the pattern of squares.

3 Take the squared-up glass and fill in one large square in the following manner: starting from the most convenient side of the square which can be seen during the operation, say the left-hand side, matt very slightly away from the cut line, with a gently rotary movement, gradually drawing the wheel towards the edge to fill in the initial gap, for the full length of the side.

4 Continue in the same way with the second, then the third and fourth side, to end with a hollow square.

5 Mop up the centre much in the manner of harvesting corn, moving gradually round the uncut edges until the very centre is left. But this implies the need for orderly matting rather than a strict system.

6 Continue with the remaining pattern of large and small squares until the matting technique is reasonably under

control, that is, smooth with no overrun edges.

Although the action of matting has been set down sequentially, the process is a continuous one of cut and recharge, of examination and recut, keeping a shrewd lookout for any deterioration of the wheel during the process. The wheel, if properly used, will keep itself flat, but the profile edges may sharpen up; when this is allowed to happen, deeper streaks will appear within the matt. The remedy is obvious; file the sharp edges back to a slight round.

Matting Exercises

It stands to reason that the larger the wheel, the greater the area of glass it will cover, but there are practical limits which only experience can determine. In the present example, a 40×3mm ($1\frac{5}{8} \times \frac{1}{8}$ in) wheel for a 20×20mm ($\frac{3}{4} \times \frac{3}{4}$ in) square of matt is considered about right, but it may be found that smaller wheels could give the engraver more room for manoeuvre, or allow corners to be entered more easily. As one progresses, methods or rules give way to experience and personal choice in how best to overcome the difficulties that arise. Suffice it to say that, at the present level of experience, the first attempts will not be very good. Overrun edges, bludgeoned corners, and discontinuous or overworked matting (ruined by attempts to fill in tiny areas of missed unmatted glass) will result in uneven, hammered, or cloud shaped patches, and will form the inevitable early disasters.

However, the main difficulties of accuracy and evenness should have been overcome in a reasonable period and, at the same time, experience in moving the glass around the

An example of matting; part of a sampler glass; a very good exercise in controlled matting

wheel will have been increased.

Matting is a very important technique and it is an exercise not to be underestimated. It is incorporated in every kind of design, as a background foil to figurative or decorative engraving, as textural effects in landscape and, perhaps most exacting of all, in the portrayal of 'fields' in heraldry.

POLISHING

This is a subject which could be separated into a chapter by itself. It is used for a great number of purposes: polishing pure and simple, the high lighting of details in engraved designs, the modulation of matted surfaces, and the removal of errors or accidental damage. Polishing wheels and abrasives vary considerably in substance and use, as does the type of engraving which will benefit from polishing. Therefore, rather than risk confusion by simply listing techniques, it is better to discuss each use as it naturally arises. This exercise is directed solely to polishing printies and olives (and small mitre cuts).

Polishing Wheels

Polishing wheels may be made up of various materials: lead, wood, rubber, cork or felt. In this instance a lead wheel is used, which in its finished state should exactly match in size and profile the copper wheel that originally cut the printy or olive. Perhaps for the most comfortable action it could be fractionally smaller, but it will soon wear to a snug fit into the printy. An oversize wheel is useless for, clearly, it will only polish the edges.

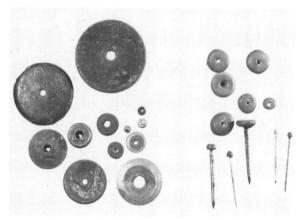

Polishing wheels. The left-hand group are lead wheels, the right-hand group are very small wheels made from expoxy resin with various abrasives

Preparing the Wheel and Spindle

A roughly shaped lead disc, approximating in size to the printy or olive but large enough to allow for trimming, is screwed directly on to a special spindle, the end of which is provided with a tapered thread. Threaded spindles are obtainable with fine, medium and coarse threads, the choice depending upon the size and substance of the wheel. In this case, with small lead wheels, it is obvious that the best grip will be obtained by the screw having the greatest number of effective 'bites' to the millimetre (or inch'. If a new spindle is not available, it is not beyond an engraver's ingenuity to file a thread on the end of an old one – certainly experienced workers would think nothing of this – but it would be worthwhile examining a professionally made one first, for the threads are similar to a wood screw, and are not particularly fine.

There is no difficulty in making lead discs. Sufficient lead can be melted in a ladle to cast several different sized wheels in a plaster of Paris mould, but the mould must be dry, and the usual precautions must be taken against accident or fire. Actually, glass engravers' apprentices did the job more simply by pouring small quantities of molten lead onto a dry board where the metal would naturally settle into circular blobs which, when cold, could be hammered flat, roughly shaped, and selected for size.

Mounting the Wheel

A small hole is drilled or punched in the centre of the chosen wheel and, with the spindle in position on the machine, is screwed tightly on to the thread. This is best done by holding the spindle firmly by the left hand and moving it backwards and forwards until the wheel held in the right hand is upright enough, and the screw entered securely enough, to continue. Whether the wheel is finally screwed on against the spindle or vice versa is a matter of choice. After a few turns, the wheel will be firmly held by

the bite of the lead on the tapered thread. Being soft, it can easily be trimmed to match the printy in size and profile by turning off the excess metal with the knife tool. If handled carefully the thread will last the life of the wheel. In the case of the mitre cut, the lead wheel may prove too soft to maintain a sharp angle, in which event the matching wheel must be turned from plywood.

The Polishing Process

Polishing medium: mix 400 grit (mesh) pumice with water.

Speed: in the middle range, about 800 – 1000rpm.

1 Select a well shaped printy from the earlier exercise. Charge the wheel as usual and enter the printy in the same direction as it was originally cut.
2 Using gentle pressure, roll the tool slightly in the cut. This will ensure even polishing and maintain the profile of the wheel.
3 Recharge the wheel as the polishing power diminishes. This may have to be repeated two or three times. Take great care to make a clean re-entry of the tool.
4 Complete the polishing by allowing the pumice-mix to dry out gradually on the running wheel, gently rolling all the time, which by the time it is just powder dry should have brought the printy to a sharp and brilliant lens.

Common defects

Several defects may be thrown up during this process:

1 White streaks in the printy indicate that the printy was imperfectly cut in the first place.
2 Black streaks of lead embedded in the surface matt may be caused mostly by excess pressure and friction, or by premature drying out of the polishing paste.
3 Rounded edges or trailing tails are due to the wheel slipping out of its cut.

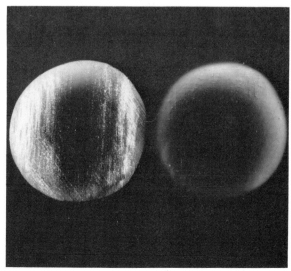

A badly polished printy is shown on the left

Detail of a late Victorian port glass, about 1880, using polished olives and printies

The only cure for white or black streaks is to repeat the whole cycle of polishing again. The last fault is virtually incurable, but it might be comforting to know that this is not an easy thing to do, and even a skilled engraver will surprise himself by producing a poorly polished printy. The lead wheel will enter well enough, but at the slightest pause in concentration, the tool will slip out of the printy with a complaining squeal, or so it seems, and with each slip some small damage to the sharp edge of the printy will have been inflicted. By polishing, printies or olives are shown up for what they really are, and it may require a return to the first exercise for new, improved samples, before satisfaction with polishing is reached.

Polishing within a Matt Area

When a reasonable level of control has been gained, take the experimental glass from the previous exercise, now matted in a pattern of neat squares, and cut a printy dead centre in each square. Polish these printies to a sharp brilliant contrast with the surrounding matt.

The shortcomings of even a decent effort are much more cruelly exposed when the polishing is set against a matt

area, for the slightest slip will polish the surrounding matt and impair the effect. All the same, there is a great pleasure and reward for the engraver even if he is only moderately successful. The counterpoint of a clear polished lens against white matt is an aesthetic element unique to glass.

EDGE CUTS

The Sharp Strap Wheel

Every wheel, so far described, has been used vertically to the glass surface, but the sharp strap wheel, which has a square, flat, but sharp profile, can be used much more flexibly. By directing the cut from the sharp edge gradually over to the full flat of the profile, a whole combination of shapes may be developed. In its full use, the strap can be considered as the detail-making tool, the work of which complements more robust sculptural cutting.

It is as well to know in advance that this is a difficult cut to control – sometimes irritatingly wayward – and is one that the professional returns to with equal caution. Further, it is useless to proceed without sharp profiles, for without them, a crisp entry to any shape is impossible.

Several different sized wheels, in diameter and width, would normally be available to the glass engraver, but the size chosen for this exercise is $40 \times 3mm$ ($1\frac{1}{2} \times \frac{1}{8}$ in). The profile must be flat, sharp and square.

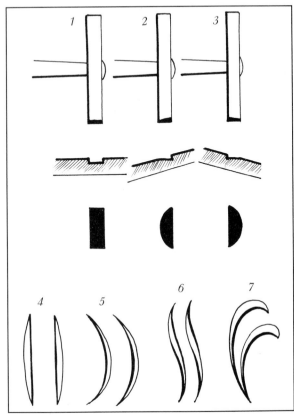

Cutting Half Moons

Abrasive: 320 carborundum/oil

Speed: medium slow

1 Make a few experimental cuts into the glass by angling the wheel about 45° to the surface. Allow the profile to cut its natural shape, which will be a half moon. Increase and decrease the angle of cut, which will determine the width of the half moon.

2 When the shape is somewhat under control, engrave a single line of continuous narrow and fat half moons. A fine line, engraved beforehand, will help in keeping the chains neat and straight.

Cutting Segments

1 Cut a few straight lines to act as a guide.

2 Enter the tool at an angle of 45°.

3 Draw out the cut, keeping the sharp edge of the wheel on the line, but gradually increasing its width by progressively inclining the flat of the profile to the glass. When half the required length is reached, continue with the cut but reverse the action. The result should be a balanced but narrow segment, narrower than that finally required.

4 Relocate the tool in the cut and repeat the action several times, leaning over a little more on each successive cut, until a nicely balanced segment of the desired width is reached, say of 2.5–3mm ($\frac{1}{8}$ in) in the centre. It is as well to enter and leave the cut a little short of the full length, as the repeated action may produce rather blunt, disfiguring ends to the segment. These can be sharpened up with a brief lick of the tool at the last moment.

5 When the technique has been mastered, engrave straight, even chains.

Cutting Crescents

This is a very similar cut but rather more difficult.

1 Line out the inner edge of a crescent, that is, part of a circumference of a circle of 40mm ($1\frac{1}{2}$ in) in diameter.

The sharp strap wheel (*opposite page*)
1 The shape and profile of the sharp strap and its vertical cut
2 The shape of cut from the right-hand edge of the wheel
3 The shape from the left-hand edge of the wheel (half moons)
4 The segment cut (elongated half moon)
5 The crescent cut
6 Reversed crescent cut
7 A widely used decorative variation of the crescent edge-cut

Cuts from the sharp strap

2 Follow the guideline with the sharp corner of the profile, gradually thickening and then diminishing the cut, outwards, to form a very thin crescent.

3 Relocate and recut and, by a series of long, continuous, stroking movements along the whole length of the shape, gradually build up the crescent to the required thickness and character. As with the segments, allow for the extreme sharp ends. The resulting crescent should be continuously smooth and of a fine, crisp shape.

Some simple shapes flow naturally from these exercises which may be incorporated into free patterns, such as those illustrated. It is not now necessary to analyse each particular element. Experience will show that these organic leaf shapes are best controlled by very sharp profiles firmly building up from the wider to the thinner portion of what might be a running design, a leaf or a reed.

Decorative variations of the edge cut

Slipping

When a strap wheel is used so that the cut started on one profile edge is allowed to slip out and move forward to the

A very fine J. & L. Lobmeyr plate, 'Morning Star', 1880, showing the control in the decorative use of the edge cut

A mid-eighteenth century English decanter, demonstrating the versatile use of the sharp strap on the flat stalk, and the edge cuts on the serrated rose leaves and the smaller crescent leaves

other edge, a shallow, flowing, leaf shape is produced. It is difficult to engrave a smooth, firm shape like the one illustrated, for as the full flat of the profile meets the glass, before it moves over to the bite of the further edge, the wheel tends to wander. However, though limited, it is a valuable addition to the repertoire, and well worth mastering.

Using the Strap Wheel

The strap wheel, of one size or another, is a most important tool. It is useful for every purpose: for lettering, for the refinement of more sculptured forms, and for the addition of all kinds of detail, from an eyebrow to the thorns on a stem or the points on a leaf. Naturally, as time goes on, it will be used with less rigidity than the exercises imply, or rather, more fluidly, but the basic disciplines must be there to underpin that freer use, so deceptive to the onlooker.

ASSESSING PROGRESS

At this juncture, it would be valuable for the independent, and perhaps isolated learner, to be able to measure his progress. Without a teacher to advise, correct and assess, he is at a grave disadvantage, but enthusiasm and application may more than make up for this loss. Roughly speaking, an apprentice at a glass school, working some 15 to 20 intermittent hours at the lathe each week, would have reached a fair ability in these exercises in about three months, but he would not have entirely mastered them. There would be many awkward shapes of glass or positions of even simple cuts to keep him anxiously on the edge of his stool.

Better than measuring time at the wheel is to assess, without self deception, the degree of confidence that has been attained. If the engraver knows what is wanted with every formal shape of cut and, without thinking, knows how to get it with a modest degree of success, he is ready for freer, more creative engraving.

The only way this can be introduced is to set a series of model tasks which the professional glass engraver would commonly face, and explain as clearly and methodically as possible the order and manner in which the job would be tackled. But it must be firmly borne in mind that another professional engraver may have a different personal approach to what is, henceforward, a matter of sculptural form and sensibility. If one glass engraver's method appears to differ diametrically from another, the proper conclusion to be drawn by the student is not that one or the other must be wrong, but that both methods must be tried so as to extract the best benefit from both.

The shapes produced by controlled slipping with the sharp strap:
1 an enlarged diagram giving the position of the wheel and the direction of the cut for a shallow slip-leaf shape
2 the different starting position and direction for a similar shape
3 slipping in serrations
4 and 5, alternative formations

Cut samples of slipping (*above right*)

The shoulder of a Victorian carafe decorated with shallow slipped leaves combined with printies (*below*)

4 Intaglio Engraving

GENERAL PRINCIPLES OF INTAGLIO ENGRAVING

Before embarking on intaglio engraving, many of its problems may be considered in advance by the close examination of good examples, particularly if one, or even a piece of one, is available for continuous handling. Apart from being a reference to accents of cutting or polishing which gives life or vitality to a design, it can be better understood how the illusion of relief is created from an intaglio cut form, in that those parts which appear nearest to the eye of an observer are, in fact, the most deeply cut and, conversely, those seen as farthest away are the shallowest.

How this illusion comes about is not easy to explain. At its simplest level, an isolated printy or lens will be seen both as convex or concave, whichever the mind seizes upon, a condition aptly described by Professor Gombrich as 'visual deadlock'. But once the lens is related, for example, to the mouth of a fish, it cannot be perceived in any other way but as a spherical bubble. Thus, once the mind is given a clue to reality – in any media – it will perceive the object in terms of past experience, even against common sense.

It is a good idea to take plasticine impressions of good intaglio work, glass or seals, so that the design method and skills may be critically appreciated. Indeed, it is a common workshop practice to make impressions of exacting forms as the work proceeds. Breathe on the glass before making the impression to get a clean release of the plasticine or putty.

Choice of Glass

The range of glass from which the wheel engraver may choose will vary from hard soda-lime glass to the very soft lead crystal. The wheel will tackle them all equally, though it is self-evident that the more resistant the material the more the cutting problems, such as time and wheel wear, will arise; for this reason the tendency will be to choose the coftest glass.

Whole full lead crystal (see the appendix) is universally used for wheel engraving, it could be said that this may be beyond the limit required for tactile pleasure; 20–24% lead, for example, is preferable to 30–33%. An engraver who had worked on hard Bohemian crystal glass would find full lead glass soapy by comparison, and the ultimate matt a little less crisp and silky. However, such predilection for hard or soft material would not be of great concern to a professional wheel engraver.

For the purposes of the earlier exercises any reasonable quality of glass would have sufficed. Indeed, it would be a surprise if, in desperation for experimental glass, beer or wine glasses had not been tried, but for intaglio work it would be sensible to search for glass of good quality, perhaps 'seconds' of either medium or full lead crystal. It is rather expensive, but there is no escape.

Marking Out the Design

There are a dozen different ways of marking out a design on glass; by chinagraph pencil, gouache or white ink directly on to the glass surface, or indirectly by tracing. The method describe is simple and rapid and may be used for any engraving purpose.

1 Make a tracing from the drawn design with a hard lead pencil.
2 Cover the back of the tracing, over the design area, with a close scribble of white chinagraph.
3 Smooth out the chinagraph with a touch of wax furniture polish on the finger, which will leave a relatively continuous film of white.
4 Place the tracing in position, tape it down and retrace, whereby the design will be clearly transferred. Use a ballpoint pen, which is smooth and sharp and will indicate when every line of the design has been covered.

A good alternative is to use a little oil or grease on the back of the tracing, taking care to remove all excess before applying the chinagraph which, when smoothed out, is equally effective.

If necessary, the design may be reinforced or extended by brush or pen. White gouache, thinned down with gum arabic and just a touch of wetting agent (such as washing up liquid), makes an excellent ink which will readily flow from a nib, provided it is applied to a dry, greaseless, glass surface. Errors may be erased with an orange stick and the finished design fixed by spraying with shellac (spirit soluble), transparent mastic picture varnish (white spirit soluble) or charcoal fixative (acetone soluble).

The Sculptural Cut

'Roughing out' of a form is almost entirely done with a rounded-edge strap wheel of various sizes. It is rather difficult to describe the gradual grinding or scooping action of this tool, but some earlier experience would have indicated the action for this basic sculptural cut. Used vertically, the cut will obviously move away from a squarish printy to a regular panel shape, but if the wheel is

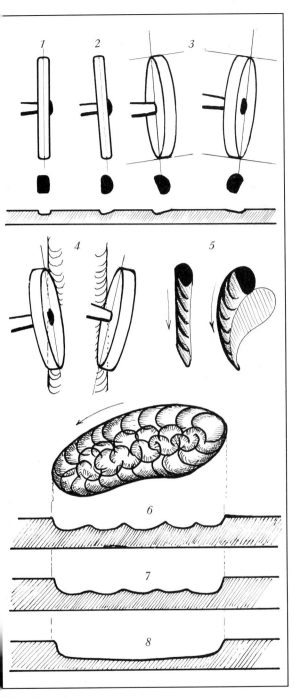

The sculptural cut.
1 The profile of the rounded strap and its vertical cut
2 The cut when the profile is leaned over
3 The wheel angled and inclined for the continuous sculptural cut
4 As 3, from above, giving the inclination, direction and angle of the wheel to the leading edge
5 The direction and rotatory motion of the cut against the wheel
6 The uneven base of the carved area
7 The base smoothed out
8 The base completely smoothed out

angled 15° to the cutting line and inclined (leaned over) to the profile edge, a softer, more variably controlled ovoid cut will be made. It is by this relatively elementary 'gouging' cut, from a large or a small strap wheel, that main intaglio shapes are initially roughed out. The illustration may clarify this description, but a little time spent on a few experimental runs ought quickly to solve the problem. It should be noted that diagrams (3) and (4) indicate the position and inclined angle of the round strap for both left hand and right hand leading edges, that is, the deeper edge of the cut.

The chances are that the engraver will, out of habit, prefer to work and observe from one particular side of the wheel and will rather turn the glass round than lean the other way. However, to be able to use both sides of the wheel with equal facility is clearly a great advantage.

FIRST INTAGLIO FORM: SINGLE-ELEMENT LEAF

The first task is to engrave a small, single-element leaf, so described because this shape, which is naturally formed by the size and width of the strap wheel, may be used to build up more complex leaves.

Roughing Out the Body

Wheel: 25–30 × 3mm ($1 \times \frac{1}{8}$ in)

Abrasive: 320 carborundum/oil mix.

Speed: medium.

1 Start engraving from the thick end of the leaf using the wheel in the manner already described.
2 Pull the wheel downward from the initial cut.
3 Re-enter and repeat the cut, pulling it out a little further each time, but with diminishing pressure. Continue until a leaf or droplet shape is almost formed. Do not at this stage attempt to form a point.
4 Should creases or ridges appear at the bottom of the cut, change the speed to dead slow and gently stroke the wheel along the whole length of the shape until they have disappeared. The depression should be smooth and the shape clearly formed with firm edges.

Engraving The Leaf Point

Wheel: sharp strap, 10 × 2mm ($\frac{3}{8} \times \frac{3}{32}$ in).

Abrasive: 320 carborundum/oil mix.

Speed: slow (half the speed used for the roughing out).

1 Slip in the point of the leaf, working from the outside inwards. This is just one half of the slipping action described at the end of Chapter 3.
2 Starting from where the point is judged to end, begin the cut from the sharp edge of the strap, but as it nears the main form, turn the wheel over towards the flat in one deft, almost instantaneous, movement. If properly done, this widening 'slip' will give a good link-up to the profile, together with a very shallow, invisible entry to the body of the leaf. It is a tricky detail to master and

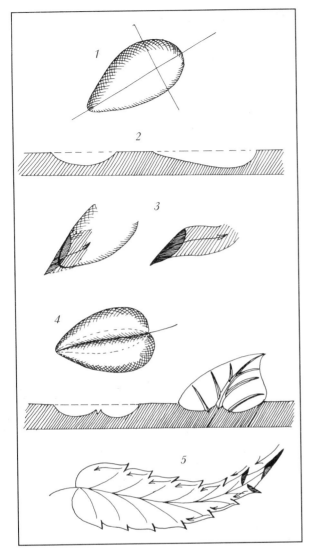

The single leaf:
1 The initial roughed out shape
2 The incised profile across the long and short axis
3 Cutting in the point
4 Construction of a leaf from two single elements, showing the centre ridge and the precarious position for the single line (vein) cut
5 Cutting in the point and serrated edges

some awkward looking points are bound to mar the first attempts.

Engraving the Vein

Wheel: line, 20mm ($\frac{3}{4}$ in)

Abrasive: 400 carborundum/oil mix.

Speed: slow

1 Cut the centre vein and stalk as one continuous line, from the outside inwards.
2 A little care is required as the line wheel meets the depression of the body of the leaf.

SECOND INTAGLIO FORM: DOUBLE-ELEMENT LEAF

In this example, a wider leaf of balanced halves is to be engraved which will be made up of two overlapping single leaf forms, but it is more than twice as difficult.

Roughing Out the Body

Wheel: rounded strap, 25–30 × 3mm (1 × $\frac{1}{8}$ in).

Abrasive: 320 carborundum/oil mix.

Speed: medium.

1 Engrave and complete one segment exactly as before. Take care that the rounded strap is in good condition, for with this particular action the profile has a tendency to sharpen up. If this is allowed to happen, a slight serration of what should be a smooth clean edge to the defined shape may occur.
2 Continue with the second element, positioning it carefully to ensure a nice parting to the base of the leaf, but with a slight lean inwards so that the points or ends of the cut coincide with one another.
3 As the second half is developed and begins to overlap the first, a ridge bettween the two will be created which will be pushed further and further over as the modelling proceeds. Ideally, when completed, this spine (the vein position) should be vertical and equidistant between the two parts. At first, it is more than likely that the second cut will push the ridge over too far, in which event the obvious correction must be made by engraving the first a little more to push it back again.

Engraving the Leaf Point

Wheel: sharp strap, 10 × 2mm ($\frac{3}{8}$ × $\frac{3}{32}$ in).

Abrasive: 320 carborundum/oil mix.

Speed: slow

1 Slip in the point as before but, since the centre spine continues to the leaf tip, this will become a little more troublesome. Hence it is prudent to finish the engraving towards the end as shallow as possible, when the entry of the slip cut will be easier to control.
2 If the point comes out of position or is unsightly in correction, practise further on open glass. To be successful the point should be achieved in one short, swift stroke.

Engraving the Stalk and Vein

Wheel: line, 20mm ($\frac{3}{4}$ in)

Abrasive: 400 carborundum/oil mix.

Speed: slow.

1 Cut a firm, continuous line of stalk and vein, from the outside inwards, to the tip of the leaf. The wheel must be in a good, sharp condition, for the cut line must move from the glass surface into the body of the leaf and ride upon the centre spine to the very end. A continuous line means a clean, uninterrupted line to the eye, for with

this particular manoeuvre tentative and careful re-entries of the line wheel are bound to be necessary in order to obtain a secure foothold on the spine, from which it may so easily slip.

2 Remember that the line wheel cuts very rapidly and that the engraver may find the control much easier at a slower speed than that specified.

THIRD INTAGLIO FORM: DOUBLE LEAF WITH VEINS AND SERRATIONS

This is an elongation of the second example but with more movement and detail. The leaf can be drawn on the glass as a guide to the general shape, rhythm and intention, but it is simple enough to engrave quite freely, which is what intaglio engraving is all about.

Roughing Out the Body

Wheel: rounded strap, $25–30 \times 3$mm ($1 \times \frac{1}{8}$ in).

Abrasive: 320 carborundum/oil mix.

Speed: medium.

1 Engrave the segments of this leaf in the same order and manner as the second example, but pull out the cut gradually to form a longer and more flowing shape. Each segment should not be wider than the natural shape imposed by the wheel.

2 Carefully and gently stroke out any creases which may have occurred in this more extended cut.

Engraving the Point and Serrations

Wheel: sharp strap, 10×2mm ($\frac{3}{8} \times \frac{3}{32}$ in).

Abrasive: 320 carborundum/oil mix.

Speed: slow.

1 Slip in the point, and then tackle the leaf edge serrations. The slipping action is the same as for the point, but the wheel is angled so that, as one side of the triangular cut gives a sharp projection beyond the leaf edge, the other side of the cut is slipped into the natural running shape of the leaf. Complete one side of the leaf with the appropriate edge of the strap before changing over for the other.

2 To be effective the serrations must be quickly and positively cut and of exactly the same size and angle, otherwise the leaf profile may finish up like a badly sharpened saw. The serrations may be sharp or blunt according to the need, but it is more important for the engraving to be rhythmically and stylistically acceptable than botanically correct. Once more, this is not so simply done, that is, in cutting from the glass suface into and over the edge of the intaglio recess. The steeper the edge the greater the difficulty and risk of disfigurement. Therefore, as with the point, it is as well to keep the main form as shallow as possible when the serrations will better merge into it.

Engraving the Veins

Wheel: line, 20mm ($\frac{3}{4}$ in).

Abrasive: 400 carborundum/oil mix.

Speed: slow.

1 Cut the main centre vein, as before, from the outside inwards to the leaf point. This could be gradually deepened towards the stalk end.

2 The side vein should flow out of the stem and be suggested rather than particularised, but it should be precise, and positioned to give a liveliness to the form. For a side vein, start the cut from outside the main stem – the join up will come later – and continue with diminishing depth, to fade away before the edge of the leaf is reached. Now return to the beginning and push the cut backward up the ridge to meet, and move into, the main vein incision. This gives a much better control and is far less hazardous than attempting to cut the side vein directly from the stem.

3 Repeat for the additional side veins.

Decorative Leaves

The difficulties which have been met and overcome in engraving these intaglio leaf forms is an extremely valuable experience, particularly in the more fluent

Engraved example of petals and leaves. Observe the confident use of edge cuts for the serrations and the supporting crescent cuts from the stem

control of the rounded and sharp strap wheels. Obviously there are many more complicated decorative leaves to be attempted, but the difference is largely a matter of degree, for in most instances they may be formed by combinations of these basic shapes. Some of these may now be well within the scope of the engraver, but for the moment it is much more important to repeat what has been learned in decorative combinations in order to prove to oneself that they can be reproduced at will to a desired size, shape and depth.

FOURTH INTAGLIO FORM: FISH

As the engraver approaches creative intaglio work, his earlier investment in drawing and design becomes increasingly valuable; indeed, as time goes by the design problems may overshadow the engraving. The balance of imagination with skill is enough for the artist-craftsman to wrestle with, but there is one other element to be reckoned with – the customer or patron. Apart from rare and privileged exceptions, it is vital for the professional worker to engrave exactly what the customer requires (in this present example a particular fish, a perch), and to do it in a way which will be decorative and sculptural, will delight the eye and give pleasure to the hands. Whatever the personal conception, a lifeless design formula must be avoided, no matter how skilfully it is executed. Alas, as most decorative forms tend to be derivative, it is not so easy to avoid this trap. Suffice it to say that he who is without sin of imitation must cast the first stone.

In the wheel engraving itself, no systematised order is possible, for as a modification of depth or shape is made in one area, a correction or more emphasis is called for in another. It is a continuously evolving process that becomes highly personalised. However, each example given here has been especially engraved for this book and any ordered method will be implicit in the sequence of actions as they actually occurred during the engraving. As with other examples, this is set down as itemised instructions for the reader to follow the identical, or a very similar, intaglio design.

Marking Out the Design

1 Make a preliminary drawing of a perch from a high quality naturalist's illustration, or better still from nature itself. Draw in the distinguishing features and details with fair accuracy, even if much of this information is later abbreviated to its most essential decorative power, much in the manner of a Japanese woodcut of a fish. It is fatal to feel around vaguely for detail imperfectly comprehended.

2 Consider the size and shape of the fish which is to fit the chosen goblet. Make a few trials on the glass with white chinagraph to determine the location and limits of the design. When satisfied, adapt the original to the size required giving the general shape only.

3 Make a firm tracing with a hard, sharp pencil and transfer the image to the glass by the method already detailed. Anchor the tracing firmly to the glass to avoid movement, and use a ballpoint pen for the overtrace so that it can readily be seen when every line has been covered; nothing is more irritating than to discover that after all the performance the design is slightly out of position or some part of it is missing on the trace. (It may be difficult to fit a flat tracing to bulbous shaped glass, but this may be overcome by cutting it into strips which will more readily adapt to the profile.)

4 When the transferred design is finally considered acceptable, 'fix' it to the glass.

Fixing a design can be done by several means, some already explored, namely redrawing in resistant ink or spraying with lacquer. However, it is better to fix more permanently by gently defining the main contours and details with the machine, using either a very small wheel – even the steel point of a spindle – or a small dental

Young perch drawn from life

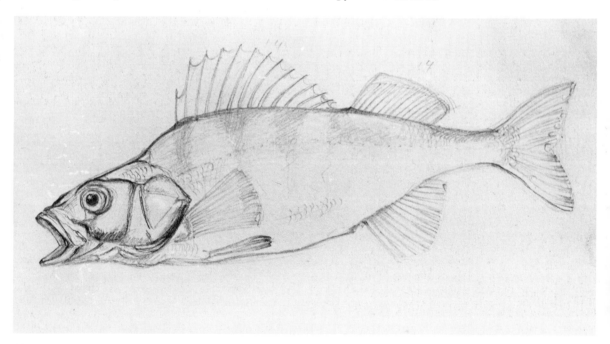

The transferred drawing outlined with the diamond burr on the inside of the outline

diamond burr held in a pin vice.

These burrs, fully described in Chapter 14, are not expensive and are extremely useful for 'slipping in' the design. Naturally, this may just as readily be achieved with a tungsten or diamond point but, except for lines which are to finish deeper and wider, this way of outlining a shape is, in general, to be avoided. The slightest cut by a diamond or tungsten point strikes deeply into glass, which may flake or break up as the strap wheel moves along it and may still be visible after the engraving has been completed.

A diamond burr was used for the present example and the illustration shows that this 'slipping in' – a dreadfully misleading term – was made just fractionally within the limit of the shape. The reason for this small allowance will become obvious a little later on.

Start of the roughing out

Roughing Out the Shape

Wheel: rounded strap, $25 \times 3mm$ ($1 \times \frac{1}{8}$ in).

Abrasive: 320 carborundum/oil mix.

Speed: mid-range.

1 Proceed as with the leaf, gradually pulling the slightly oblique cut downwards, wheel wide, along the marked contour of the fish, from tail to nose, tackling one side at a time.

2 On reaching the nose, fix the position of the gills by engraving the area a little deeper, moving the tool round and round until the shape is roughly defined.

3 Once the main outline has been secured, rough out the entire body area. This is a simple extension of the basic cut and, as with all this roughing out, is a robust movement. Follow alongside the first channel from end to end, and spiral from side to side by turns, taking care to angle the tool for its most effective action. There is a lot of latitude in this operation, but the more recklessly it is approached the more work will be needed to smooth out the irregularities later on.

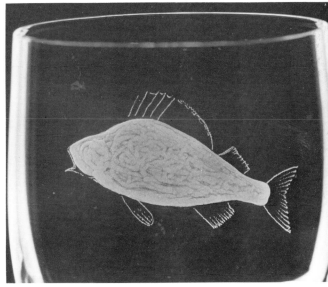

Body roughed out showing the uneven texture

Smoothing out the Form

Wheel: rounded strap, $25 \times 3mm$ ($1 \times \frac{1}{8}$ in).

Abrasive: 400 carborundum/oil mix.

Speed: as slow as possible.

1 At this stage the roughed-out form will have unevennesses to the base of the intaglio cut, no matter how well done, which must be evened out before further modelling can be considered. Using the same wheel and engraving technique, but with an altogether gentler rubbing action which the slower speed permits, gradually stroke and circle the incised form over and over again (as with matting) until a nice, smooth finish

The body smoothed out, the head modelled

Fins and tail modelling. Note different texture

throughout the shape of the fish is obtained.

2 At the same time as this refining takes place, push the contour out to the desired outline, for which a very small allowance has already been made when 'slipping in' the design.

3 Compare the drawing with the engraved shape. Without tail or fin detail it is a little difficult to judge, but no serious amendment should be necessary. The final edge should be continuously clean and crisp, dipping smoothly – not precipitately – into the intaglio body. Do not be tempted to improve corners or engrave subsidiary detail for which the wheel is unfitted. This must be left to a smaller wheel.

Engraving the Eye, Gill and Mouth

Wheel: round strap, 15×1.5 mm ($\frac{9}{16} \times \frac{1}{16}$ in)

Abrasive: 400 Carborundum/oil mix.

Speed: medium slow.

1 Clean the glass and with a pencil draw into the matt engraving the position of the eye, mouth, gills and gill fin.

2 Gently engrave – just indicate – the position of the eye socket. Cut in the top and bottom lip firmly. As this is a strong forward detail having precise sharp edges, the wheel, for once, may be used directly, vertically, to fit the shape, and cut rather deeply. Conversely, the distant detail of the inside of the mouth must be only lightly engraved.

3 Continue modelling the cheek and gills using the small wheel exactly as with the earlier modelling but angling the wheel one way or another to give vigour or softness to the plastic form.

All this intermediate modelling must be deeply considered, thinking in the round, constantly guarding against the dangers lurking in the reverse order of cutting.

All depths must relate to one another, for overemphasis can produce swollen parts which become an eyesore – and quite incurable. This is where complete familiarity with the subject has its effect, for the depth and boundaries of the modelling is instinctively felt. In short, again, one should only attempt to engrave what one understands.

Engraving the Fins and Tail

Wheel: rounded strap, 40×3 mm ($1\frac{1}{2} \times \frac{1}{8}$ in).

Abrasive: 600 carborundum/oil mix.

Speed: medium slow.

1 Engrave, say, the dorsal fin, delicately, with not much depth, moving from the outside into, or just touching, the body without offending the profile of the fish. Engrave in the direction of the bony ribs of the fin but completing it as a general shape only.

2 Continue with the tail and other external fins.

3 Cut the gill fin separately and deeply, which, being within the body and the nearest member, needs to be thrust forward visually. Still keep to the general shape; the final detail will come later. Naturally, where the fin is seen to have a long leading edge, the wheel is manoeuvred to give a more incised edge.

The engraver may consider that it would be better to engrave the fins first and cut the body across them, which would avoid the risk of deforming the outline; he could be correct. It is a matter of preference and available skill. With this example it was a matter of personal convenience in wheel and abrasive changing, and it could be different next time.

Engraving the Scales

Tool: Use the smallest wheel possible, spindle end or diamond burr, possibly the one used for 'slipping on' the design in the first instance.

Abrasive: 600 carborundum/oil mix, (where the wheel is used).

Speed: high speed.

Gently suggest the curved scales on the body of the fish. The only thing to add is that, whether the scales be small or large, weak or strong, naturalistic or stylistic, make certain they are comfortable to the swimming fish – that is, facing the right direction.

Engraving the Eye

Wheel: small rounded profile, 4–5 × 2mm ($\frac{3}{16} - \frac{7}{32} \times \frac{3}{32}$ in).

Abrasive: 400 carborundum/oil mix.

Speed: medium.

1 As this feature is formed by two printies, one within the other, there is no problem apart from placing them in the correct position. Engrave the largest shallower printy, but before changing the tool to complete the tiny inner pupil, sharpen up one or two details which will improve vitality, for example the folded skin under the lower jaw or the stronger leading edges of the front fins.

2 Complete the eye with a very small printy for the inner pupil, using the smallest wheel, burr or pinhead.

Fine Detail Finishing

Wheel: sharpened for fine lines, 15mm ($\frac{9}{16}$ in).

Abrasive: 600 carborundum/oil mix.

Speed: medium slow.

1 Much good work may be undone at the last moment by a reckless impatience to fill in the final details, but it is sensible to draw in what may still be missing – the fin ribbing – rather than attempt to engrave it freehand. Starting with the dorsal fin, engrave the fine ribs from just within the limit of the fin up to the body, but without breaking into the edge.

2 Reverse the glass and re-enter the ribs to neatly extend the spines to the right length and weight. The ability to re-enter a fine line will now be fully tested.

3 The other fins are different in form, having feathered ends, hence the main ribs are single cuts made heavier as they approach the body, with added multiple fine lines at the tips to complete the effect. Do not risk a start on these delicate lines with a blunted wheel. It is useless to hope that the wheel which has been used for the main ribs will be sharp enough for the ultimate cuts. Make sure and use a finer 800 grit if necessary.

4 To complete the design, change to a small strap and engrave the small crescent link of skin between each spine of the dorsal.

Polishing

The purpose of polishing is to give accent, change of tone or texture to the intaglio form. The engraving can exist in

Linework detail in fins and tail completed. Scales, bubbles and water weed (with edge cuts) included

its own right, without polishing of any kind, but a contrast of tone within the matt, or the slightest 'touch' to a particular edge of modelling, can lift the whole design to a further dimension.

The novice is very likely to allow the newly found polishing technique to run away with him, an enthusiasm which must be severely restrained. But perhaps one overpolished, bald disaster is really the best restraint of all. For this particular purpose the polishing wheel should be made of cork. Natural cork bark is unsuitable. It is better to cut the disc from a table or bathroom mat made of compressed cork. Choose one, if possible, of a medium aggregate. Centre hole the cork wheel and attach it to a screw-ended spindle for trueing, profile forming and working. It is, of course, much better to obtain cork wheels for polishing from a manufacturer who takes the precaution to choose cork of the right quality and completely free of grit.

Wheel: cork profile edges soft rounded, 40 × 10mm ($1\frac{3}{4}$ × $\frac{1}{2}$ in).

Abrasive: 320–400 pumice/water paste.

Speed: slow to medium (40mm ($1\frac{3}{4}$ in) is fairly large and therefore will have a high peripheral speed which determines the setting of the machine).

1 Begin with the fins and tail. Charge the cork wheel with the pumice/water paste (applied on a small piece of sponge) and tackle the conveniently isolated dorsal fin first. Notice that the matt becomes progressively darker as the polishing proceeds. Continue until the right degree of transparence (darkness) is obtained, but as the wet paste makes it difficult to see this, frequently dry up and remove all powder from the engraving to examine the progress and effect against the unpolished areas.

2 From this experience complete the other fins and tail

Completed fish on the goblet. Fins and body and eye polished

with more or less polishing according to the need. The action of the soft wheel and abrasive is very mild so that the wheel can, without fear, be passed completely over the whole fin. Any encroachment on the open glass may result in a slight bloom, just visible, but easily removable at the last moment. However, overlapping into what should be virgin matt can result in a quite unpleasant appearance, and where such accents of shadow are wanted the polishing wheel must be carefully applied and turned over to the sharper edge, or a smaller wheel should even be used.

3 Gently polish the head detail. The polishing wheel will inevitably catch the boundary edges of deeply cut modelling; consequently the slightest amount will quickly raise the contrast. Once more, do not over-polish, but as this, like sin, is never recognized until it happens, cease if possible, in time for redemption.

4 As the back of a fish is always darker than its belly, polish until the matt is reduced to the correct feeling of contrast, and (if the fish be a perch) carry the dark tone in characteristic streaks around the body.

5 To form the pupil of the eye, polish the inner printy using a small lead wheel with water/pumice paste; if it happens to be too small for this to be possible, use a rounded orange stick held in a pin vice, with oil/carborundum 600 abrasive instead.

6 Finally, any slight bloom which can be observed, due to polishing over the open glass, may be removed by a light polish using the felt wheel, with cerium oxide and water as the polishing paste (see Chapter 17).

Background Decoration

The worst or best of this exercise on larger and freer intaglio modelling is over. Decorative embellishment beyond the basic fish form is open to every variation. In this example, a flowing weed made up of simple line and crescent cuts, confidently positioned to the swelling shape

of the glass, freely cut at the time when the emerging linear detail suggested it, is all that is needed. The addition of bubbles and a small fish imparts a little more excitement.

The Sculptural Form

It is hoped that the description has not been over-long. It seeks to anticipate and answer questions which an apprentice might raise while engaged in the task, but such instruction cannot do everything. It could be that the example is a little too elaborate at the present stage of skill. No matter, well or ill, the real value has been in the building up of an understanding of modelling depth relationships particular to intaglio engraving. If the body of a fish is simply opened up and smoothed nicely, with fins and details positioned in a simpler, more stylistic form, this is quite an achievement.

One last point: intaglio form may be cut deeply or shallow – within reason – without affecting the three-dimensional, sculptural, plastic effect. It will become a personal preference out of habit, caution or vigour as to which form one should choose. But there are practical considerations; the deeper the engraved form the more difficult it is to include details within it, or to bring other work up to the edge without damage. This danger is greatly reduced by engraving shallower but, in compensation, the edge of the main shape should be a little more abrupt (vertical) to catch the light.

FIFTH INTAGLIO FORM: CLEMATIS

All the wheel engraving so far has been of a tight, disciplined nature – it is not often otherwise – but some subjects naturally allow a little more latitude; the clematis shown in the illustration is chosen as a good example, where the design and the engraving may be approached in a more relaxed manner.

The Flower Design

The design is very important and it is worthwhile examining flower compositions of all kinds, on tapestry or porcelain, or early watercolours and engravings, in order to profit from that powerful combination of economy in design and information which was so beautifully understood in the past and is so difficult to emulate.

The engraver has learned all that is needed to tackle such a project which in the designing, setting out and engraving, free from particularised instructions, should give a deal of pleasure. However, the accompanying photographs showing the simple stages of development, together with a few associated comments, may help in measuring one's own progress.

Roughing Out

It is obvious that the sizes of the strap wheels are determined by the area of the petals or leaves to be engraved. In the initial roughing out the engraver may be alarmed by the large size of wheel 45mm (1¾in) chosen for this purpose, but it is only a small segment of the wheel that is being used. The only danger arises when a large wheel is pushed beyond its capacity.

It is imperative to move over the entire area, feeling one's way to the sculptured form before committing oneself too far. Some modification to the shapes may be made as the work goes along, but the outline should have been reasonably accurate to the design and not too much modification should be called for – unless the first shapes prove less lyrical than they should be. Once satisfied that the plastic forms promise to be lively and decorative, the modelling can be continued until everything that can be done with that first wheel, flower and leaves, is done.

The transferred design, superficially outlined with a diamond burr and the flower and buds roughed-out

Intermediate Modelling

Ordinarily, the next immediate step would be the refining of the now vigorous form and the addition of smaller modelling followed by linework detail. In this particular case, however, it is difficult to use the sharp line wheel along the ridge of the veins within the leaf and so, instead of leaving the vein to the last, in one risky irrevocable cut, it is prudent to 'fix' the position in advance. Even if this pilot line becomes partially obscured by subsequent modelling, there should be enough purchase left for the wheel to engrave a firm and confident line.

Common sense must determine when veins or similar details should be handled this way, and equally whether to be soft or sharp. Softer, more indeterminate lines may be slipped in from a very small wheel or even from the turned end of an old spindle. Lines within the modelling which become too strident or wiry may gradually be ground down to the desired emphasis.

Apart from this diversion, all improvements or additions to detail modelling in, say, the turnover of a leaf or the undulating edge of a petal, must be formed by smaller wheels, though the wheels must be large enough to avoid niggardly overworking. Stems and tendrils of various thickness speak for themselves, but it should be remembered that diminishing circles, from which spirals are formed, can only safely be engraved from wheels of approximately the same diameter. Hence, with curled or spiralled tendrils, to stay overlong with one wheel risks – invites – an eyesore.

Fine Detail Finishing

When all intermediate modelling has been fully completed, little should remain to be done beyond engraving the stamens and accenting the stalks or veins. If there remains any uncertainty about the quality of the modelling, that it is too violent or ridgy, then a further smoothing out or softening with the rounded strap may be necessary – but it must be run at the slowest speed. Equally, the thrust forward of the stamens should be anticipated by engraving the shape, in which they rest, a little deeper than the surrounding area.

Nothing at this late stage should be taken for granted, for a badly grouped cluster of stamens could suddenly halt all the earlier creative pleasure. It could be worthwhile drawing the stamens in the matt – or any other such detail – before the almost final act of engraving.

The inclusion of veins and finer detail within the modelling

Polishing

Polishing is optional and depends on personal preference,

The completed goblet with polished details

and there is no guide other than sensibility as to how far it should be carried, or even if it should be done at all. Some engravers may prefer to leave the engraving in the matt condition and consider polishing a retrograde act. In this example it was thought that some accents of polished tone would give an added interest, which the final photograph should illustrate.

As a footnote to this work, it is clear that the quality of the intaglio matt is determined by the hardness of the glass and the grit substance and grade. Similarly the polish or sheen given to that matting will be dependent on the substance of the wheel – or other means – by which

various polishing pastes are applied. This polishing is open to every expediency from the cork wheel to a blunt stick, another piece of glass, or the constant wipe away of the fine engraving paste with the thumb each time the glass is removed from the wheel. No doubt much of the subtle sheen seen on eighteenth and nineteenth century glass is due to the last of these. The engraver should experiment with materials that might improve an effect. However, until he knows better, it is wise to rely on the traditional use of cork, grainless limewood, poplar, willow or the knotty section of elderberry wood.

5 Heraldic Engraving

THE HERALDIC TRADITION

For the artist engraver or designer there is much to be learned from heraldry. Apart from its historic importance in the recording of pedigrees, armorial bearings are rich in medieval symbols, which, used as visual notation, are unsurpassed in graphic inventiveness. Indeed, one would be hard pressed to invent any similar symbolic system with equal decorative lucidity. Considering the rigidity of the conventions which are used in emblazoning, that is, in the portrayal of heraldic devices, the vigour and ingenuity is astonishing. It is not surprising therefore that armorial bearings or some borrowed symbols are common to engraved glass, particularly commemorative glass.

Chief features of a coat of arms

The Royal Coat of Arms. Part of a silver gilt table centrepiece engraved by Peter Dreiser and presented to H.M. the Queen on her Silver Jubilee 1977, by the Silversmiths and Goldsmiths Association. (By gracious permission of Her Majesty the Queen)

Conventions of design

There is a wide range of technical and historical information available on this absorbing subject for specialist study, but as far as engraving is concerned it is only necessary to understand the limits imposed by convention and where decorative innovation can be admissible. Very briefly, no coat of arms may be reproduced without permission, and all the conditions of the convention of shape of shield, quartering, type of helm and all symbolic language must be met. But it is obvious that within these requirements the differences between carving, painting or engraving must allow a wide freedom of treatment. providing each element is tastefully and appropriately portrayed.

For the most part, the engraver will be asked to reproduce an established coat of arms of an approved design and he would not be expected to depart from it, but with some shapes of glass it would be right to handle the design much more freely, extending the mantling or motto ribbon in lyrical flourishes to fit the form of the glass.

Tinctures

Virtually all colours, metals and furs, ('tinctures' as they are called) have long since been graphically represented by a series of lines, dots or simple abbreviations, as are shown in the accompanying illustration. Although much heraldic work ignores this convention, it is important to know how this particular problem was handled traditionally. Certainly, as regards intaglio engraving, the inclusion of these details greatly adds to the information and quality of the finished work, but there is nothing to prevent an engraver from handling the same design very much more simply.

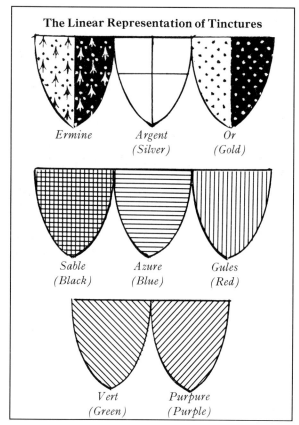

The linear representation of tinctures

The Commission

In this example, which is an actual commission, the tinctures will be included and the problems involved with them will be discussed as they arise. No attempt will be made to explain every detail of the engraving since so much of it is repetitive and has already been covered in earlier exercises. All the same, the sequence of engraving, matting and polislhing a coat of arms may be quite involved and confusing at first sight, so before starting the commission two enlarged quarters of the shield have been separately engraved and photographed at different stages so that the method and reasons behind it may be closely understood.

It must be said that this is a very advanced exercise

The original (embossed engraving)

which would stretch the capabilities of the best, and there is no room for error or stodgy modelling. However, difficult as it may be, a great deal can be learned from attempting these two examples either whole or in part, for when heraldic work and lettering have been mastered, all that remains is a widening of the engraver's repertoire through professional experience.

QUARTER SHIELD: THREE COUCHANT LIONS ON A GULES FIELD

Preliminary Outlining

1 Make a sketch of the three lions and the surrounding framework and transfer it to the glass.
2 Slip in the outline (profiles) of the lions to just within the limit of their final sizes with a small burr.
3 Engrave the frame surround with a line wheel (the larger the wheel, the easier for straight long lines) as a pilot guideline.
4 Strengthen and deepen this line with a large 50mm (2 in) wheel, with the profile appropriately rounded to give the increased width. It should have been a habit by now to start the line fractionally away from the corner.
5 Complete the corners with a small wheel of the same profile, by pushing the cut carefully into the angle.

Matting the field

Wheel: large strap.

Abrasive: 400 carborundum/water paste.

Speed: slow (creeping).

From the chart it is seen that gules (i.e. red) is represented

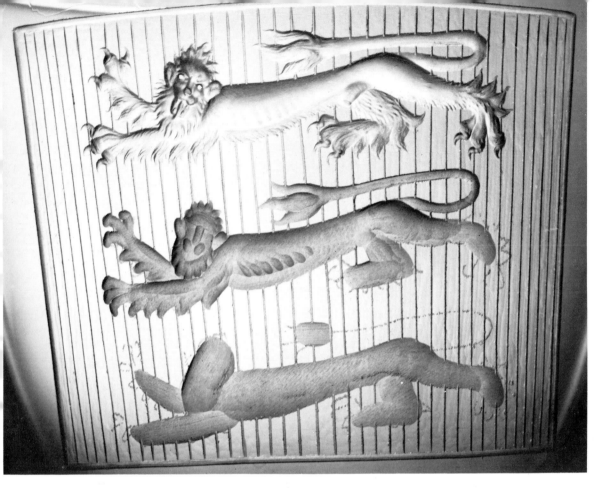

by vertical lines. However, lines against open glass is a trifle bald, and it is aesthetically more pleasing if some small difference is held between the open glass and the shield itself, so the background to the lines is matted and polished back to a nice sheen.

Matt over the entire area within the frame using a large strap wheel at creeping speed. Refer to the section on matting in Chapter 3 for the general approach to this problem. Matting a large area of about 75×50mm (3×2 in), as in this example, is rather a long job with a copper wheel. The outlines of the lions should not be obscured by the gentle matting.

(It may be known that this operation may be speeded up with corundum (aloxite) wheels instead of copper, but this is a shortcut which has its own technique and is best dealt with at a later stage when every use of the copper wheel has been fully explored.)

Lining the Field

Wheel: line, 40mm ($1\frac{1}{2}$ in).

Abrasive: 400–600 carborundum/oil paste.

Speed: slow.

Using a large line wheel firmly and slowly in action, cut a series of fine, parallel and evenly spaced vertical lines.

It is very important to be certain that the wheel is charged with enough abrasive to engrave a full line without pausing, since this is likely to cause 'knots'. It

The first introductory engraved example of one quarter (three couchant lions) illustrating the order of the development of the design. *Background*: the engraved framework, matted background overcut with fine vertical lines (to represent red), the whole matt polished back to a light sheen. *Bottom Lion*: preliminary roughing out. *Middle lion*: intermediate modelling included. Note the general development of the structure of head and claw. *Top lion*: the fully engraved version

must be repeated that a very close watch should be kept on the sharpness of the wheel, as any thickening will quickly alter the character of the lines.

Engraving fine, even parallel lines is not an easy task, even if pencilled guidelines are drawn in the matt. The aim is to cut in one continuous sweep, apart from the short return portions which can be handled by a smaller wheel, which gives better control at the very ends. One last reminder: the finer the cutting medium, the more difficult it is to control.

Polishing the Field

Wheel: cork, 75×40mm ($3 \times 1\frac{1}{2}$ in).

Abrasive: 400 pumice/water paste.

Speed: Slow.

It has already been said that the aim is to produce a continuous sheen as a background to the intaglio ingraved lions, so that the matt must be evenly polished back to the desired strength. To do this efficiently the largest area of the polishing wheel must be brought to bear on the glass, therefore the wheel must be large and wide, and evenly and firmly applied, taking the obvious precautions against local overheating and the exhaustion of the polishing abrasive.

All polishing is best done in short bursts which allow for examination and cooling at the same time. When finished, the panel should be of an even sheen with the lines cleanly superimposed, but with the outline of the lions still faintly visible through it all.

The even reduction of relatively large areas of matt is an important part of 'architectural' intaglio engraving, where several changes of tone or texture must be shown in one plane as against another, so that it is as well not to dismiss this aspect of polishing too lightly.

Roughing Out the Lions

Wheel: rounded strap, 25×3mm ($1 \times \frac{1}{8}$ in).

Abrasive: 320 carborundum/oil mix.

Speed: medium.

Beyond that of scale and the greater accuracy required in engraving fine decorative detail, there is no difference in handling the sculptural content of the heraldic lion from that of the earlier examples of leaf or fish. All are based on wider or narrower elongated oval cuts. By now it should be second nature to visualise flat pattern as three-dimensional form, so that in the initial roughing out the deepening of buttocks, rib cage or shoulders, or the setting of the related depth of the head or the near and far legs, ought to be one continuous, instinctive action.

Modelling the Body

Wheel: rounded strap, 10×2mm ($\frac{3}{8} \times \frac{3}{32}$ in).

Abrasive: 320 carborundum/oil mix.

Speed: medium/fast.

1 Emphasise, perhaps exaggerate, the modelling of rump, belly, rib cage and shoulder, dragging out the cuts into the nearside legs so that they join the torso in a natural way.
2 Mark out the edge of the skull and deepen its forward shape.
3 Position the ears.
4 Engrave the fur tags to the legs, blending them into the main form.
5 Apart from the head, which requires special attention, the bulk of the modelling should be corrected at this stage, gently softening out ridges which might have occurred where different depths of modelling came together too abruptly. At the same time carefully correct the outline.

Modelling the Head

Wheel: rounded strap, 4×1.5mm ($\frac{3}{16} \times \frac{1}{16}$ in) (larger or smaller according to the need).

Abrasive: 320 carborundum/oil mix.

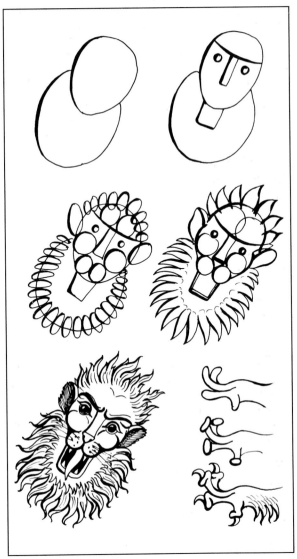

The structural development of a head and claw from the basic shapes formed from the rounded strap, the printy, olive and sharp strap

Speed: medium-fast.

Whatever the animal, it is invaluable to have observed the natural structure on which the heraldic form is based. It makes it so much easier to determine the order and shapes on which the more difficult details, such as head or claws are built up. Note that all cuts on the head are crucial, so it would be prudent to try out the widths, shapes and depths on a glass first.

1 The dome of the forehead having been engraved earlier, cut in the nose with the appropriate strap wheel, its full width.
2 Engrave the cheeks and muzzle.
3 Accurately locate the position of the eyes.
4 Engrave the two sides of the dropped open jaw, and pull out the approximate shape of the ears, hair and mane.

5 Model the bony prominence and curved shape of the forehead. Smoothen out and soften the cheeks and muzzle. Improve the forward thrust of the nose and muzzle by engraving more deeply if necessary.

6 From this point, the completion of the details are obvious and should, if the dominant features of the mask have been correctly positioned, easily fall into place: teeth, tongue, lower eyelid and detail of ears and fur. All can be formed with a small line wheel when the other associated details on the body are being worked.

Engraving the Foot

Wheels: Small olive and printy.

Abrasive: 320 carborundum/oil mix.

speed: medium fast.

Having studied the decorative organisation of the heraldic clawed foot, which might vary in the number of claws or in their positions, choose the style which best suits the present design.

1 Engrave each separate segment by pulling out an olive – no wider than the form permits – outwards from the leg to the position of the pad. The method, wheel size and shape must by now be intuitive; engraving the furthest, and shallowest, bony protuberance first and deepening the others progressively as they come forward. All details of the foot must melt into the leg so as to give a natural appearance.

2 With a small printy wheel improve the swelling, rounded shape to the pads and the profile of the knuckles.

Engraving the Claw

Wheel: small sharp strap.

Abrasive: 400 carborundum/oil mix.

Speed: medium fast.

This ultimate detail should grow out of the pad. It is really a part of a crescent cut which should softly merge into the pad. To ensure this, it is best tackled in two stages.

1 Secure the correct exit from the pad by tentatively slipping outwards from the broad section of the crescent, partway towards the point. This arc is critical, and so this first cut is really feeling its way.

2 Having positioned the cut, re-enter from the pad and complete the claw as a clean, sharp crescent. A very small line wheel may be useful to sharpen the point still further.

Engraving the Tail

Engraving the tail should present no difficulty. All the same, its width and movement is an important element in the design, which may easily be marred by a sudden clumsiness with a wheel too large or too wide to handle the curve.

Finishing the detail

When the modelling has been completed and most of the detail added, it may be found that the intaglio form is too muscular, or abrupt, for pleasure. This is due to the tendency to create ridges where the differing depths of modelling overlap or meet each other. These high spots, or any other surface imperfections, should of course be carefully smoothed over with a very slow-running wheel, but in very small areas it may be too difficult or even dangerous to do it in this way. The simple alternative is to rub them down gently, manually, with a smaller finger of copper, or copper wire, with the same grit as that used for the modelling. In a short time a more natural texture is obtained without altering the overall character of the matt.

Modelling Problems

Emphasis has been given to this first section of heraldic work, particularly the head and claws, for many of the difficulties of intaglio engraving will be met here: the attempted correction of ill-positioned shapes which will drive the frantic operator deeper and deeper into – and possibly through – the glass; the retribution that comes from a careless choice of condition of wheel; the confused modelling or oversized features, all of which may result in a creature resembling not so much a couchant lion as a newborn mouse!

The difficulties are great enough without inviting more, and many may be circumvented by not assuming too much – for example, that the drawing is understood or that such and such a wheel or grit or speed will perform a certain task – and by putting everything to the test in advance on a practice glass. Even so, the going will be rough and some disasters are inevitable. But they should not be disheartening for they will highlight weaknesses in technique which should perhaps have been earlier overcome.

Suffice it to say that even an experienced engraver will approach such projects with a breathless excitement – if not trepidation.

QUARTER SHIELD: SCOTTISH RAMPANT LION ON AN OR FIELD

Transferring the Design

1 Draw the design to the correct size and transfer it to the glass.

2 Strengthen or improve the design and parallel lines with white gum arabic ink as a protection against the oil abrasive paste. Scrape away and improve any clumsy work with a hardwood point.

It is always worthwhile giving this extra attention to a difficult detail before starting the engraving, no matter how skilled the engraver may be. Designs larger than the example may need protection from moist hands with a shellac lacquer spray which, when thoroughly dry, will withstand a deal of rough handling, protecting both the design and the glass surface from abrasive scratches.

Preliminary Outlining

1 Outline the lion and fleur-de-lis with a burr.

2 Lightly engrave the parallel lines of the framework to fix their position.

3 Repeat the lines with a slightly thicker line wheel and strengthen them to precise, clean lines. The outside frame line could be a little wider to give a degree of variation.

Keeping long lines square, straight, and parallel is particularly difficult, but if the earlier exercises have been mastered this should not be too troublesome. However, as all one has to go by are drawn lines, some initial problems should be expected, hence the reason for the pre-cautionary pilot cutting. Again, the larger the wheel the easier the task, but extra care must be taken not to over-run the corners – a mistake very easily made.

Corner Motif: Fleur-de-Lis

Wheels: 15 × 3mm ($\frac{5}{8} \times \frac{1}{8}$ in) mitre; 4 × 1m ($\frac{3}{16} \times \frac{3}{64}$ in) sharp strap.

Abrasive: 400 carborundun/oil mix.

Speed: medium

1 Engrave the centre leaf of the fleur-de-lis with the mitre wheel at a 90° angle. Allow the wheel to cut its natural shape and then smoothly pull out to the required length, avoiding creases or irregularity. This is one of the rarer occasions where a mitre profile is of great use, that is, in cutting a balanced shape of sharp facets.

2 Engrave the curled side leaves with the sharp strap wheel. These can be engraved in one of two ways.
(a) As with the crescent cut, lay the strap wheel over and cut the curved form, bit by bit, from the sharp to the broader part of the profile, and back again.
(b) The wheel can be slipped (as explained in the section on the use of the sharp strap in Chaper 3) to give an effect similar to that obtained with a reed pen. It is wise to make a light, pilot slip-in before being committed to the final cut, which should be one continuous move-ment, hardly changing the position of the angle of the glass to the wheel. The first method gives the more precise cut shape but is rather more difficult.

Engraving the Rampant Lion

Engraving this lion follows exactly the same pattern as those on the first quarter, though the added experience will perhaps allow the engraver to give more attention to the refinements of drawing and intaglio modelling rather than the physical difficulties of engraving. It is some comfort to know that the side is easier to engrave than the front view, where the risk of overcutting to obtain the right contrast of modelling is very great. In any event the side view has more decorative power. Naturally, all the basic shapes which form the structure of the lion-or any

The second engraved heraldic example, a rampant lion on a gold background (the Scottish lion): the framework and fleur-de-lis engraved and the lion partly developed (*below*)

The completed quarter with the matted background which has been engraved with small dots (representing gold) (*opposite*)

other animal-must be analysed in advance. The progress, too, should be gauged by plasticine impressions.

Engraving the Field

There are two acceptable ways in which the gold field or background of this second quarter may be represented. The finished matt lion may be set against a clear glass background with dots, which is the convention for gold, cut in as matt printies. Alternatively, the finished and polished lion may be set against a matt background with dots of polished printies.

It is a matter of taste. The latter has been chosen in the example illustrated to give a change of tone or contrast against the other quarters. But the whole thing must be thought out in advance, for the choice affects the order in which the job is tackled. In this instance the lion, and the inserted matt printies, for obvious reasons, must be polished first; and again, since it has been decided to have the frame polished between the parallels so as to add a further interest, this also must be countersunk and polished in advance.

Polishing the frame

Wheel: cork, 75 × 20mm (3 × ¾ in).

Abrasive: 320 pumice/water paste.

Speed: slow-medium

Charge the wheel with the pumice/water mix and, holding the glass firmly in both hands, apply it to the wheel in bursts of no more than two or three seconds in every direction.

Polishing the Lion and Printies

Wheel: dental brush, 125mm (5 in)

Abrasive: pumice/water paste/(or tripoli powder paste)

Speed: very high.

It will be understood that very small details preclude the use of cork wheels. It is possible to polish such details with tiny lead wheels and the like, but this is extremely tedious. It is better, therefore, to use a brush wheel, made particularly for polishing, in the following way.

1 Apply the polishing paste at the very moment the wheel touches the glass. This means holding the glass securely with the left hand and applying the paste on a small rag pad with the other, giving whatever further support is possible with the free fingers. Take great care the rag pad is not ripped from the hand by slipping between the glass and the wheel.

2 Use the full width of the brush, polishing in every direction so that the bristles enter every interstice of the engraving.

3 Guard against rapid overheating, which may be caused by the high speeds, by polishing in very short bursts.

4 To examine the progress, lightly brushed away residual pumice. Do not be tempted to wipe away the dust with soft paper – it always scratches.

Matting the Background

Wheel: 40 × 3mm (1½ × ⅛ in).

Abrasive: 320 carborundum/water paste.

Speed: dead slow.

Carefully matt over the background using the wheel as described in Chapter 3. There should be no pressure at all; the tool should gently ride on the surface of the glass, otherwise the printies will become distorted. They will of course be reduced slightly, but not seriously. The lion, being much deeper, ought to remain unaffected. If it has been well handled, the matt will give a fine contrast to the polished design.

FULL SHIELD: THE COAT OF ARMS

Returning to the original commission, it is apparent that there is a good deal more in it than lions and tints to think about but, fortunately, other supporting features, generally speaking, present the same interpretative problems. If anything is omitted in this chapter, such as

The basic outline of the shield and ribbon transferred to the glass and engraved

mantling, crests, or helms, it is because the process of engraving is virtually a repetition of what has gone before. For example, by overcoming the engraving difficulties of the motto ribbon, the mantling, though different in design flair, may equally be mastered. All the same, each element must be understood and well drawn in advance so as to extract the most lively and decorative value from it in the engraving. The bowl photographed in various stages of development should give a very fair idea of the treatment

of any other heraldic device or pattern.

Much of the appeal of early intaglio heraldic glass is created not only by the design but by the embossed vigour of the engraving itself. If this effect is to be sought after, certain areas (in this example, the shield, ribbon and book) must be countersunk in advance. This gives the illusion of embossed platforms, of greater or lesser degree according to the depths of countersinking, upon which the added symbols or lettering will sit up more interestingly. Not to do so will risk a certain flatness. Naturally it is an added task which the engraver might wish to avoid, but it should be done, or seriously considered, for even the untutored eye will pick up the difference.

General Procedure

1 Draw out the finally approved design, trace and accurately transfer it to the glass or bowl. Amend any inperfect detail, or correct for curvature, with white ink, paying particular attention to the main verticals and horizontals to the shield. Fix in the design permanently with a point or dental burr. As the handling of a large bowl at the lathe with moist fingers may damage a carefully prepared transfer, the important outlines (of shield and ribbon) can be carefully drawn in, on the bench, with a tungsten carbide point. However, before doing so, the glass must be known to have been evenly annealed (see Introduction). Fire polished rims can set up uneven stresses which make any mark, particularly horizontal marks, on an expensive bowl very hazardous. Most engravers have experienced the horror of a circlet of glass gradually detaching itself from the main body, all started by a scratch at the maximum stress point.

   All other details can be sketched in at the lathe, using a spindle-mounted diamond burr.

2 Cut all the main outlines with a sharp line wheel: the shield, ribbon and outline of the book – all the areas which need countersinking.

3 Fix the position and deeply outline the main forms of lions, harp and frame.

Countersinking the Shield

1 Working from the edges (which should have been cut a little deeper than usual) towards the centre of the shield, smooth out the whole area to a shallow, convex lens. The centre should remain almost at the original surface level. With large areas it is sufficient to countersink in this manner. It gives the same embossed effect but avoids the labour and difficulty of engraving a flat smooth recess, and it allows further intaglio work within the shield without the danger of cutting too deeply into the glass. Once in a while the engraver may surprise and shock himself by going right through.

2 The main forms of the symbols in these countersunk areas should still be plainly visible, but if in the process of smoothing out there is some danger of losing them, obviously some corrective deepening is necessary.

Countersinking the Ribbon

1 Pay great attention to the overall flow and movement,

nking glass. Bohemian, about 1835. Blue glass, amber stained,
aglio wheel engraved. Where the motif has been engraved the
ber stain has been removed to expose the beautifully engraved
e glass in various depths of blue. Height 150mm (6in), by John
tton of Berkhamstead

e Pilgrim'. White glass overlaid with warm brown, deeply wheel
raved. Some windows are completely cut through to suggest a
aying medieval cloister in which monks are moving in one
ction, with one dissident pilgrim facing the other. By Peter
iser. 125mm (5in)

2 Goblet. Ruby cased glass which is a rarity for mid-eighteenth
century. Probably from northern Bohemia or Saxony. The very
spirited and well executed engraving is typical of that period. Height
200mm (8in)

4 'Frozen Cascade'. A lead crystal paper weight, carved with diamond
and small stone wheels, mostly a strap wheel. The larger facets are
polished, the others are left with a silky matt finish which adds to the
contrast and brilliance. Diameter 80mm (3in). By Peter Dreiser.
(Victoria and Albert Museum)

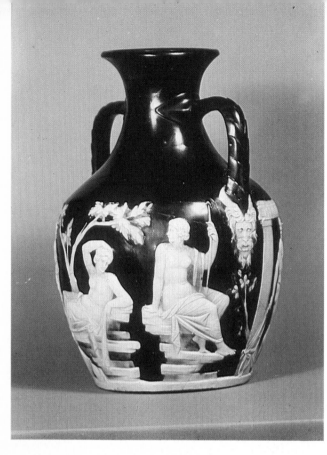

5   The Portland Vase. Roman, first century AD. Dense blue transpa[rent] base glass cased with opaque white, cameo engraved. It has all [the] signs that it was the work of a gifted hardstone cameo engra[ver]. Height 245mm (9½in). *(British Museum)*

6   Lycurgus Cup. Roman, fourth century AD. An outstanding exam[ple] of deep carved and sculptured glass. The relief figures are [so] skilfully undercut as to almost stand free of the main form. [The] material has a strange dichroic quality, being ruby by transmi[tted] light and olive green by reflected light. Height 165mm (6¾[in). *(British Museum)*

7   'The Cycle of Life', 1978. A ruby cased glass on a golden base. H[igh] relief engraving on which both orthodox copper wheels and mo[dern] diamond wheels have been used. Height 200mm (8in). By P[eter] Dreiser

8   A small green vase cased with opaque purple. Emil Galle, ab[out] 1890. Relief (cameo) engraved showing the mark of the whee[l on] the glass surface

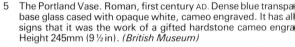

and keep sharp turnbacks to the folded ribbon at the appropriate depths to maximise the three-dimensional effect.

2 It is not always possible to engrave and smooth out a flat narrow band or channel, as this should be, without some unevenness or ripple showing. To avoid this, contrary to the usual practice of moving lengthwise along the edge and working inwards, a 40mm (1½ in) rounded strap wheel may be used *transversely* to the direction of the ribbon, which, by stroking backwards and forwards along and between the parallel outlines, will form a level, gentle depression. This together with strengthened outlines, gives a good embossed appearance, and the depth (which is controlled by a large strap) will not inhibit the insertion of the lettering later. However, at the first fold of the ribbon, the corners must be square, the edge sharp, and it must be flat at that particular section, so that it is necessary to melt one area into the other.

3 The progress of this detail, as with all others, should be checked with a plasticine impression, for it is very easy to baffle oneself by the varying order of depths required to create the correct sculptural illusion.

Countersinking started after the main linework has been strengthened

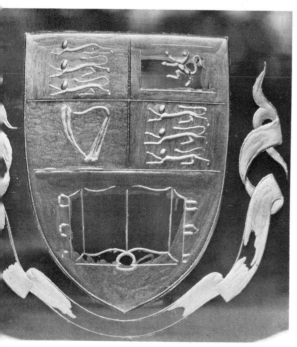

Engraving the Rampant Lion

1 As described earlier, this detail is to be polished out against a white matt, so it is best to complete it first. Cut all the vertical and horizontal 'field lines through their appropriate quarters. The backgrounds to these will be gently lightened during the next step.

2 Polish all the details requiring it at this moment; polish the lion and all matt backgrounds to the correct tone.

3 Re-matt the surface surrounding the Scottish lion with a water/abrasive mix. (Earlier matting was effected with an oil/abrasive mix.) The superior whiteness of the water matt gives a fine contrast to the lion and the small polished printies, and a change of colour to the other matted areas.

4 Engrave the small dots, representing gold, to the background of the rampant lion. Because of the scale, these dots are necessarily very tiny and in this case are engraved as miniature printies with a pinhead into the matt surface, using an abrasive fine enough (about 800 grit) to leave them polished, or rather of a sufficiently polished appearance.

Engraving the Three Couchant Lions

These are handled exactly as before but, because of their smallness, in a sharper, more abbreviated scale of modelling depths.

Engraving the book

In preparation for the overall modelling, countersink the

The countersunk shield and ribbon slightly polished. Matted background to the lion half completed. Lettering positioned. Red and blue tinctures (vertical and horizontal lines) inserted

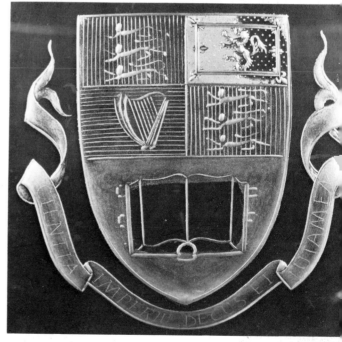

flat, open pages into the cover. Engrave the flat planes of the book edges. Keep a firm grip on the modelling as the engraving proceeds.

There is quite an amount of labour in this harmless looking detail. The planes of the book edges must be level and sharp with the right depth relative to the deeper open pages and the shallower cover. There is no short cut to this; each flat recess or corner must be patiently worked in

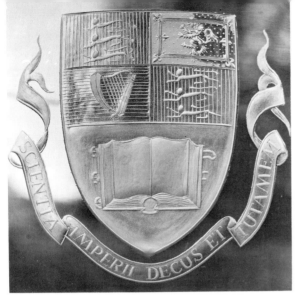

The book countersunk, modelled and detailed. The harp and lions improved

the orthodox manner with small, sharp, and rounded strap wheels. The modelling of the open pages, where they slip into the spine of the book, should meet in a clean, forward mitre.

Other details such as the clasp of the lines representing the edges of the pages speak for themselves.

Engraving the Harp

Model this feature in the same manner as the book, countersinking the main frame as a purchase for the smaller details. This cannot be a success unless tackled with a little vigour. It is a tricky detail which needs to be right first time. The receding planes of the main structure should be cut firmly, and of level depth, and held together with sharp supporting lines. Any surface decoration should just be suggested, or hinted at, rather than be struggled with. The matt harp strings, cut firm against the slightly polished background, should give a fair feeling of depth.

The finished engraving. Note the polished accents of light and the two versions of the gold background

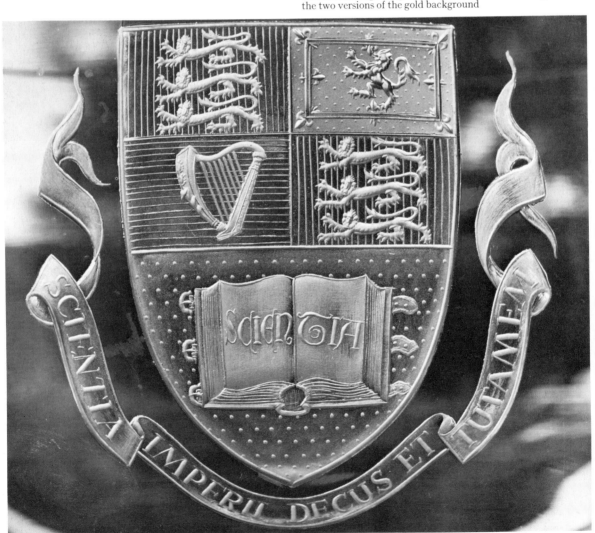

The Flow of Work

Although the approach to this commission has been described as proceeding in a particular order, the work will actually flow creatively from one part of the design to another, according to which process of wheel is in use at that moment. Obviously, all sharp corners, or similar completing details, will tend to be finished at the same time, while the line wheel will be intermittently re-defining peripheral linework throughout the task. No matter how organinised an engraver may be there is always some obstacle he will eagerly wish to overcome, or some area of work will sieze him, defeating his innate sense of order – and quite properly so.

The lettering on the book and ribbon has been omitted at this juncture because the problems involved are better dealt with in another section. Suffice it to say that it is built up with very small line and sharp strap wheels, of which quite half a dozen will be called upon. Enough has been experienced in engraving small curves, say the tail or claw of the lion, to enable the engraver to know how to tackle the job, but there is no room here for a slip which in other circumstances might be turned into an embellish-ment, or for bad spacing and shape, even where the engraving itself is perfect.

HERALDIC LINEAR ENGRAVING
Engraving with Dental Burrs

As a useful sequel to the previous work, and much less difficult, another example of heraldic engraving, completely linear, is included here. While intaglio engraved, heraldic presentation pieces are always very desirable, they take a long time to complete, are very exacting and therefore costly; they may demand a higher price than a customer wishes to pay. The linear design illustrated is a very good alternative and, because there are less constraints in the engraving of such a design, it could gain in decorative invention what it loses in sculptural quality. And of course it is quicker and cheaper.

Detail of a Nüremberg goblet engraved by Hermann Schwinger, 1681, depicting a coat of arms

The linear design illustrated was engraved at the lathe with dental burrs, pin-vice held, mounted on a spindle. The method of tentatively sketching a design into the surface of the glass as a preliminary to intaglio engraving

A coat or arms, engraved in linework only (height: 50 mm, 2 in). Right hand side, an even strength of line. Left hand side showing the linework slightly flared (widened). Engraved by Peter Dreiser

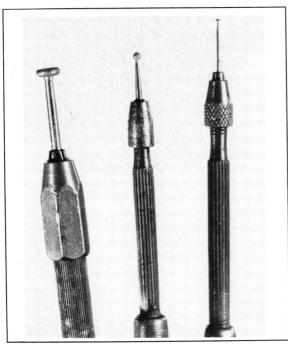

Pin vices mounted on spindles. The two on the left are small dental burrs, and the one on the right is a shaped pin for very fine work

is now commonplace, but in this instance the engraving is firmer, more confidently accurate to the drawing.

Before the time of the dental burr, the only quick alternative in handling linear work – etching apart – would have been the diamond point or by the prepared end of a spindle on the lathe. However, concentrating on the lathe at the moment (for the diamond point has special characteristics) the dental burr is superior in most respects, giving a cleaner, whiter line than the abrasive-fed spindle. But in saying this, a distinction must be drawn between work of the kind illustrated, which is rapid and effective enough, and linework cut with very fine wheels to form a continuous line which is altogether more elegant, sharp, clean and regular.

Egermann Glass

Superficial linework may be engraved with a tiny, rounded strap wheel which, by being moved around the design with hardly a change of angle, gives broader or narrower lines roughly in the manner of pen lettering. Engraving of this type, known as Egerman glass, was widely executed – perhaps that is the appropriate word – in the early part of the nineteenth century. Friedrich Egermann (1777–1864), a man of many parts, experimented with coloured glass of all kinds, but the kind of engraving referred to was applied mostly to a surface stained glass (as distinct from cased or flashed glass) upon which the slightest slipping of the wheel exposed clear glass beneath. It had its attraction for the cheap end of the market but in no way approached engraved cased glass. No doubt the engravers were deft enough since any overwork would be disastrous, but the general level of quality – even in the best examples – is rather poor.

Adding Decorative Emphasis

The drawback to straightforward linearity is its tendency to be flat, even boring, so that it is as well to strengthen the design quality if possible, or at least give some decorative emphasis to small details, so as to impart a little life. Some flow and rhythm can be added by fastidiously varying the width of line, a procedure best handled with an inverted cone-shaped burr which increases in width as its cuts deeper. Where to start is a matter of common sense, entering the tool at the point chosen to be the widest part of the line and stroking the tool one or both ways until the right flare is obtained.

If the engraving still appears a little stark, it does not take much time to add a small amount of tone or stipple as a final embellishment, but it should not be so much as to detract from the overall linearity, which can be a very powerful design factor, existing in its own right.

In conclusion, though cut on the lathe, this design could just as well have been engraved by the flexible drive method. Indeed, in some positions, or because of its weight, a glass can only be more safely controlled by this means. Whatever the work, if the engraver feels more secure with any alternative method, for instance in engraving lettering on an awkward foot, he would be foolish not to use it. But it is wise to recognise not which tool will do it easier but which, in fact, will do it better.

6 Wheel Engraved Lettering

THE ELEMENTS OF DESIGN

In any skill, whether wood, stone, brass or glass it is a first priority to have a firm knowledge of lettering in all its aspects: alphabetic, calligraphic and typographic. It is not possible to be 'good' at lettering without earlier experience with pen or brush. Even when the elements of shape and spacing have been mastered, problems of rhythm and design for its applied purpose remain. It is a lifetime's study and the engraver is fortunate who, in early training, was disciplined in pen lettering, or Roman alphabets.

However the newcomer should not be discouraged by early difficulties with lettering which after a time may be more a question of style rather than engraving skill. Once mastered it will become, as it does with most calligraphers, an obsessive pleasure. Hopefully then, the engraver will approach this almost separate art with the necessary patience and application rather than avoid the effort and ignore its importance.

The ceremonial, sentimental and commercial reasons for the demand for lettering or glass have been evident through the centuries and should the modern engraver neglect or find this part of his task too intimidating, the ever developing technology for applying designs to glass will quickly fill the gap. It hardly needs saying that such encouragement to commercialism is not in the interest of the craft when the best mechanical performance could well be good enough for the undiscerning client.

This book is concerned basically with the mechanics of engraving so, apart from hinting at the underlying aesthetic problems, no attempt will be made to answer the question of what is good or bad in lettering; it is better to consult the many excellent books on the subjects. However, some examples have been included of conventional and freely formed lettering engraved by wheel, flexible drive and diamond, which should be enough for the engraver to measure himself against in terms of design, flair and skill. With many commissions the lettering will be a simple reproduction of some supplied copy, but where there is no constraint, and particularly where lettering is the main element, it must be reiterated that success is heavily dependent upon the drawing and designing skills of the engraver. And the freer the style the more considered must be the design; there is no easy lettering.

Early Examples

As far as early wheel-engraved glass is concerned, it might

A wheel engraved, dark green, trumpet-shaped glass, by Herman Schwinger. 1683

be wondered what all the fuss is about, for the lettering, particularly on English glass, is crude enough to set a calligrapher's hair on end. The main virtue-as with some early examples of woodcarving – is that the unselfconscious mark of the tool is clearly to be seen in the construction of the lettering, which is entirely consistent in vigour and individuality – in naïvety – with the overall design. There are, of course superb examples of wheel-cut lettering to be seen, mostly from Europe, but in the main it can be said that the quality of early lettering falls behind the standard of other engraving skills.

It is hard to guess the reason for this, for at that time (the seventeenth and eighteenth century) lettering was as accomplished as any other skill; one does not need to go beyond the local church gravestone or brass, or even the face of a long-case clock, for the evidence. It can only be concluded that lettering was the last vexed thing a glass engraver learned and by then it was too late; or, more simply, perhaps a sculptor does not necessarily make a disciplined letterer, or a lettering artist a good sculptor.

METHODS OF ENGRAVING LETTERING

There are obvious cramping difficulties in handling tight curves at the fixed head of the lathe, consequently the methods by which 'cut' lettering may be formed are quite limited. Apart from the use of the burr (see heraldic linear engraving), which abrades the surface rather than engraves, the wheels used for lettering are restricted to the line, sharp strap and mitre.

Line and Strap Wheels

By using the basic cuts of the line and strap wheels the elementary shape of the letters may be crudely built up. The resulting angularity can be seen on many a Georgian glass. As lettering, apart from its almost reckless vitality, it gives more pain than pleasure and can hardly be justified on any modern glass of merit. The only exception to this is old English or German Gothic script which, because of its structure, cannot be engraved by any other means.

Though very simple in structure, it is imperative that the individual cuts be accurately positioned, of equal weight, regular and precise. Thus the wheels must be very sharp and as large as possible; that is, large enough for the arc of the cut to allow a little manoeuvring at the end of the stroke, but not so small as to be obliged to fidget up

and down the length. Some help may be given to the curves in letters such as 'B', by leaning the strap over on its edge so as to give a rounder entry and exit to the cut. This, of course, will be more effective the smaller the lettering, when a simple half moon will fill the need. Where thick cross-strokes occur, as with 'A', a blunt square end may result, so the strap should be slipped out to give the correct angle.

A much better formation is obtained by first engraving the running outline of the lettering in one single cut line, subsequently adding the stronger strokes to the letters as they should apply. The smaller line wheels necessary for the continuous line must be fitted to this exacting task. Each wheel must be absolutely sharp and not larger in diameter than the section of curve it is attempting to engrave naturally, and where the line is straight or the curve slight a larger wheel should be used. Each curve or part of a curve must be patiently built up, entering and re-entering the line wheel as it follows each individual letter. There is not much room for error.

The strap wheels used for strengthening the main strokes and curves can be a little larger than the line wheels and must be very edge-sharp so that the location for the crescent-type cuts, which make up the curves, can be 'felt' to be secure. The strengthening takes place at the thickest point, the wheel stroking the angled cut both ways to lead into the thinner portion of the letter. The curves are enlarged from the inner outline outwards, so some allowance should have been made in the initial outline engraving for this.

1

Samples of wheel cut lettering:
1 Simple line and strap lettering
2 Lettering built upon a line framework
3 More fluent use of the flat strap

4 Gothic lettering: line and strap
5 Old English lettering in various stages of finish
6 and 7 further examples of decorative orthodox script.
   Engraved by Peter Dreiser

5

6

7

Mitre Wheel

The mitre wheel is a good alternative to the strap. It is rather easier to locate and control within the engraved outline and imparts a fine, prismatic, chisel-cut effect, which in some cases – particularly in long flowing lines and gentle curves – may be considered very superior. But in engraving tight curves there is a danger – almost a certainty – of producing a feathered outer edge. Selectively used, say in an intertwining monogram, the sharp brilliance of the cut can be entrancing. Naturally, the sharper the mitre the more incisive and brilliant the cut.

Diamond Burr

Any well-formed lettering, however produced, is extremely difficult. Indeed, the reader may have long formed the impression that everything is equally difficult. This is not so. It is simply that each separate task has its own inbuilt problem. With lettering, although every stroke may have been mastered, any imbalance of shape or angle will stick out like a sore thumb. In general it must be admitted that engraving lettering by the wheel is very inhibiting, so that until some real confidence has been built up, the engraving of the lettering, such as that within the ribbon of the heraldic

A reproduction of a J.S.Bach 'mirror' monogram, 1740, engraved with the mitre and sharp strap (edge cut). A fine model to practise. By P. Dreiser. Engraved size height 50mm (2 in)

Lettering engraved with a diamond burr on the lathe. By P. Dreiser

design, may better be left to the multi-directional cut of the diamond burr, in combination with the flexible drive which allows more freedom and control over lettering curves.

The use of the dental burr on the lathe was introduced in Chapter 5 in the engraving of a linear coat of arms. The burr is dealt with at greater length in Chapter 14.

Comparing the Method

It will now be evident where the main obstacles lie: that, size apart, the more formal the lettering the more difficult it is to engrave; that a letter made up of straight lines, the Roman 'A' for example, is easy enough until the serif is reached, but a Roman 'O' or lower case 'g' could hardly be faced without some trepidation. But not all lettering is formal, and there are many freer or more decorative shapes, as may be used in a monogram, which can be handled with much greater panache by the wheel. After all, when well done it has one advantage over all other processes: the facility to cut clean-edged, evenly-incised lines of varying widths, which, because of the greater depth, will catch the light in a much bolder fashion than can be captured by the burr or diamond.

7 Engraving Architectural Subjects

DESIGNING A THREE-DIMENSIONAL SUBJECT

Engraving architectural subjects – manor houses, civic centres, churches, buildings of all kinds – is among the most exacting, and perhaps the most unrewarding, of commissions which the engraver must face. The opportunity for decorative innovation is very limited, while the engraving difficulties involved in satisfactorily interpreting three-dimensional architectural details, such as windows, within a perspective framework, makes it a very daunting task. (All this, of course, does not apply to diamond point engraving, where a freer, more beguiling style may be used.)

The type of building to be engraved makes a great difference to the attraction of the finished engraving; a rococo facade, for example, will allow a greater variety than, say, a flat Georgian front, but the choice of the subject is seldom that of the engraver. Ordinarily the engraver will be supplied with a series of photographs to work from, and very inhibiting they may be too, for average photographs seldom impart the character or essence of anything. If photographs are to be used then the engraver is better served by doing the job himself, photographing the subject from different angles so as to understand fully, or to be stimulated by, the most outstanding features. If he can sketch the building and its surroundings at the same time, so much the better, for the concentration will add to the interpretative information.

Nineteenth-century engravings of urban and rural England, based as they were on artists' drawings, have a decorative power which is difficult to equal, it may be that the quality of design in these early examples of engraved glass depicting buildings stems from the fact that glass engravers worked from similar copper plate engravings used in printing. This is not to denigrate photography; but it is safer to use it to verify information than as an aesthetic tool. Naturally, the decorative quality of the intaglio reproduction will gain if the building can be drawn in a rural setting, when trees, paths, and a distant vista will add to the interest of the scene, or at least offset a plain façade.

Here again, some earlier experiences in landscape drawing should have been gained, or the countryside should have been studied very closely before attempting to add such decorative subjects, for nothing is more damaging to an otherwise competent work than the inclusion, out of desperation, of some ill-formed feature.

Choice of Glass

If the engraver has any choice in the matter, he will select a cylindrical glass or flat decanter for work of this nature, for on both surfaces the uprights will remain upright from any reasonable viewpoint. However, working on large flat surfaces brings its own difficulties, for in some positions the spindle may foul the glass. On the whole, for comfort and looks, the preference will usually be for a cylindrical surface.

Unless a design is very small, a globular vessel should be avoided at all costs. Design problems are complicated enough with cone-shaped glass where the engraver must choose between two evils: that of plotting his uprights on the true vertical axis of the glass, in which case the buildings will appear to splay outwards from a fixed viewpoint, but look reasonably acceptable in movement, or that of drawing the verticals from one fixed position, when the opposite visual effect will occur. Either way, a

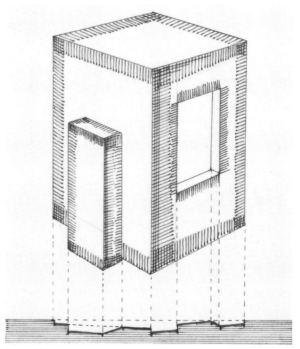

An architectural model describing the practical intaglio treatment of the main planes. Note the avoidance of an internal mitre for the most forward vertical, and the relative depths of protruding porch and recessed window to their particular planes

An original steel engraving copy

little compromise is necessary, and with too many uprights the result may always be a little uneasy.

Engraving Problems

Many of the practical engraving problems which apply to architecture have already been met in the chapter on heraldry, therefore only the order and method of the work will be given here. This, together with sequential photographs, will be reference enough for any project of a similar nature. However, unless the wheel engraver has had previous experience of architectural subjects, before starting some ambitious piece, it would be worthwhile experimenting first in order to understand the principles involved. Consider, or indeed cut, a simple architectural model with its recessive planes. Taking the two facing sides (assuming that the framwork had already been outlined), it could be assumed that the forward-looking vertical would be formed from a sharply incised mitre, with the two sides gradually diminishing in depth to the surface of the glass.

This can be done, but there are practical impediments to tackling the job this way: firstly there is the actual difficulty of forming perfect internal mitres, and secondly there is the need for all planes to be as shallow as possible to allow for the entry of other, deeper details. Hence it is expedient to recess one facet to a sharp, deep, forward edge and to bring the other place, halfway in depth, to meet it as a step rather than a mitre. By these means, together with some selective emphasis to the framework, the illusion of reality is sufficiently created for other work to continue. Apart from the obvious leading corner, where and how the 'steps' occur in the actual subject can only be decided by experience; certainly, all sunken planes must

be engraved with caution for the final depths will be dependent on what further details must be engraved into, or left proud of, the surface.

ARCHITECTURAL STUDY: A COUNTRY HOUSE

The design

The commissioned engraving to be considered is based on a line engraving. In it the artist has beautifully grasped the architectural details of a building, which is still partly existing, for his own illustrative purpose. Apart from the need for reduction or enlargement, many of the design difficulties have already been solved for the glass engraver. It still must be translated into intaglio form, but the artistic spirit in it may, hopefully, be held.

Outlining the Design

Wheel: line (various sizes).

Abrasive: 400 carborundum/oil mix.

Speed: slow.

With the appropriate size line wheels, firmly outline the main structures of the building.

Engraving the Background

Wheel: rounded strap.

Abrasive: 320 carborundum/oil.

Speed: slow.

Lightly engrave the clouds or any distant landscape in advance of any other work. It is better to complete the background so that any polishing subsequent to the soft strap work does not interfere with the building. Naturally, all trees or foreground detail, being nearer, will be engraved last of all.

Starting at the top, engrave the first layer of clouds. Complete and polish back the underside shadows before superimposing the next layer, and so on, until the right perspective quality has been reached. Extend the clouds under any proposed overlapping details, such as trees, but polish back to a dark tone any engraving immediately near the rooftops in order to give a good profile contrast. All this depends upon the background design. The clouds are a matter of judgement – it is so easy to produce a series of cauliflower heads.

Countersinking the Forward Planes

Wheel: sharp strap.

Abrasive: 320 carborundum/oil mix.

Speed: slow.

Determine the leading edges and start countersinking the main forward planes accordingly as a scaffolding for the other perspective masses.

Continue countersinking, carefully emphasising forward details such as the porch and gables. Work around the windows, leaving them at the original level so as to appear recessed. Conversely, recess the bay windows so

that they give the impression of thrusting forward.

At this stage a good deal of unevenness is to be expected, but it is much more important to develop the right depth of relationships between planes than bother with imperfections. Smoothing out should not begin until this main structure modelling has been satisfactorily completed.

Smoothing Out the Planes

Wheel: rounded strap (various sizes).

Abrasive: 320 carborundum/oil mix.

Speed: slow.

Remembering to reduce the speed of the strap wheel, smooth down and soften the texture of the countersunk planes. This is a long drawn out process, for, after the initial smoothing, smaller wheels have to be employed to enter and clean out neglected corners or the angles of towers and gables (indeed every countersunk area) until the recesses are cleaned-out and level.

Linework Detail

Wheel: line (large and small).

Abrasive: 400 carborundum/oil.

Speed: medium to slow.

When all the countersunk planes have been defined to give the best three-dimensional base likely to be obtained, redefine the main structure or framework which would

The first stage roughing-out (*above*)

The main planes countersunk. The trees delineated (*below*)

The planes smoothed out, the structure redefined and the trees improved in shape (*above*)

The finished decanter showing the improved detail in trees and house. By Peter Dreiser

emphasise any important enclosed shape, such as gables or windows. All confirming lines should be cut just *within* the edge of the countersunk plane using wheels as large as the line will support without risk of over-running.

Continue with the subsidiary details (tiling, window bars, tops of columns or finials) until the whole design begins to take shape. At this point the engraving will swing from one detail to another and as the wheels became too blunt for one purpose they will be systematically used for another; for example, the bushes and trees.

Adding Patterns and Textures

Wheel: rounded strap.

Abrasive; 320 carborundum/oil mix.

Speed: slow.

Add the surface patterns of woodwork to the outbuildings and, as with any other surface textures, do this gently otherwise it may attract attention rather than harmonise with the structure. Carefully insert the foreground path on the right perspective curve. When satisfied that everything which is important has been included or sharpened up, add the deeper decorative form to the bushes and trees, to give distance and movement, but without allowing them to dominate the eye.

Polishing

Wheel: cork.

Abrasive: 400 pumice/water paste.

Speed: slow.

Finally, with a cork wheel of the appropriate size (wood is rather too harsh), polish a few strategic shadows: to the sides of the towers, gables, windows, porches, bushes, and within the form of the tree which, if adroitly done, will greatly add to the tonal contrast. If, by mischance, an edge is overrun, the tone may be put back, manually, with a ball-ended dental burr.

The Importance of Accuracy

Architectural subjects of this kind are the most demanding of all tasks. Akin to lettering, there is no decorative escape from an ill-directed cut, for that which in many other projects may be hidden or disguised will become an abomination in both perspective design and lettering. It is pointless to complain that the glass decanter was too heavy, or so large that it fouled the spindle, or that the details were too small for the line wheels to cope with, or that one eye needs correcting for astigmatism – one's skill is stripped naked. All is revealed.

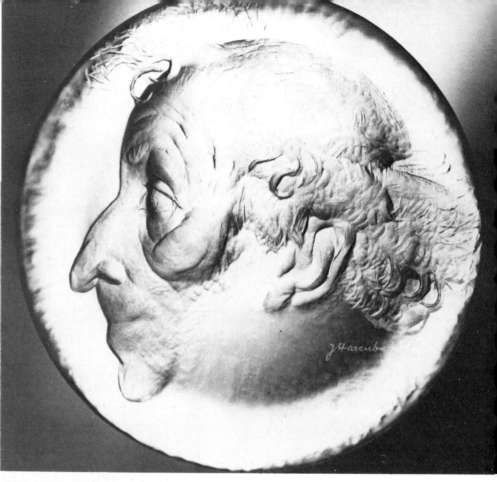

A general view of Baden Baden, possibly from Gagenau, abou 1840. Tumbler height is 150mm (6 ins) (*below left*)

Four fine examples of modern wheel engraving
Portrait of Marc Chagall, I Harcuba, Prague, 1977 140mm (5 ins) (*above*)
'Europa and the bull'. Curved optical glass, Jane Webster Width 250mm (10 in) (*below*)
'Iguana', Michael Fairbairn, 1975. 300mm (12 in) (*opposite*)
'Dragonfly'. Design by Sheldon Fink, engraved by Steuben Width 400mm (16 in) (*opposite*)

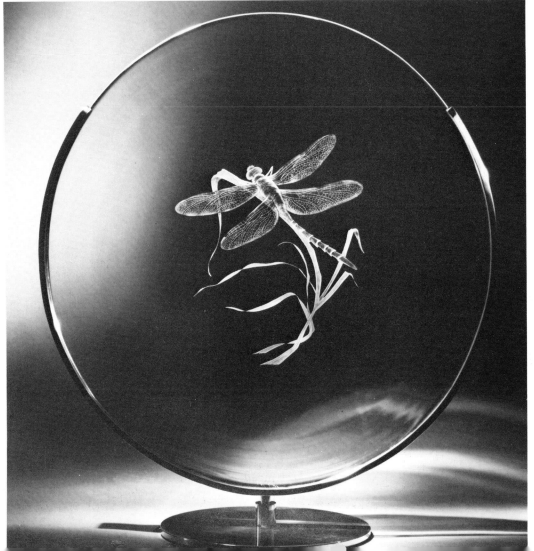

8 Synthetic and Diamond Wheels

No doubt the engraver is well aware that synthetic and diamond wheels exist as a modern alternative to grit-fed copper wheels, and has been perplexed that these have not been introduced until now. The reason for this is that, for the greater part of the developing skills at the lathe, the traditional copper wheel offers the best training in terms of patience, control, feel and flexibility, which only a quick glance over past engraving skills should confirm. However, equipment does change, for convenience if not always for the better, and it would be a foolish purist who did not accept improvements in lathes, materials and methods.

Natural stone and synthetic abrasive wheels have been in use for a long time. They have an advantage over copper in speed and convenience which increases as the work becomes larger and broader. There is one category of wheel engraving – so-called *intaglio* (described in the next chapter) – in which stone and synthetic wheels are used exclusively, up to 180 mm (7 in) or more in diameter, which by the nature of the engraving need to be fast in abrasion and resistant to profile wear. It is these characteristics, together with the convenience of water lubrication, which make similar wheels attractive for small scale average wheel engraving, but within reason.

THE ABRASIVES

Synthetic grinding wheels are, for the most part, based upon three abrasives: aluminium oxide, silicon carbide and diamond. Although it would be far better to refer to the materials alone, namely, aluminium oxide and silicon carbide, which does occur in some catalogues, the terms corundum and carborundum have such wide currency that the terms have been kept throughout the text.

Aluminium oxide (Corundum, Aloxite) (9)

Found naturally as bauxite, and in its purest crystalline form as the gemstones ruby and sapphire, aluminium oxide may also be found in one of its impure forms as black corundum or emery. High quality corundum is now produced synthetically.

Silicon carbide (Carborundum) (9½)

Universally known as carborundum, this substance is a synthetic combination of silica and carbon, first made in the United States 1891.

Diamond (10)

Diamond, the hardest known mineral, is a crystaline form of carbon. Its gem forms may be transparent, brilliant and colourless; other forms may be blue, black or yellow. Industrial diamonds may now be produced synthetically.

Scale of hardness

The bracketed numbers given above represent the hardness of the materials on a scale of 1 to 10 (known as Mohs scale), hence they are very hard indeed. Quartz crystal, for example has a hardness of **7** and glass approximately **5–5½**.

CORUNDUM AND CARBORUNDUM WHEELS

The advanced technology which is used in the manufacture and grading of these abrasives guarantees a very high standard of reliability of the components from which they are formed.

Grit or Grain Size

The particle size on which the grinding efficiency depends is determined by the sieve mesh through which the abrasive is passed; the number of spaces per linear inch. The standard range is **8, 10, 12, 14** etc., in regular increments up to **1200**. For engineering the range would roughly fall between **12** (very coarse) to **130**, for the glass engraver from **100** (coarse) to **400**, and for the lapidary from **60** to **600/1200** for final polishing.

The Bond

The matrix, in which the grit is held and formed to shape, may be ceramic – that is the material is vitrified with clay and other fusible materials, synthetic resin, rubber or shellac. The two used by engravers, vitreous and rubber bonds, are code marked 'V' and 'R'.

Grade

The grade or hardness of the bond on which the cutting efficiency depends varies from soft to very hard, and is alphabetically coded from A (soft) to Z (hard), of which the medium range M, N, O, P would be used mostly by the engraver. Other qualities such as the density of the grit must be left to the manufacturer.

Ordering Synthetic Wheels

By using the accepted standard coding, synthetic wheels may be ordered to specification and repeated with certainty, for example:

Abrasive	Letter code	Grain size	Grade	Bond
Carborundum (Silicon Carbide)	C	100	K	V
Corundum (Aluminium Oxide)	A	180	M	V

In abbreviated form, the above example would read C 100 K V and A 180 M V.

Although wheels of all sizes may be ordered to coded specification, this applies more to large than small wheels. Wheels below 60mm (2½ in) are much more easily obtained 'off the shelf' as general purpose wheels, limited to coarse, medium and fine grades, the greatest range of which are supplied by the dental trade. They are very valuable tools but do suffer – as does the engraver – from the variation in quality from one manufacturer to the other.

A selection of synthetic wheels: carborundum, brown bauxite (corundum,) and high quality white synthetic aluminium oxide (aloxite). All have been lead bushed

DIAMOND WHEELS

Early Use of Diamond Abrasive

The use of diamond grit appears to be a relatively recent development. Artisans of the past were well aware of the use of emery or crushed garnets as abrasives and knew that their simple tools worked much better, in drilling for example, when the grit had become embedded in the grinding end. Whether the glass engravers at any time deliberately incorporated diamond grit into their wheels cannot be known, but they must have tried everything in sight in order to extend the life of the cut. Although the physical quality of the diamond was known to the Greeks, it is not until **1456** that is appears to have been used for a practical working process. The Flemish lapidary, Ludwig van Berquem is said to have been the first man to use diamond dust for polishing gems.

However, experience in engraving hardstones leads one to the opinion that if the diamond was not used earlier something very near to it was, perhaps crushed rubies. Natural black corundum (emery) or quartz makes very little impression on semiprecious stones, leaving a burnished condition quite unlike the structure which is evident on intaglio hardstone cylinder seals. As for pumice, it would be as useless as 'rotten-stone' (decomposed limestone) for hardstone engraving.

While the requirements of scientific investigation must rule out attempts at romantic speculation, considering the close association which would have taken place between the gem engraver and the lapidary, if diamonds had been available, it would have been uncharacteristically obtuse of the engraver not to have used them in one way or another. At the very least, surely from Berquem's time forward, some enterprising engraver must have incorporated diamond dust in his abrasive paste. Copper wheels can be embedded with diamond grit by simply physically rolling it under pressure into the profile, and this will lengthen its useful life by many hours. Yet it must be remembered that once the grit is embedded it becomes difficult to reshape the profile, so it is prudent to limit any experiment to just one or two selected wheels.

Composition of Modern Diamond Wheels

Modern impregnated diamond wheels are high precision grinding tools made to exact limits for the engineer. Above 25mm (1 in) diameter they become preposterously expensive, but can cover a vast amount of work, and do it so quickly that most engravers will be eventually invest in

A small sintered diamond wheel showing the normal limit, about 3mm (⅛ in) thickness of impregnated diamond grit at the outer edge

one or two small wheels.

Diamond grit (which may be graded in micron sizes) of precise specification is distributed in a metal matrix which is formed by welding the powered metal and diamond grit mix together ('sintering') at very high temperature and pressure. The metal is usually phosphor bronze, but it need not necessarily be so. A nickel steel diamond sintered wheel, in some respects, is superior to phosphor bronze. But the engraver must take what he can find.

WHEEL SELECTION

The following choice of wheels has been suggested for the main, but overlapping, categories of work: roughing out, intermediate modelling, detail modelling and work requiring polishing.

Roughing Out and Coarse Work

Carborundum wheel: 120 grit, medium bond, L,M,N

Whether L, M or N bond is required will depend on the hardness of the material. The harder the glass, the softer the bond; the softer the glass the harder the bond. Hence a soda-lime glass may need an L bond, and a full lead crystal glass an N bond. Carborundum is fast cutting but rather messy, breaking up rather rapidly so that the profile is difficult to preserve. However, it is very useful for heavy shaping, and if speed is essential it is the only alternative to the diamond wheel.

Diamond wheel: 180 grit, phosphor-bronze sintered, $50 \times 8mm$ ($2 \times \frac{5}{16}$ in)

The diamond wheel at 180 grit cuts fiercely and fast, and is resistant to wear for many years. This grade should be used exclusively for roughing out.

Intermediate shaping and modelling

Carborundum wheels: 220 grit, medium-bond, M, N

The sizes can be a repeat of those copper wheels found most useful for this purpose.

Diamond wheels: 400 grit, phosphor-bronze sintered, $25 \times 4mm$ ($1 \times \frac{3}{16}$ in); $12 \times 2.5mm$ ($\frac{1}{2} \times \frac{7}{64}$ in); $5 \times 1.5mm$ ($\frac{7}{32} \times \frac{1}{16}$ in)

Select all three of the sizes given, or as near as can be purchased. If one only can be afforded, the best choice would be $25 \times 4mm$ ($1 \times \frac{3}{16}$ in), for this size wheel will do the most work.

Final Detail Modelling

Copper wheel

There is no alternative to the orthodox copper wheel.

Work Requiring Polishing

Corundum wheel: 220 grit, medium bond, M

In general, this wheel can be used for all printies, olives, lines, mitres, matts and any cut which may require polishing. The wheel may be of any size commensurate with the task. The glass, soft or hard, has much less bearing on the choice of bond for corundum wheels. It is the actual quality of the cut that is important. Where a relatively large area of glass is to be ground to a near polishing condition, for example a large shallow printy or olive, the best finish will be obtained from an L or M bond. A line or mitre wheel could be much harder still – nearer to the grade limit.

SETTING UP THE WHEELS

Synthetic Wheels: Making a Lead Bush

All wheels are supplied with centre holes, and some may have lead centres, but neither of these conditions is of use to the wheel engraver. Each wheel must be provided with a secure lead bush, so that it can be rapidly screwed on and off the tapered screw-ended spindles. It is a nuisance but not too difficult a problem to solve.

1 Prepare a disc of good plywood, rather larger than the wheel to be bushed, and countersink the centre, say 12mm ($\frac{1}{2}$ in) diameter × 3mm ($\frac{1}{8}$ in) deep depending on the size of the wheel to be bushed

2 With the spindle set in the lathe, screw the disc onto the spindle end, keeping it as vertical as possible until it is quite tight. Allow sufficient of the spindle end to protrude to secure the bush eventually.

3 True up the vertical face of the revolving plywood disc. Leave it on the spindle.

4 Chip away the centre of the synthetic wheel leaving any irregularities which will act as a key to grip the lead bush.

Setting up – centering – the wheel on the spindle support

5 Remove the spindle and secure it upright. Place the wheel on the face of the disc, where it should allow the spindle end to protrude about 3mm ($\frac{1}{8}$ in) beyond the wheel and have a space of not less than 2.5mm ($\frac{7}{64}$ in) around the screw through which to cast the lead bush.

6 Pre-warm the wheel to remove moisture or coldness in order to prevent cracking-particularly with thin wheels.

Pouring the lead

breaking a thin wheel, or use the punch against a sloppy wheel. At this stage correct any which are out of alignment.

The bushes made as described can be as neat and professional as desired. All they need to be is tightly embedded on the wheel with a well-formed thread, and in balance. If the casting has been uneven and lumpy the excess metal can easily be turned back on the lathe with a knife. Obviously, the large wheels will be better accommodated with a course-threaded spindle and, conversely, small wheels with a fine. (Professional equipment for casting bushes is shown in the illustration.)

7 Melt a little lead in a small ladle and gently pour it into the space around the centre of the wheel until the excess metal rises to form a small button. Thin light wheels may be 'floated' out of close contact with the plywood base, therefore it is best to hold it down, for the few seconds it takes with a file tang or anything which keeps the fingers away from danger.

8 Unscrew the chilled wheel from the spindle, which should now be provided with a perfectly good taper threaded bush. However, as the lead contracts on cooling, a slight movement may be felt (sometimes hardly perceptible) which must be remedied.

The bushed wheel released from its support mould

Professional equipment for casting lead bushes

9 Replace the wheel firmly on the lathe-held spindle, and with a blunt punch gently tap all the way round the bush centre, both front and back, until the wheel is securely gripped. As the tightening progresses the bush may be loosened on the spindle, in which event the wheel should be screwed up firmly, hand-tight, before continuing. Do not endanger the spindle thread, or risk

Diamond Wheels: riveting to the Spindle

Diamond wheels are manufactured to precise limits. In order to perform efficiently they must be firmly and accurately set up at dead centre, run at a fairly high speed and copiously lubricated with water. If any unevenness or eccentricity of the smallest kind occurs it will be a fault in the setting up, not that of the wheel. As it is beyond the layman to amend the shape, unlike all other wheels which are trued to the spindle, the spindle must be tailored to the diamond wheel. It is important, therefore, to prescribe the size of the centre hole most suited for the spindle, that is, if there is any choice in the matter.

It follows that more than usual care should be given to the preparation or selection of the spindle, which should have a cleanly, shallow-tapered and accurately-centred end, and in riveting the wheel to it. All the actions which have been described earlier in the setting up of copper wheels should be meticulously followed. Diamond wheels larger than about 6mm ($\frac{1}{4}$ in) are unlikely to be made with a band of sintered diamond grit more than 3mm ($\frac{1}{8}$ in) in from the circumference, so that making a taper to fit the spindle is as easy as setting up the copper wheel, except that the phosphor-bronze core will be tougher. Small, completely-sintered wheels must be riveted against a

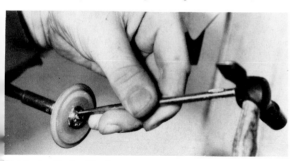

Tightening the lead bush

small shoulder which, if the spindle can be accurately turned to fit the centre hole, is the best way of mounting all diamond wheels.

If, in a running test, the wheel revolves out of centre, there is no other recourse than to correct the spindle with the bending iron, which at this late stage should be handled with the greatest care and patience.

CORRECTING THE PROFILE

Freshly bushed synthetic wheels need correcting for balance or concentricity, as do new copper wheels, but it is more difficult to acomplish. Being compacted of hard and dense materials, there are limited means by which high spots on an accentrically running wheel may be reduced. Each material is handled differently.

Carborundum Wheels

As silicon carbide is nearly as hard as the diamond, it should be no surprise that an efficient dressing tool would incorporate the harder material. Several such diamond dressing tools are illustrated, but the cost almost prohibits their use for the average engraver unless a great deal is being undertaken with synthetic wheels. And, as the main action of dressing consists of tearing away the softer bonding to allow the grit to loosen and break away, cheaper, if slower, metal alternatives to the diamond are also available.

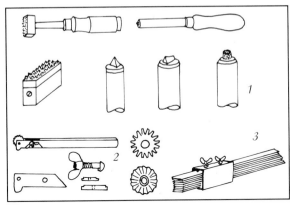

Dressing carborundum wheels:
1 Professional diamond dressing tools
2 The spur dressing tool
3 An effective improvised tool made from hacksaw blades

Diamond dressing tool

1 Improvise a frame or bridge-rest of wood on which to control the tool, with the lintel, so to speak, parallel to and just below the level of the spindle.
2 Initially set the machine at medium speed, for if the wheel proves to be badly off-centre the pressure of the dressing tool may set up a damaging and unpleasant vibration.
3 Start the water feed.
4 Hold the tool securely on the rest and apply it to the running wheel at or just below dead centre. Continue until the worst of the jarring unevenness has gone.

5 Increase the speed and continue until the wheel runs smoothly concentric.
6 Shape the wheel to the appropriate profile.

As diamonds are prone to fracture under heavy shock, it is common sense and economic sense to respect the expensive tool by reducing the high spots gradually. Undue vibration may be absorbed by resting the tool on a piece of felt or thick cloth. The whole operation takes a matter of moments.

Spur wheel dressing tool

The professional tool is made up of a number of hardened steel spur-wheels, set up in parallel, which can move freely on a simple axle. When held almost vertically to the running wheel the spurs revolve, causing the points to 'chatter' and tear away the outer carborundum layer. Although it can be hand-held, it is better to secure it firmly on a rest similar to that suggested for the diamond tool. The 'attack' angle is slightly below centre.

Improvised metal dressing tool

There is a simpler alternative to the foregoing tool which is, perhaps, more effective for small wheels; in fact this homespun method could very well handle most of the carborundum wheels the average engraver might acquire. It consists of three or four old hacksaw blade ends, firmly bound together with wire to within 25mm (1 in) of the end. It is better held in the hand than on a rest, and should be directed to the underside of the running wheel at about 15° to 30° from the vertical. There is a critical position beyond which, instead of the vibrating blades scraping away the carborundum surface, the wheel begins to grind the steel instead, but the feel is quite different and easily adjusted to.

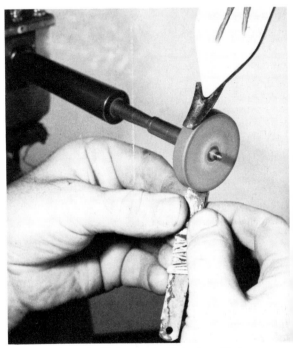

A carborundum wheel being trued with hacksaw blades

Corundum Wheels

Carborundum lapping stick

Corundum wheels are best shaped with a carborundum lapping or dressing stick which is manufactured for the specific purpose. Two are required, a coarse **80** grit for the greater part of the work, and a harder, finer **220** grit for the finishing. In lieu of these, broken pieces of carborundum of the appropriate grade will suffice, but the bonding and grit density of the correct lapping stick which is particularly formulated for the task is obviously better.

Diamond burr

A much more efficient method is to use the flat side of one or other of the dental diamond burrs of the shape illustrated. They are relatively cheap and will give a fast, positive cut that will do the job in half the time, leaving a precise profile, needing only a slight wipe over with the fine lapping stick, and it is an added pleasure to find a use for a part of a burr which is seldom used. To dress a sharp strap wheel, for example, assuming that any imbalance or unevenness has been dealt with, complete the following stages.

1 Direct the flat of the tool to the wheel at approximately 7 or 8 o'clock.

2 Starting from the centre of the profile, and with the flat very slightly inclined away to the right, wipe the profile gently to the right-hand edge of the wheel.

3 Reverse the procedure – from the centre to the left-hand edge – with the 'flat' inclined away to the left. By moving from the centre outward in this manner the danger of suddenly digging into the profile with the full flat of the tool is avoided.

4 Continue until the profile is square and sharp.

5 Stroke the sides of the wheel, from the centre towards the periphery, so as to give a final sharpness to the wheels.

Smoothing the profile

A short test cut at this stage would give a rather coarse grain, most probably with parallel burn streaks within it. This indicates that the profile is not uniformly smooth and is unfit for use – a condition after the initial dressing which can be taken for granted.

1 To smooth out the imperfections, run the wheel for a minute or so with plenty of water into hard bottle glass. Press hard and keep the bottle glass in a fixed stationary position. It must not be moved otherwise the particles of grit will break out against each other, which would defeat the object.

2 Continue until the (dried) profile has a fine, even sheen, when it should give a precise, flawless, silky cut and last for some hours. Until this condition is reached it is important that all dressing and test cuts should be stationary to the running wheel.

Mitres of any shape are handled on the same principle as the strap wheel but from the outside inwards to the sharp mitre point. The procedure for handling round or amended straps is self evident.

Diamond wheels

It is virtually impossible to change the shape of a diamond wheel, since no other substance is hard enough to make any impression on the profile. If special profiles are required they must be specifically ordered. The best that can be done is perhaps slightly rounding, or rather, blunting an edge which is too sharp, by running it into an approved lap (generally corundum) which, after about 40 minutes, may have modified it slightly.

THE COMPARISON OF QUALITY

Only by experience can the value, quality of cut or the feel of synthetic wheels be determined. They have been discussed here under specific categories, but the actual choice is nowhere so simple. Apart from speed and efficiency, texture too is important, and a coarse wheel which is too rough for many purposes may give just the right granular effect for a particular design. Again, a corundum wheel of the correct grade will give a distinctive, almost translucent matt as a finished decorative cut, very different from the oil or water matt of the copper wheel.

In general, artificial stones are harsher, more intractable and, as they must be run at higher speeds, much more dangerous than copper wheels. The random distribution of the grit in these wheels means that they will cut in any direction, and perhaps it is for this reason that they are inclined to a wilful movement away from the direct cut. Oddly, this tendency to wander does not occur to anything like the same extent with copper which, once started in its cut, will want to push forward in the same track.

Cut for cut, within the appropriate grade, there is not much difference in the quality of cut between a diamond and a carborundum wheel, but of course the carborundum will wear very much more rapidly and need frequent redressing, either for the correction of the profile or to remove the 'glaze' from the workworn surface which will gradually reduce its effectiveness. The sintered diamond wheel may smooth out a little and lose its bite after long use, but a slight dressing with the appropriate carborundum lap will quickly abrade the phosphor-bronze to expose more grains of diamond.

Corundum has an altogether different cut from the other wheels. It needs the same firm handling but gives a much cleaner, smoother matt. An olive formed from a well-conditioned corundum wheel should be silky and have a clean, sharp edge to it, but an olive cut by diamond or carborundum, even under careful control, is liable to have a sharper edge to the entry of the wheel than its exit. However, apart from these tendencies, the variables in hardness of glass, grit size and bonding in a host of available wheels make it dangerous to generalise. The wheels suggested above, which the engraver must acquire sooner or later, required for speed or large scale work, will quickly fit into the repertory of tools, but the copper wheel will remain the supreme tool for all engraving of refinement and delicacy.

9 Relief Engraving

Relief engraving, as one would suppose, is the very opposite of entaglio engraving. The design is engraved so as to be raised above the background, as does the head on a coin, with the modelling following the natural configuration; that which is nearest to the eye in engraved to be nearest. There are many inspiring examples to be seen in museums, among which perhaps the most famous of all such pieces is the Roman cameo engraved 'Portland Vase', earlier known as the 'Barberini Vase'. It is formed of dense blue glass cased with relatively opaque white glass which has been gradually engraved away, so as to leave the modelled design in silhouette relief against the polished blue base glass. The white low relief is so skilfully controlled as to allow the under blue to show through and give supporting tonal modelling to the figures. Other amazing and baffling work such as the Lycurgus Cup or dietreta glass (cage glass) represent the very pinnacle of engraving skill. But ingenuity is one thing and art another, and the engraver may face a lifetime of aesthetic uncertainty in the assessment of the balance of skill with design, which leads to beauty, and skill for its sake alone.

The physical difference between intaglio (used in its widest sense) and relief engraving is quite marked. With intaglio engraving the cutting arc of the wheel conforms sympathetically to the inward modelling of shapes, say, of thigh or thorax, leaving the edges sharp against the untouched glass. With relief work however, in the very act of removing background glass in order to allow the design to stand proud, and in forming rounded, convex relief shapes from a concave cutting wheel, an altogether different character is imparted to the glass.

This may be better understood by comparing a printy, which is so simply formed with the appropriate profile, with the same shape and volume engraved – carved – in relief, a much longer and more difficult task. No matter how well the background is removed and smoothed out, the marks of the tool can be detected on the polished surface. Even were it possible to remove them, it would be

A simple printy. On the right, the equivalent shape in relief. Note the laborious method of forming it.

an aesthetic loss to do so, as it would be to oversmooth wood carving or remove the unobtrusive mark of the hammer on beaten precious metal.

It is a matter of taste or temperament which form of engraving one prefers, but that restless light which comes from every polished surface of relief-engraved natural rock crystal or crystal glass, the residual imprint of the strap wheel which gives a life and vitality to the whole surface, can be an addictive personal pleasure.

A very fine Silesian relief engraved goblet, about 1700, from Hirschberger Tal. Height 185mm (7¼ in)

student at work polishing a cut-glass vase with pumice and water
ste. The Rheinbach school of Glass

dern (about 1950) Bohemian glass. Pale ruby glass, freely
med, the whole surface of which has been modelled on the
ting wheel. Practically all evidence of the wheel has been
oved by polishing. Height 125mm (5in)

10 Victorian cut glass dish, about 1840, exemplifies the fine control of
the basic cuts: slanting pillars (the fan shapes are left in relief),
printies, olives and faceted edge cuts. Width 250mm (10in)

12 A vase designed, formed and deeply etched by Maurice Marinot,
1930

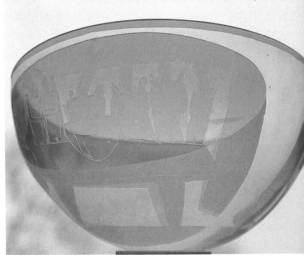

13 A small panel leaded into a clear panel etched skilfully and with great care through a multiple coloured casing. By Ann Wärff, Sweden

15 Another example of the work of Ann Wärff. A very large cased gla bowl etched to different depths to achieve subtle variation in ton and shapes. 500mm (19¾in)

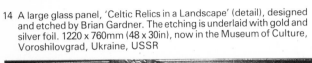

14 A large glass panel, 'Celtic Relics in a Landscape' (detail), designed and etched by Brian Gardner. The etching is underlaid with gold and silver foil. 1220 x 760mm (48 x 30in), now in the Museum of Culture, Voroshilovgrad, Ukraine, USSR

16 'Dream Fantasy', 1978. A full lead crystal bowl, designed , form and sandblasted by Ray Flavell, Height 175mm (7in)

DESIGN CONSIDERATIONS

The big advantage of relief engraving, high or low, it that it follows the natural order of things, so that a little experience in clay modelling, or wax or plaster carving, will soon acquaint the engraver with the main planes or elements of the design. Certain conventions or limitations must, of course, enter into the design. For example, the front view of a face presents considerable problems which a side view avoids (and has generally continued to avoid for many centuries) and the full scale of related depths must, of necessity, be greatly compressed and emphasised in some way to reinforce the effect of full relief.

Sculptured relief work is a very beguiling occupation in which the imagination can shoot ahead of achievement. Even with well advanced skills it always takes much longer than anticipated. Therefore, initially, it is as well not to be too ambitious, but to tackle some simple motif in which the main problems and pitfalls may be met, and the work completed within a reasonable time, instead of becoming disillusioned by exhaustion or exasperation with some larger and too imaginative project.

Choice of Glass

The Strömberg crystalline decanter which was used for the following example is made of a rather harder glass than the average lead crystal. Obviously, soft, full lead crystal is easier to engrave than hard glass, but this is less important than the shape and thickness, which should support and augment the essential sculptural quality of relief engraving. The shortage of simple but boldly interesting, thick-walled blanks is perhaps the greatest impediment to experimental design, but one or two pieces may be discovered and treasured for an 'occasion'. In the meantime, ordinary thick-walled 'seconds' are sufficient for early efforts.

Decanters (indeed, all blown glass) can be treacherously uneven in thickness, and it should be a habit to check the substance of any area to be deeply engraved before starting, to avoid a disastrous break-through. Some uncertainty may be removed by placing a spot of easily removable white paint on the suspected area on the inside of the decanter; then, by holding a pencil point on the outside, the thickness may be roughly guaged.

SCULPTURED RELIEF: BIRD WITH OUTSTRETCHED WINGS

The relief design chosen for this example is of a bird with outstretched wings, the overall form of which may readily be separated into simple relief planes. It is bold enough to give sufficient room for the strap wheel to remove the surrounding glass.

There is a limit to the information which can be transferred to the glass, for the obvious reason that the development in one part eliminates or affects another. Thus, apart from the profile of the design, or its main components, the engraving becomes a matter of controlling an emerging sculptural shape which nearly always has a will of its own. In the struggle there is a strong tendency to erode the outer edge of the relief which makes the enclosed area much smaller than an intended and perhaps fatally unacceptable. This is the opposite tendency of intaglio forms, where the boundaries of the incised shapes are very liable to be pushed out further and further. Hence it is important to make allowance for this by starting *outside* what is intended to be the limit of the relief design.

It is impossible to describe adequately all the processes through which the decanter shown in the illustration passed. The whole exercise, which took over 40 hours to complete, has here been telescoped into five stages of development. However, the accompanying photographs should give a fair indication of how any relief engraving should be approached.

All the wheels, large or small, copper or synethetic, have been dealt with. No holds are barred in their use for any form of engraving, so there is no further need to discuss the choice of wheel, speed or abrasive for any purpose. But as this may be first time the engraver has met with relief work, the size of the most used wheels are given. The comments are brief, but should be of sufficient help to allow the engraver to tackle a similar project.

Transferring the Design

1 Complete a detailed drawing of the proposed design.
2 Make a tracing and transfer the main elements of the design to the decanter.
3 Modify the design where necessary with white gouache until it balances the shape of the decanter.

The design transferred and drawn up with white ink

Engraving the Outline

1 'Fix' the design with a diamond burr.

2 Deeply engrave all the important outlines with a line wheel, 25mm (1 in).

3 Change to a diamond strap wheel 50×5mm ($2 \times \frac{7}{32}$ in), 180 grit. Make a strong cut around the main shapes, keeping slightly outside the outline. Give more emphasis (greater depth) towards the cut outline. The diamond wheel is used on this occasion because of its faster cutting speed, thus a great deal of time is saved in removing the rather large quantity of glass. Obviously the orthodox copper strap wheel may be used, but it is slower.

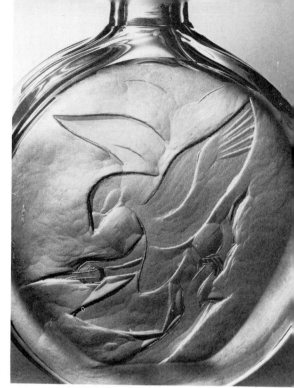

Roughing completed. Note the mark of the action of the strap wheel on the wing

The initial roughing out

Roughing Out the Shapes

1 Continue with the same diamond strap wheel until the entire background to the bird and branch has been removed to a depth of 2–3mm ($\frac{3}{32}$ in $\frac{1}{8}$ in).

2 Pre-model the bird; that is, separate the main planes of the wings, tail and body from each other. Start from the nearest leading edge and work back step by step leaving the furthest part until last.

This is perhaps the most important structural part of the work. It is not only a question of separating planes but engraving each one so as to give the impression of a greater volume (depth relationship) than actually occurs. For example, an intermediate plane may be made to appear further away by dipping it deeply as it meets the

next forward plane. In this way the tip of the further wing need not be too much lower than the original surface of the glass.

The background smoothed and partly polished

Smoothing and Polishing the Background

1 Patiently smooth out all the undulations and unevenness in the background with a corundum wheel,
50×2mm ($2 \times \frac{3}{32}$ in), 220 grit, N bond. With a copper
wheel use a 400 carborundum/oil mix. Reduce the size
of the wheel as necessary to enter the sharp corners of
the relief.

2 Before proceeding with any other modelling, polish the
whole background with wood and cork wheels, from
150×15mm ($6 \times \frac{5}{8}$ in) down to 12×6mm ($\frac{1}{2} \times \frac{1}{4}$ in) in
size, using pumice/water paste.

The polishing was completed at this stage (one illustration
also shows it at the halfway state), because if it had been
left until after the bird had been engraved there would
have been a certainty of overlapping its edge. Some
intermediate detail modelling may be seen on the near
wing of the bird, but this was premature and had to be
remodelled.

Engraving the Intaglio Background

It is seen that although the main design is cut in relief,
some contrasting intaglio engraving is applied to the
polished background. It is common to mix these two
techniques in this way.

1 Draw in the branches, leaves and berries on the polished
background with white gouache in the best decorative
position.

2 Engrave the thin branches with a line wheel, 25mm (1
in), stopping just short of the raised body in case it
damages its edge. This is the reason for attending to the
background first. Return to the line with a very small
line wheel, 3mm ($\frac{1}{8}$ in).

3 Engrave the leaves by 'pulling out' an olive to a pear
shape. Cut in the serration with a minute line wheel,
2mm ($\frac{3}{32}$ in).

4 Engrave the berries as printies. Two differently profiled
wheels are needed: one for shallow printies, 3×2mm
($\frac{1}{8} \times \frac{3}{32}$), which is used for the distant berries, and the
other deeper forming wheel, 2.5×2mm ($\frac{7}{64} \times \frac{3}{32}$ in), for
the nearer and overlapping berries.

5 Polish the printies with the appropriate lead wheels.

Modelling the Relief Detail

Using the same strap as that which was used for roughing
out the sculptural form, engrave all the intermediate
modelling. As before, start at the nearest point and work
back, step by step, to the deepest part of the relief bird.
Move the cut in the direction of the modelling (say, the
large feathers), and when the wheel becomes too big for
small detail modelling, change to a smaller strap
commensurate with the task.

   All modelled details must be handled in the same way as
their supporting planes, that is, inclining the cut so as to
give an edge contrast against the next shape. Thus each
feathered shape is modelled around, and up to, each other,
in the same way as tiles may sit upon a roof. It is a long
and patient business allowing no short-cuts; for example,
the eye is treated as a relief ball, and not a small printy.

The finished decanter: modelling detail completed and intaglio
engraved background leaf and berry decoration inserted and
selected highlights polished

Engraving the Linework Detail

Engrave all supporting sharp linework detail. Choose line
wheels which will fit comfortably into the shape without
fouling the surrounding work.

The Problems and, Limits of Modelling

While the distance travelled between the fourth and the
fifth photographs in this example may appear formidable,
apart from the relief aspect there is nothing new to learn in
the use of the tools. Practically all the work was done with
three straps, whereas the intaglio background occupied
five or six different tools; therefore, providing some
experience has been gained with the use of the large strap,
there is no reason why the engraver should not pursue
such work.

A high relief glass. By Fritz Glössner, 1928, Rheinbach. Height 120mm (4½ in). The background to the relief form has been removed by sandblasting and subsequently 'acid polished' to leave a sculptured base for the following copper wheel modelling

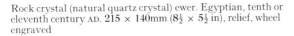

Detail of finished decanter

It is not necessary to carry detailed modelling to the same length as the present example. Indeed, overworked detail may prove to be a curse – too late for exorcism – by emasculating the original sculptural vitality of the form. Also, a glass does not have to be big to impart an intense sculptural effect, but it is exciting to tackle a large blank and watch the form gradually change direction from the original intention to a better, more instinctive, plastic shape. Every type of design, whether natural or abstract, can be indulged in.

No doubt the modern student would prefer to follow the path of the Czechoslovakian artists whose imaginative work has for a long time excelled in this field, but, occasionally, a look back at rock crystal engraving – some of the noblest engraving ever done – or Roman cameo cutting should rapidly adjust any myopic vision.

Rock crystal (natural quartz crystal) ewer. Egyptian, tenth or eleventh century AD. 215 × 140mm (8¼ × 5½ in), relief, wheel engraved

10 Small Stone Intaglio Engraving

ENGRAVING/CUTTING WITH LARGE SYNTHETIC WHEELS

The synthetic wheels which have been discussed so far should be considered as auxiliaries to the copper wheel for the purpose of speeding up the roughing out or intermediate processes of modelling. For the light traditional lathe they would reach the limit at about 65–75mm (2½–3 in) diameter. But even so, the bearings could be expected to be under some strain, so it would be wise to restrict their use to intermittent work. Beyond this a sturdier machine is required.

The modern lathe illustrated in Chapter 1 is robust and versatile. It will handle both orthodox wheel engraving and the heavier form of stone (synthetic) wheel engraving, for which the bearings are strong enough to take wheels of up to 175mm (7 in) in diameter. However, as the wheels increase in size beyond the range required for the copper wheel, the larger, more incisive nature of the cuts tends to impose its own design form. As a consequence, the character of the work changes from engraving in the accepted sense partway to that of glass cutting, though the glass is still handled in the same traditional manner – under the wheel – which is the very opposite position for facet glass cutting. Having said this, although such work has an unmistakably dominant 'cutting' quality about it, it should not be thought of as a separate limited category of engraving but as a natural creative development of the copper wheel.

THE 'INTAGLIO' STYLE

In general the design content is free of any modelling and is almost entirely wheel dominated, built up with simple or convoluted curves formed from the basic cuts of the sharp and rounded strap and mitre wheels; the strap wheel profile is sometimes so shaped as to produce multiple parallel lines. To the confusion of the newcomer, engraved glass of this kind is known as 'intaglio', a term which has wider significance.

John Northwood supplies the reason for the currency of the term 'intaglio' in his valuable book on his father, dedicated to the Craftsmen of Stourbridge. It also gives so rare an account of outside economic pressures on an established glass decorating workshop, necessitating a change of direction, methods, skills and machines, that the relevant paragraphs have been quoted in full.

Typical high quality Stourbridge *intaglio* 'cased' engraved glass

'After the decline of public demand for cameo glass J. and J. Northwood's had to re-arrange their workshops to enable them to resume their principal business of etching tableware and other fancy glass. They, however, did not find it too easy to obtain the quantity of business which they formerly had on account of the great increase of imported glass into this country. The reason for this being that the foreign glass was considerably cheaper due to its lower cost of production. Moreover, as there was no more cameo to be engraved, alternative work had to be found for their staff of engravers.

The manager of J. and J. Northwood's at that time was the late Mr. W.O. Bowen and he was very anxious to retain their services if possible. He consulted John Northwood about this difficulty and in the course of their conversation on this subject John suggested that to help the etchers *and* the engravers, why not try to combine the efforts of both. He advised Bowen to see if he could introduce some cutting effect to be part of an etched design. As of course the firm did not have any cutting shop or glass cutters, he suggested putting small stones on the engraver's lathe in place of the copper wheel and see what they could do. They proceeded to try this but it was some time before they could obtain results, mainly owing to the engravers being unaccustomed to the use or preparation of stone wheels. They had a difficulty in obtaining stones suitable in size and quality and the fitting and trueing them up on their engraving spindles needed some practice before a stone could be used to give a satisfactory result. Eventually, they got over their difficulties and started to "Stone-engrave" small additions to etched designs already prepared for them. They were soon producing small ornamental stars, rosettes, small flowers, etc., which, when polished, gave the etched pattern quite a new look. The process of polishing these additions to the etchings was by lead wheels and whitening powder, followed sometimes, by small wood wheels and putty powder.

They became very adept in this new departure; particularly, Joshua Hodgetts delighted to use his skill in this stone engraving. It soon became apparent that owing to the very small power which could be executed by the foot-operated lathe the size and depth of the cuttings were comparatively small and therefore limited the extent of the engraver's art.'

John Northwood saw the need to design an entirely new machine strong enough to take stone wheels.

'This they did, and although the lathe was primitive and crude it yet gave the desired power to stronger spindles. These spindles carried larger cutting stones far in excess of those which could be worked on the old engraving lathes. Joshua Hodgetts soon found that he had now an opportunity of experimenting with new patterns and effects which were unobtainable on his engraving lathe.'

The initial success of this project encouraged the setting up of an independent stone engraving department at Stevens and Williams where the engravers could make full use of their skill. However, improvement to the lathe was required to give it the same speed flexibility of the treadle but much more powerful in control.

'A lathe headstock was cast in iron of a sufficient height and length to take in a horizontal position two wood cones about 12 inches long by 4 inches diameter to 2 inches diameter taper. These were fitted in the lathe, one directly over the other with their taper in reverse directions. That is to say, the wide diameter end of the one over the small diameter end of the other, the top cone having a mandrel projecting from the right hand end of the lathe frame some little distance. In this was fitted a spindle which had a small diameter-threaded end to take the cutting stone. The varied sized stones had a cast-lead centre with thread to fit this spindle. The shaft of the bottom cone extended outside the left side of the lathe frame sufficiently to take two small pulley wheels, one the driving pulley, the other the loose pulley. These two pulleys had the usual forked guide for stopping and starting and could be controlled by the worker. The two cones were connected by a small narrow endless belt running over the outside faces of both. A small bar of square section was fitted in the front of the lathe and extended from end to end in a sloping position to run in a line with the slope of the cones. On this bar a clip was fitted to slide along it. This clip had on it a small guiding fork through which the endless belt ran. By this, the operator using his left hand could easily and quickly slide the belt along to any position on the cones to give the desired speed to his cutting wheel and a thumb screw would hold it there. The spindle of course could take any size of stone.'

The Stourbridge 'Tag' lathe, about 1890

Over the years many other mechanical arrangements were experimented with but the general construction remained the same until the system was superseded by the electric motor.

'As this was a new departure from the existing styles of decoration, a name for it was very desirable. Eventually the name "Intaglio" was chosen and so it has remained ever since. This is abbreviated into "Tag" by the workers.

Intaglio has been an established branch of the Stourbridge Glass Industry for many years and its craft and style has spread to many other countries. By the nature of the process, a much wider and more important field for his skill was opened up for the old-time engraver. This he has amply demonstrated by the great variety and richness of the work produced by him over the past years. The free-flowing character of the engraver with the depth and sharpness of the glass cutter's skill has given a style distinct from both, yet preserving the fine qualities of each. From the first idea of combining these branches and the patience in the stages of its development, came this happy result. Stevens and Williams can very justly claim to be the original producers of Intaglio decoration.'

Such stones had been in use long before this innovation took place and engraving-cutting of a very similar nature may be seen on European glass two hundred years earlier. But there is validity in this particular claim for the 'Tag' lathe in as much as it pioneered an altogether bolder, deeper stylised form of engraved/cut decorative glass which found its way into most homes and is now a part of the art history of that time. At its best it is work of superb verve and skill. At any level the late nineteenth century engravers had, and still have for the present day engraver, an unnerving capacity. *Intaglio* engraving is only one facet of an amazingly creative industry which appears to have been full of restless innovative energy, – happily before the time of 'feasibility studies'. It had the good fortune to be led by artist-craftsmen cum teachers, managers and entrepreneurs such as John Northwood and Frederick Carder of Stevens and Williams (Frederick Carder joined Steuben at Corning, New York state, in 1903). It was a period of confidence and creative vitality which is unlikely to be repeated.

ENGRAVING

Wheels and Spindles

The stone wheels, along with the 'tag' lathe, have long since been overtaken by carborundum and corundum, though new natural stones are still being supplied and old ones being sought for the discriminating studio engraver.

Typical Corundum stones, illustrating the basic profiles: printy, olive, mitre and strap

The range of grit and bonding is the same as that prescribed for the smaller synthetic wheels in the previous chapter, but engraving of this kind which requires clean, sharp edges and a near-polished quality of cut is almost completely dependent on corundum 220 grit, M bond, or thereabouts. Diamond wheels are a luxurious alternative but are so prohibitively expensive beyond about 75mm (3 in) that they are ruled out of our consideration.

It has been said that the modern lathe will accommodate wheels up to 175mm (7 in), but the bulk of them will run between the useful sizes of 12mm ($\frac{1}{2}$ in) and 100mm (4 in), of widths which only experience with the copper wheel can determine. But none would ever be likely to be wider than 12mm ($\frac{1}{2}$ in). As each wheel is likely to be formed for some specific size of cut or purpose, it will find its place in a bank of wheels to be drawn upon for a similar job. In this way 20 or more may be accumulated, at the ready, for the same spindle.

Although used for a much bolder and broader form of engraving, they must be set up with as much care and precision as the wheels used for fine engraving; indeed, while at times a little liberty may be taken with, say, a 60mm ($2\frac{1}{2}$ in) copper wheel, none is possible with a stone wheel. All wheels, even quite large ones, are screwed directly onto the spindle via lead bushes which are prepared and corrected in the same way as their smaller counterparts, except of course that the securing spindles will be stronger, of solid steel, and the tapered, threaded end coarser.

Wheel Profiles

The familiar profiles of the copper wheel are used: printy, olive, sharp and rounded strap, and mitre. As very thin synthetic wheels are liable to fracture under heavy usage they will need to be thicker than the corresponding copper line wheels, consequently the extra substance must be turned back to a high, sharp mitre.

Speed

The variables of grit, size of wheel and quality of glass make it impossible to prescribe which speeds should be selected for a particular task. At a rough estimate it would be about twice that of a copper wheel of the same size, or as fast as possible without producing burn marks, which would be a clear signal of excess, bearing in mind that too much pressure or insufficient lubrication can also contribute to burn marks.

Lubrication

Plain tap water, fed from a small reservoir, is all that is wanted. Engineers' cutting fluids used for metal grinding is of no value to the glass engraver. The lubrication should be free but not so much as to flood the wheel or cause the water to run down the arm. No doubt some additive may be found that will facilitate the grinding of glass, but for the engraver the lubricant must not froth or otherwise obscure what is already difficult to see.

The condition of the residual water is a good guide; if it becomes so thick with superfine particles of ground glass as to obscure the engraving, then the supply should be increased until a thin, milky consistency is reached.

Engraving Procedure

The general grinding principles are the same for large wheels as for small. Deep or shallow olives or printies will be engraved from the appropriately sized and shaped wheels, but the feel and pressure at the wheel will be rather different. Over a diameter of 25mm (1 in), the stone will want to create a vacuum and will tend to hold in the cut; consequently, in moving it out, the wheel may inadvertently slip. With the engraving of designs based on wide, sweeping crescents, the slightest tilt of the strap is always a treacherous manoeuvre, and the changes of direction and angle of the wheel for the curve is very liable to create a series of creases which must be smoothed out.

Much more physical energy is required to control the glass at the wheel, and this will obviously vary as the tool moves from the sharp cutting angles to the flat of the profile, and considerable experience is necessary before full freedom of movement can be gained over flowing curves. Undoubtedly it is an entirely different environment of engraving and before the best combination of wheel, speed, lubrication and pressure can be found some repeat practice with larger olives, printies and crescents will certainly be required.

POLISHING

Polishing Wheels

To enter and polish a deep cut, indeed any cut, effectively requires a polishing wheel of the same size and profile as that which originated it. Good sandstone or corundum wheels should leave a texture so silky and fine that little effort is required to bring it to a good surface. With very small cuts lead wheels such as those used for polishing printies must be employed, but in general the wheels would follow a standard order: wood and cork for directional polishing, that is, following the length of the cut, and felt for multidirectional finishing.

Speed

The use of polishing wheels has been discussed in the earlier chapters on copper wheel-intaglio (modelling) engraving of the fish, flower and architecture etc., and the general instructions apply equally to *intaglio* work. But it must be remembered once more that the larger the cut motif or area of glass to be polished the larger the wheel and the slower it should run, in order to avoid localised friction heat, which builds up surprisingly fast. It is a matter of common sense.

Polishing Agents

All polishing compounds are water-bound. They may be limited to pumice for the bulk of the work and cerium oxide for the final lustre polish with the felt wheel. Intricate patterns may be better handled with the bristle brush (see page 111) using tripoli water paste, which may give an overall polish sufficient to leave as the final treatment, but a lick with cerium oxide will remove any bloom and restore the polish to its virgin condition.

Hedwig beaker, engraved with small stones below the wheel. Islamic, twelfth century (British Museum)

EVALUATION OF *INTAGLIO ENGRAVING*

Two wars have intervened since the 'tag' lathe was developed and glass engraving has changed, perhaps inevitably, so that we now have a cultural climate where, metaphorically speaking, one must clamber over a dozen accountants to reach one creative artist. All the same, to

Stourbridge 'rock crystal' type glass, *intaglio* engraved

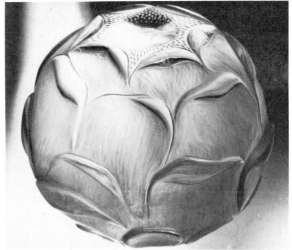

A relief engraved glass. The design is based upon a Visigothic capital from the Naranco Palace (Spain). Showing the use of small stone wheels which fall comfortably within the range of the modern lathe. By Peter Dreiser, 1976. Height: 175mm (6¾ in)

'The Rose', paperweight engraved with small 'stone' wheels. By Peter Dreiser

'The apple', Pavel Hlava, Prague, 1962. Height 140mm (5½ in). A vigorously designed glass, wheel engraved with coarse carborundum stones, which has been selectively polished to expose a lively granulation

An engraved plate. V. and M. Plâtek, 1965. An abstract design of interlacing patterns which gives a strong three-dimensional effect, although it is engraved on one side of the plate only

be fair, a large amount of skilful *intaglio* engraved glass (but of limited design) is still being produced for the cheaper end of the market, for which the lathe must be grateful. Fortunately for the individual engraver, the use of the heavier side of the lathe, so to speak, need not be all grapes and crescents.

This bold form of engraving, either alone or in combination with other processes, has a much more spirited decorative potential, which should be seized upon if only as a stimulating release from the confines of orthodox work. The use of large sweeping cuts in formal or asymmetric shapes, sometimes combined with cut textures, has long been a feature of Czechoslovakian creative engraving, and it is still under active tuition. Little can be seen at the moment which approaches the vigour and inventiveness of design shown in the glass which has been coming from the European engraving schools since the 1940s.

But with the widening interest in every form of glass decoration, running concurrently with the increase in free-formed glass from individual furnaces, the future possibilities for the designer craftsman are boundless.

11 Cut Glass

THE DEVELOPMENT OF WHEEL CUT GLASS

At times it is difficult to justify the categories into which wheel cut glass may be placed – high relief, *intaglio* or cut glass – particularly when a deeply slicing cut made by the same sized wheel may be featured in each. But in the main, cut glass is so separate a process that, even when it is combined with other forms of engraving, it should easily be recognised by the geometrical patterns of strong facets or incised shapes of which it is mainly composed.

A glass cutter at work in about 1900. Roughing out on an iron wheel

It should now be well understood by the engraver that the larger the facet or area of glass to be cut the larger must be the wheel, and the greater must be the pressure and energy needed to drive it. Thus, by scrutinising any facet one can form a shrewd idea of what was involved in producing it. The size and shape of some Roman wheel-formed designs indicate that quite large wheels had been used requiring a fair amount of power to turn them. But there is nothing very remarkable in the mechanics of the grinding wheel, which would have been improvised horizontally or vertically for any purpose a millenia earlier, and it is easy to imagine a large, hand-cranked sandstone wheel having picked up enough momentum to take a tiring and careless apprentice round with it.

However, it is not known how the Eastern craftsmen turned and hollowed out the harder natural rock crystal; whether the wheel or drilling tools were turned against the crystal, or the crystal turned, in part, against the tool. Nor is it known how far metal wheels, solid or tyred, may have been used together with loose abrasives to aid the task.

But as far as the physical act of cutting glass is concerned, one can feel fairly secure that little has changed. The skills which may have fluctuated over the centuries have always been available and waiting. What is rarer for the artist-craftsman, sometimes more important than technology, is that combination of skill, energy, confidence, investment and patronage which seems to be a pre-requisite for any renaissance.

Such an invironment happened to flourish in Bohemia and Silesia during the sixteenth, seventeenth and eighteenth centuries, in almost feudal extravagance. From these already established centres of natural crystal and hardstone carving, superb glass cutting skills were developed which dominated European trends, and from which in time Britain was to benefit. As the glass cutting of this period remains unsurpassed, a brief description of the traditional method is given here.

Early Glass Cutting Lathes

As with the loom or the woodturner's pole lathe, early cutting machines would have been constructed of sturdy timbers. Cast-iron framed machines which were designed for greater utility appeared in the second half of the nineteenth century, either as a very strong variation of the orthodox lathe with insertable spindles or as a more simplified version with a very solid, single, screw-ended mandrel to which the cutting wheels could be quickly attached.

Such lathes were not stronger or better or more accurate than the ones with a centred shaft running between hardwood bearing blocks, just more convenient. In the cutting shop it is very likely that they would be augmented by large wheels, centre-mounted in the ancient manner. From a review of these machines the changing workshop practices may readily be imagined. Thus, when the cutting became too resistant for the treadle, a hand-operated flywheel became a natural alternative, and as that in turn proved inadequate for the workload, the ubiquitous waterwheel, and later the steam engine, provided more than enough energy to run a series of subdivided departments independent of horse or man power.

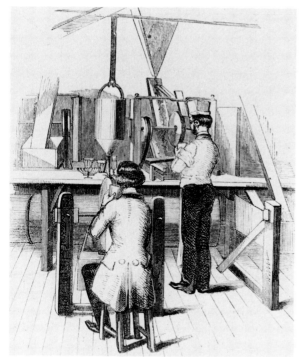

Glass cutters at work. Notice the sand hoppers over the simple lathes. The seated figure is cutting on the upper part of the wheel while his colleague appears to be trimming the edge of a glass from below. The lathes are driven by steam via crude shafting. From Pellatt's *Curiosities of Glassmaking*

The Position and Direction of the Cut

Glass cutting is distinguished from all other engraving by being worked for the greater part towards the top of the wheel instead of the bottom. Changes of this kind are always made for a good reason, and were perhaps due to a mixture of advantages with regard to sighting, and the weight of the thick-walled material which, together with the leaning stance of the operator, would tend to do part of the work.

The cutting is almost universally made against the push of the wheel, that is, as it revolves *towards* the operator. However, there is an opposite instruction of 'moving *from* the operator' by Duthie in 1908 (in his book *Decorative Glass Processes*) which means that this must have been the habit of about that time. Wheels can still be seen running this way in Britain, but no conclusions can be drawn from this.

The Cutting Wheels

The cutting followed in the order: soft iron wheels (sand fed) for the rough cut, sandstone for smoothing, and willow or poplar wood for polishing. The size of these wheels was obviously determined by the size of the facet or motif to be cut, and could vary from **75–900mm (3–36 in)**. Some larger facets which appear almost flat, perhaps with the cut being made transversely to the wheel, would

require much larger wheels, so that any cutting shop handling a variety of flutes, printies, crescents and the like would need to draw upon a stock of **50 to 100** wheels, and a multiplicity of machines.

Very large flat areas were ground as a separate operation on a horizontal sandstone wheel, which can be detected by the undistorted reflections.

The Wheel Profiles

The common profiles of the iron wheels would have been shaped by some simple turning tool. The simplicity of old methods always comes as a surprise, and within living memory both wooden and iron wheels are said to have been trimmed with flint flakes bound in a split wooden handle.

Sandstone wheels were no doubt formed as they have been for a long time, by holding an iron bar against the profile edge as it is fed with sand and water, and were brought to the essential silky finish by running the well-lubricated wheel against a stationary piece of quartz, hard porcelain or glass.

Rough Cutting with the Iron Wheel

The iron wheel was fed by sand from a tray or hopper into which a crudely regulated trickle of water could fall, to carry some sand with it to the wheel. Spent sand and debris would fall into the reservoir beneath the wheel. Except for the roughest type of cut, new sand is too coarse and granular and has limited usefulness, but when after a little work it has been broken down into smaller and sharper fragments the grinding action becomes much more efficient. Therefore the whole of the debris would be stirred up in a settling tank, when the coarser particles would sink to the bottom for retrieval, and the finer granules separated off to be used for polishing.

Smoothing with the Sandstone Wheel

After the initial rough cut, a sandstone wheel of about the same size as the soft iron wheel, but of identical profile, was entered into each facet cut until it was smooth enough to take a polish. It was lubricated by water alone. Being a natural material, the stone varied from quarry to quarry from grey to ochre, and in fineness and feel of cut.

From the aesthetic (tactile) point of view, eighteenth-century craftsmen may have had a greater variety in 'grit and bonding' with natural stone than can now be obtained with synthetic corundum. Thus it was said of brilliant cutting in 1908: 'The stone used for cutting is a carboniferous sandstone, obtained from the Craigleith Quarry near Edinburgh, no other seeming to give the necessary combination of qualities.' But it must be added in all fairness that these stones could contain treacherous imperfections. All the same, as more glass engraver-cutters experiment and the cost of synthetic materials increases, many an ancient garden path will be turned over for the treasure trove of discarded stone wheels.

Polishing with the Wooden Wheel

The polishing of facets was effected entirely with wooden wheels, usually of willow or poplar, which is strong and fibrous and open enough to hold the wet pumice or tripoli paste without disintegrating; but oak for small sharp wheels, and the use of leather, must not be ruled out. The wheel would most likely have been fed with the loose paste or fine sand sludge at the bottom of the wheel with the glass held, as it is today, rather towards the feeding position.

The negative evidence of the disappearance of polishing 'bloom' from cut glass seems to suggest that the bristle brush did not come into general use until the end of the nineteenth century. The work which has come from these simple materials and methods commands a respect hardly to be accorded to much of the present-day output.

MODERN STUDIO METHODS

The Design

There is an endless variety of examples to draw upon; indeed, the sheer volume can become an obstacle to detached judgement as far as design is concerned. While there is a great deal that is refined, inspired and enchanting, an equal number of examples abound which show an extravagance, even vulgarity, of style and taste in cut glass. To begin with, therefore, rather than emulate some complex geometric pattern that may give uncertain pleasure, it is better to make some simple, personal arrangement of olives or printies, perhaps augmented by flutes or mitre cuts.

Choice of Glass

Lead glass is the natural choice. Being soft, and highly refractive it is eminently suitable for glass cutting. Indeed, it was the development of this quality glass by George Ravenscroft in 1674 which had by the late eighteenth century turned the market advantage away from European soda-lime crystal glass in favour of the more brilliant 'English glass of lead'. But it must not be forgotten that Bohemian and Silesian cut glass was famous long before the English thought of producing it.

The Indexing Machine

Equipment is available which simplifies the problem of subdividing a glass, but a system may be improvised without much difficulty. It consists of a turntable, upon which the glass is centred, that can be locked (indexed) in any reasonable number of subdivisions. A vertical surface plane in line with the centre of the glass acts as a guide for the brush or ruling pen. Obviously the ruled lines must be waterproof. Any white paint free enough to run from the pen will suffice, but a suitable ink is easily made from white pigment, gum dammar (a natural gum resin) and turpentine or white spirit.

The ruling pen should be wide-bladed and of more parallel construction than the average tool, so that it can hold enough ink without exhaustion or blobbing on a long run, and it should be mounted in a wide, flat handle so that it may be held securely to the vertical surface as the pen makes its passage down the profile of the glass. The modern felt-tipped waterproof marker is a valuable alternative to this. For horizontal lines the base may be set free when, by holding a brush against the circulating

glass, lines may quickly be marked out round the circumference. Some professional indexing equipment provides for the upright plane to be set at any angle from which diagonal lines may be drawn on the glass.

Only the scantiest information is marked out by the professional – just the geometrical position for the primary cuts. Virtually all other work is cut freehand on the glass.

A modern indexing machine, with ruling pen. Made by Spatzier

The Modern Lathe

Apart from a few mechanical refinements, the modern machine has scarcely changed since the 1900s, and can be seen to be of orthodox construction, with a very solid drive, integrated mandrel and spindle, for interchangeable wheels ranging approximately from 90–600mm ($3\frac{1}{2}$–24 ins) diameter and from 12–25mm ($\frac{1}{2}$–1 in) thick.

The Wheels

Both iron and sandstone wheels have virtually departed from the scene, though independent workers still treasure sandstone for a particular finish unobtainable by any other material. Sandstone and iron wheel remain superior for horizontal grinding. The synthetic wheels which have replaced them – carborundum and corundum – have been dealt with in Chapter 8. All are prepared with threaded lead bushes to fit the spindle end.

The Wheel Profiles

Trueing, dressing and shaping follow earlier procedures. The profiles are straightforward mitres, olives, printies and flutes, and sharp straps for half moons and crescents. For some difficult positions an offset mitre may be resorted to.

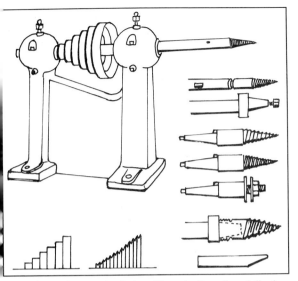

A popular modern cutting lathe with a selection of specialised spindles showing the alternative pulley systems

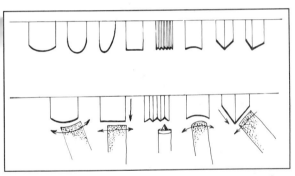

The profiles of glass cutting wheels; note the offset mitre and olive. The arrows indicate the direction and action of the dressing tool

Speeds

The operational speed will depend on the size of the wheel and cut, the material and the grit of the stone. At a very rough estimate, a wheel of 250mm (10 ins) diameter would be run from about 700–800 rpm. Carborundum, being a freer, coarser and quicker abrasive, would be worked faster.

Rough Cutting with a Carborundum Wheel

The glass is held near the top of the wheel (not quite on top) with the profile – say, a mitre – registered to the marked position which can be observed through the glass. Water is fed to the top of the wheel via a piece of rag or leather (anything to even out the water on the profile) with enough flow to give a good grinding action and to wash away the debris without flooding. A good deal of

Ivan Kolman dressing a large carborundum wheel with a spur wheel tool

Some simple shapes cut freehand. Note the stages of finish in the printies and the offset mitres. By Ivan Kolman

physical energy is needed to overcome the push of the wheel against the glass, particularly with large broad sandstone or corundum wheels, so it is sensible to provide some anchorage for the forearms.

Once the cut has been started, the glass is moved against the wheel from the top of the segment or line to the bottom, riding gently back to repeat the operation until the cut is deep or wide enough which, as it will be rather granular and broken edged, should stop a little short of what is wanted. It goes without saying that the cutting should be as even as possible in order to avoid creases or ridges, and that the profile must be kept in trim if a consistent character of cut is to be maintained.

Glass cutting in action. The end of the spindle has been 'stepped' in order to accommodate a large range of small stones. The absence of a splash guard indicates the wheel is running in a clockwise direction, the surplus water being removed by a sponge just below the wheel

Smoothing with a Corundum Wheel

The profile of the smoothing wheel should be identical to that of the carborundum but slightly larger in diameter, so that by the time it has fully entered the first roughly ground shape to the very bottom of the flute or mitre it has not only smoothed out the carborundum marks but slightly enlarged the cut shape with a new sharp edge.

When changing from carborundum to corundum every precaution should be taken to wash the hands and glass, and to change the rag and support, for the smallest grain of carborundum could cause havoc. The corundum smoothing movement is exactly the same as for carborundum, but as the finer profile beds into the cut the vacuum that tends to be created causes quite a degree of suction. A large wide flute will require a good deal of muscular effort to keep the glass under control.

To remove any ridges formed in the rough cut, the corundum wheel must be moved slowly and smoothly up against the pressure several times, riding back lightly at each turn. When completed it should have a delicious, silky appearance, free of any ripple or striations which indifferent work may reveal after polishing.

Polishing with a Wooden Wheel

The wooden polishing wheels are turned to the same pattern of the preceding wheels, but no matter how well they are finished and fit the cut facet, there is always a tendency to overlap the edges. The mitre is particularly difficult in this respect because, unless it is sharp, it will never reach the apex of the cut. Consequently wheels are manufactured which are built up of triangular segments of selected wood joined together so that the long grain runs from the centre to the edge at every position, and this naturally gives a much more manageable, sharper and wear-resistant profile.

The action is the same as that for the original cut, but requires a rather slower speed – about 200–400 rpm for a 250mm (10 in) wheel – moving up against the direction and pressure of the wheel and then quietly riding back again. This action should be repeated until a good polish is obtained. However, this operation takes place slightly below the centre (seven or eight o'clock) for the reasons that the polishing medium in its slurry state is more conveniently applied to the bottom of the wheel, and because in this position the 'pull' is away from the glass and not against the operator. Thus, if the wheel fouls a facet – as it may do with a slender stem – the glass is thrown clear of the wheel and not towards it.

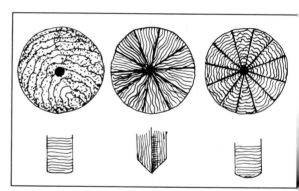

A selection of wooden polishing wheels. From left to right: Solid wood, selected for the maximum consistency of grain; A wheel made of segments with the grain running radially for maximum resistance to wear; A segmented wheel with the grain running circumferentially, more usual for large wheels

Polishing with a Bristle Brush

The bloom which is always left behind by the pumice polish is removed by a hard but flexible bristle brush, which has the advantage of reaching into every inner crevice of multiple cut facets. It is a messy job, for, as the wheel must run at high speed for the bristles to be effective, the polishing compound is spun off in all directions. For this reason where there is much polishing of this kind to be done separate equipment is set up within a shield or booth to give protection, as far as this is possible, to the operator and the workshop from the flying particles. The speed is commensurate with the size of the wheel; as an example, a brush 300mm (12 in) in diameter would be run at 2500 rpm.

In operation the tripoli powder, which is the polishing medium commonly used (cerium oxide is too fine and too

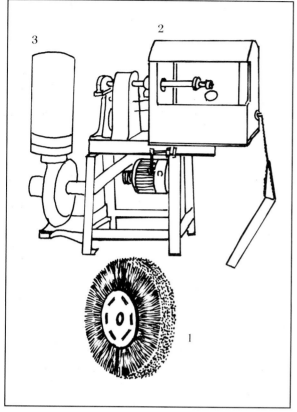

Modern polishing equipment:
1 The bristle brush
2 The polishing chamber
3 The dust extractor

Polishing with Cork and Felt Wheels

Cork and felt wheels, using pumice and cerium oxide respectively, are alternatives to the bristle brush, but it is a personal judgement which method should be used. There are other wheels, for example impregnated rubber, and also other polishing compounds such as putty powder, rouge, and tin oxide; but those already discussed set a reasonable practical limit.

It may be that, if the wooden wheels were strictly kept within the cuts, provided that the preceding smoothing had been well done, the work would be sufficiently polished if left in that state. Equally, if the condition left by the corundum wheel is sharp and fine, the wooden wheel may be omitted and the polishing completed entirely with the bristle brush. It depends on the complexity of the cutting, the position on the glass and the critical level of the polish desired. It is a matter of experience. But there is a repeated warning for all polishing: at no time should the friction heat of the glass be allowed to rise much above blood heat.

THE APPLICATION OF CUT GLASS METHODS

The foregoing outline of glass cutting as a technique deserves more detailed attention than has been given to it for, after all, over the years it has produced the main bulk of decorated glass. However, the main intention is not to tempt the engraver to emulate the nineteenth century

A fine example of a Roman cut glass beaker (faceted cut). The upper and lower rim has been left proud from a turned thick base glass. Olives have been cut on a fixed lathe to form lozenges which, in all, makes it into a powerfully designed glass. (*British Museum*)

expensive for large-scale work), is kept as a slurry in a sump below the brush, into which enough natural fibres (such as short pieces of teazled hemp string) are thrown to enable the hand to dredge up a fistful of mixed fibre and tripoli powder to load the revolving bristles. This is a very unlikely carrier, but it is the best means of holding a mass of loose polishing paste. Other material would in time disintegrate and clog the slurry.

The brush, which is at its best when it is about half-way worn, is applied vigorously in the direction of the cuts, and this allows the swirling bristles to make a searching penetration of every sharp incision. The bristles come from the agave cactus plant, a native of Mexico, and have remained unequalled for this task for well over a generation. The polishing takes place towards the bottom of the brush wheel, the glass being held to the bristles with the right hand while the other feeds the slurry just below it. Modern machines are equipped with a foot pedal which semi-automatically applies the paste to the brush, and this allows a much better control of the glass, but without such an aid, when large or heavy glass is being polished, some 'feeder' helper must be recruited. When the polishing is seen to be almost completed, the brushing is continued, without paste, until it dries out on the glass, after which a few light passes with the powdery residue should leave the whole glass with a brilliant lustre.

glass cutter, but to show how the cutting techniques may be applied to the strong, modern, copper wheel engraving lathe. What has been described for wheels from 75–1500mm (3–60 in) in diameter applies equally to wheels from 15–175mm ($\frac{5}{8}$ – 7 in) diameter and so, within these limits and the size of cuts they may make, there is no reason why cutting should not be pursued by the copper wheel engraver, either as a traditional end in itself, so to speak, or more experimentally as a support theme to free-formed glass. It is a fertile area virtually untouched by British engravers.

Apart from a few isolated examples, it is as well to keep away from modern, run-of-the-mill cut glass. Though skilful, it is for the most part boring and unrewarding, having in many cases come from a two-step (sometimes merely a one-step) diamond wheel cut, through the hydroflouric acid polish dip, direct to the table with blunted brilliance. As such, cut glass leans dangerously towards the all-embracing technology of pressed glass and programmed automatic cutting machines, which is now a reality. But beyond this need to satisfy the mass demands, to which we all subscribe, there is enough space and oportunity left for the studio glass engraver to take his own short-run design risk which, understandably, manufacturers would not dare to do.

A modern vase, cut designed by Lord Queensborough. Webb Corbet Glass, about 1960. (*Victoria and Albert Museum*)

Typical example of shallow faceted cut glass of the second half of the eighteenth century. Observe that the star base has been cut with a sharp strap (edge cut) rather than a mitre, and note the beautifully formed scalloped rim

A dish of strong abstract design formed from dominant, very sharp and deeply-cut interlacing 'mitres'. The design is augmented with a little sandblasting. 36cm (14 in). By Ivan Kolman, Liberec, Bohemia

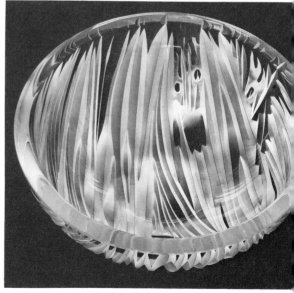

12 Flat Glass

FLAT GLASS DECORATION

Architectural decorated glass is a wide-ranging subject, and this particular section will not attempt to give more than a very brief outline of its development and the methods employed in its decoration.

Flat glass for windows and mirrors had been made as 'crown or broad' glass since before 1600, but it was not until 'cast' glass was invented, by Perrot in 1688, that large, thick, 'plate' glass could be manufactured in sufficient quantity to meet the increasing, but narrowly privileged, demand of the time. But at that moment there was little, apart from noble patronage, to satisfy the wider social and domestic need for glass. This did not happen until the begining of the nineteenth century when improving technology and entrepreneurial energy expanded the production of plate glass a thousandfold, allowing its almost profligate use for every architectural and decorative purpose.

But the appetite of the Victorians for decoration of all kinds could not be satisfied by the methods which had been used for glass heretofore, consequently alternative, broader and simpler processes were developed – brilliant cutting, etching, and (later) sand blasting – which continued to fill the need until the First World War. These techniques could vie with one another, or were combined with the cutting wheel, to give contrast effects of great brilliance and beauty.

All artifacts suffer from the savage action of time and none more than glass. That which has survived gives no more than a glimpse of the intellectual energy and artistic capacity or production of the past and, as regards architectural glass, the very recent past (this has no reference to stained glass). The dreadful damage of war and demolition combined have largely destroyed the visual evidence and the records by which the advancing artisan skills and methods could be traced. However, enough glass remains to know that such very high levels of skill and competence can only come from well disciplined workshops, and it is intriguing to speculate on the environment of, say, 1890; the number of shops, the subdivided skills of artist-artisan, apprentice and labourer, and the associated trades on which they all depended for stones, wheels and polishing abrasives.

THE DEVELOPMENT OF BRILLIANT CUTTING

Small Glass

In technique, early wheel engraving on flat glass did not differ in any particular from that of hollow-ware of the same period, and undoubtedly would have been worked in the orthodox manner. However, apart from the more insecure grip on a flat plate, the separated hands (almost in line with the wheel) would run the constant risk of fouling the machine, which would make delicate modelling, so dependent on the flexible use of small wheels, difficult or impossible on flat glass of a size much larger than 300×200mm (12×8 in). For bigger areas there would be every reason to change to a light cutting lathe when, by working from the top of the wheel, a little more freedom would be gained and the progress of the work better followed, but by this time it is no longer copper wheel engraving.

A copper wheel engraved commemorative glass by H.G. Köhler illustrating, among other trade symbols, a light treadle-operated glass cutting lathe in use at the time, 1774. (*Victoria and Albert Museum*)

Such a lathe is depicted on an interesting and lively piece of engraved glass by Heinrich Göttleib Köhler of 1774. It is basically a water-fed sandstone grinding wheel centred between simple bearings; a cutting and grinding system centuries old. But the advantages of working this way are still limited, for the larger shaft-mounted wheel, and the overall difficulties in handling a plane surface, tend to cramp the cutter. Even where the glass cutting lathe was most effectively used on flat glass, the constraints imposed a stylistic rigidity on the designs, as indeed the *intaglio* lathe did on hollow-ware 100 years later. However, as long as engraved glass remained acceptable in small units, the wheel engraver could satisfy most decorative demands, and there remains some fine, mid-eighteenth-century, wheel engraved (mixed with cutting) mirror glass which exhibits a skill and flair as excitingly fresh as the day it was cut.

Copper wheel engraved apple-green cased glass door panel. William Reckett, 1780. (*Victoria and Albert Museum*)

(*Below*) The crowning piece, and one cross panel, of the Mentmore mirror. It is a remarkable achievement for wheel engraving on flat glass of that size 600mm (24 in)

An English mirror with Jacobite emblem. Small stone wheel engraved, mid-eighteenth century. (*Victoria and Albert Museum*)

Large Glass

As decorative glass panels increased in size to architectural proportions – that is, for windows and partitions – the grinding wheels and the design elements formed by them grew in scale. By the mid-nineteenth century a

unique environment of specialised glass decoration, termed brilliant cutting, had been created.

It is alleged that 'brilliant cutting' evolved in America, and was first introduced into England by Mark Bowden of Bristol in 1850. Whatever the claim, neither the sandstone wheel nor the balancing steelyard on which the system is based can be said to be revolutionary, and perhaps it would be more realistic to see this as the almost end result of a gradual development which had been anticipated in many a workshop, or crudely innovated to solve the heavy handling problems of the glass. 'End result' may appear to be an extravagant statement, but this system has continued virtually unaltered from 1850 up to this very moment. (Brilliant cutting can still be seen in action in the decoration department of James Clark & Eaton Ltd at Bracknell.). As with most traditional craft developments, it is difficult to think of anything simpler or better. Some brief details are given to supplement the illustrations, which almost explain themselves.

BRILLIANT CUTTING TECHNIQUES

Handling Plate Glass

The glass plate, contained in wooden side runners, is bound tight by a rope across the front of the glass (roughly halfway), so that when hoisted it is near enough in

Two brilliant cut and etched pub windows. *Left*: 'The Orchard Tavern', Askew Street, London. *Right*: 'The British Prince', Goldhawk Street, London

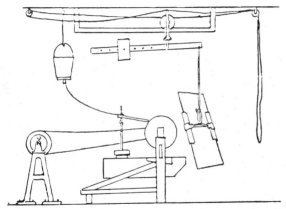

General layout and counterbalance for brilliant cutting. Duthie, 1907

balance. This in turn is centrally suspended by another rope to an overhead beam which, by the simple and ancient expedient of moving weights towards or away from the fulcrum, is able to counterbalance any variation in weight which might arise. The suspended panel may be anchored against any (or too much) movement, but the balanced position is such that the operator can, at a gentle pressure, move the glass to the wheel. Sideways and forward adjustments are provided.

The Lathe

The cutting equipment is an enlarged version of the glass cutting lathe figured on Köhler's Glass. The bearings are hard beech or oak blocks held into position by wedges or screw clamps, enabling the changeover of the fixed shaft wheels to constitute a very easy operation. The shaft ends are cone shaped and located into recessed counterparts in the bearing blocks. Hence, providing the shaft is accurate and the wheel properly assembled, this seemingly crude equipment becomes an efficient, fixed, centred lathe – accurate, quiet and vibrationless. Wear is taken up simply by tapping the bearing forward.

The wheel which revolves clockwise over a trough is fed with water, but any excess is wiped free by a sponge or rag fixed between the reservoir and the cut. Speeds are generally quite slow, about 200–300 rpm, but may be varied by two-stage pulleys on the motor and inter-mediate drive. Whatever the mechanics, the link up with the wheel is by a pulley which is attached to the shafting of each wheel. The wheel pulley and shaft is an integrated unit.

The Wheels

The wheels first used for brilliant cutting were of the same sandstone as that currently used for glass cutting. Corundum is now the alternative, and since the cutting is very shallow it is the only material used. Two or three grades would suffice for most work, say from 120–240. It is more important to have a wide selection of sizes and shapes to draw upon, which may number as many as 20 or 30, ranging from 75–600mm (3–24 in) and 12–50mm ($\frac{1}{2}$–2 in) wide.

Synthetic stones have been discussed in more detail in

Chapter 8. That which applies to small wheels is also true for large wheels, within the sensible limitation of speed; the bigger the diameter the slower it must run for a manageable control of the profile.

The Profiles

The profiles echo the shapes of those required for hollow-ware glass cutting, but there is a much greater reliance on the mitre, of one angle or another. For example, it is hardly possible to lay the plate glass over far enough to use the strap wheel for a semicircular crescent. Consequently, in order to obtain better control over similar sculptured forms, or for turning tight corners, an offset mitre is used. This profile permits the formation of a series of crescent and scalloped shapes upon which a wide variety of designs may be based, but at a much shallower angle of glass to the wheel.

The Cutting Technique

At first sight the scale of the cutting is innerving. The large panel of glass is held so that it rides gently on the stone, patiently allowing the profile to form its shape beneath, while the progress is vigilantly inspected from above. The whole action denotes a quiet satisfaction best expressed by the following quotation from a brief treatise on the subject in 1908 (*Decorative Glass Processes*, A. L. Duthie):

'... running which is delightfully smooth, so smooth that the contact with it is of a very sensitive nature and almost as much is done by feeling as by sight in following the patterns ...'

But the very scale and inherent difficulties of brilliant cutting tend to restrict lyrical freedom, to say the least, and even the best of the remaining partitioning or panel glass repeat formulated patterns which – nostalgia apart – can be aesthetically oppressive. However, as glass cutting, examples reach a level of mastery over the material hardly to be improved upon.

It is quite a long step from copper wheel engraving via *intaglio* cutting to brilliant cutting, and it is unlikely that many engravers will wish to attempt it, but it is very important to understand every decorative development even if one is temperamentally set against it. It has a much greater potential than that offered by the Victorian formula. In a glass school it could be a relief and a release from what could be a small-glass-outlook. Both intaglio and brilliant cutting constitute an incised technique from which the mastery of the tool over the medium can be seen at a glance.

In some forms of engraving on panels of the same scale, where the surface is used as a transparent canvas, free and emancipated as that may be, it could be contended that it is not until the glass is well bitten into, to add a third refractive dimensional quality to the design, that this unique medium of glass can be said to be satisfied.

Polishing

Polishing wheels are used exactly as earlier described: of the same size and profile as the corundum wheel, using pumice/water paste.

A completed architectural panel, 'Space Cathedral' (with a little sand blasting), by Ivan Kolman, now in Toronto. 1000 × 1000mm (40 × 40 in)

Panel 1000 × 300mm (40 × 12 in). 1950, Rheinbach

The brilliant cutter at work today

BRILLIANT CUTTING WITH THE DUAL-PURPOSE LATHE

Due to the cumbersome nature of the equipment with its multiplicity of expensive wheels – other than in one or two specialised workshops it is virtually impossible for the student to widen his experience in this field. However, with the modern copper wheel lathe, which can cope with wheels up to 150–175mm (6–7 in) in diameter, experimental cutting from the top of the wheel is readily possible.

Panels up to 600 × 600mm (24 × 24 in) may be handled either as single designs or as units of a large integrated pattern. Obviously the size that can be managed will depend on the strength of the wrists, though much of the weight is offset by the riding action on the wheel. The lathe must not be pushed too far. No traditional machine has been idly developed and the Köhler machine (wheel centred) will sustain more pressure and hard work than an interchangeable wheel of the same size screwed to a spindle, no matter how strong. But apart from the extra vigilance required to keep the wheels running true, some fine design opportunities are open to the engraver in creating an approach to glass which is now missing from the English scene.

Free-formed glass of the most stimulating and exciting design has in the past few years released a new energy which can do nothing but good. In the same way a broader, more recklessly adventurous use of the larger wheels, perhaps reinforced by other techniques, may beat a new path in glass design.

13 Diamond Point Engraving

THE DEVELOPMENT OF DIAMOND POINT ENGRAVING

A number of early Roman and Syrian glasses exist which have been 'engraved' by being cut into the surface with some very hard material. The designs, mostly geometric, were crudely executed by any standard, but from the skills available at the same time for other forms of decoration: enamelling, seal cutting and jewellery making, it is hard to have to conclude that the artisan did not have the capacity or the better means to pursue this form of decoration than with a sharp flint. Even some wheel work appears surprisingly and unnecessarily elementary when in the same period the hardstone cameo engraver was so astonishingly versatile. It may be that the isolated glass worker, with his tactile mastery and innate sense of form, rebelled agaist the use of applied decoration, and that surface embellishment was left to some outside unskilled innovator. More likely, the system

Linear diamond point engraved. Humpen: 'Arms of Nüremberg', 1592, German. Height 270mm (10⅝ in). (*Victoria and Albert Museum*)

of the 'closed shop' prevented the cross fertilisation of skills in a hierachy of prestige, which, as it does at this very moment, protects each group economically but debars and stifles ingenuity.

The quality of diamonds had been known to the Greeks but, strangely, glass and the diamond point did not come together for linear decoration until the mid-sixteenth century. At least, that is when we first see it as a developed technique. The method was almost certainly introduced to England by the Venetian, Giacomo Verzelini, who secured a monopoly to produce cristallo in 1574. There is strong evidence, however, that the group of glasses known as the Verzelini glasses, dated from 1577 to 1590, is the work of an immigrant Frenchman, Anthony de Lysle, a pewter engraver. All glasses of this period, English and European, in the organisation of design and the free, almost casual, use of the diamond, bear a close similarity,

Enlarged portion of one of the earliest existing English engraved glasses (Verzelini) which illustrates the very free and lively use of the diamond point. (*Victoria and Albert Museum*)

work towards a controlled, broken linework used to simulate tonal change, to end, inevitably with stippled tone. Copper plate engraving has followed the same deterministic course, progressing beyond mezzotint to photogravure. Let us hope that glass decoration of the kind under discussion stops short at stipple!

This brief introduction to an absorbing period cannot be left without some mention of Dutch calligraphic glass such as that engraved by Anna Roemers-Vischer (1558-1651) and Willem Jacob van Heemskerk (1613-1692), work of great individuality, freedom and decorative beauty. It could be expected that linework built up of tiny diamond strokes would be limiting, but the calligraphy of these early masters swirls and wraps itself around the bottle or glass as though the glass had been made for the lettering. It is a reminder to all calligraphers who think they may be breaking new ground.

Line used tonally. A very lively engraved glass which shows a spontaneous treatment. Dutch, 1720 by Frans Greenwood. (*Victoria and Albert Museum*)

A fully stippled glass showing complete tonal control. The highlights are given an enhanced vitality by joining up and overlapping the stipple with fine lines. It is a painter's glass. Aert Schouman, Dutch. (*Victoria and Albert Museum*)

as though they had all issued from the same workshop. But one may easily be deceived by engraved designs, once an idiomatic pattern and method has been adopted.

The use of the diamond point for stippling the surface of a glass with lighter or heavier dots in clusters to produce subtle changes of tone is almost exclusively a Dutch development of the eighteenth century, and is said to have been introduced by Franz Greenwood (1680-1721). He and his followers, painters such as Aert Schouman (1710-1792) and D. Wolff (1732-1810) and a host of ensuing gifted amateurs, brought this technique to the highest level of pictorial skill. This independent development was helped, no doubt, by the use of softer English lead crystal – imported for this purpose – and the availability of diamonds or diamond chips, Holland being the centre of diamond trade and technology.

Some suggestion has been made that the earlier invention of mezzotint, a copper plate printing process giving very rich, soft tones, may have sparked off the stippling process. This would have been an inviromental influence, but it would be more correct to regard stippling as the result of a natural progression from plain linear

Calligraphic engraved romer (drinking glass) by Willem Jacobz van Heemskerk. Dutch, **1685**

Enlarged detail of a calligraphic glass. Dutch, **1660**. (*Victoria and Albert Museum*)

TOOLS
The Diamond Point

At a reasonable guess the early European engravers used diamond chips, small natural diamond crystals or polished diamonds, perhaps set in shellac or hard solder in a simple metal handle – very much like a glazier's writer'. The etcher's hardened steel 'dry point' is the only alternative.

The present day tool consists of an industrial diamond that is, a diamond unfit for decorative purposes, brazed into a steel mount and polished to a sharp cone, generally between the angles of 60° and 90°. But while the diamond is the hardest of all known substances it is relatively brittle and may under shock or rough treatment break away at the point. Consequently manufacturers do not recommend angles much below 90°; they will make them down to 60°, but very reluctantly beyond this.

All the same, 90° is a large angle for a cutting point, and when mounted forms a blunt and clumsy end to the tool, which rather obscures the engraving action just where it most needs watching. The glazier's cutter, which houses a tiny natural diamond crystal, is a much lighter tool, but as would be expected the point of the crystal is much more directional in cut. Mostly workers use coned diamond points, and there is a fair selection of these in angle, size and weight from which to choose; 60° is the most useful angle.

Any diamond tool is expensive, therefore it would be sensible not to order carelessly but to select what is best suited to the hand and general purpose. Whatever the hazard of chipping, diamonds can be repointed by the manufacturers, providing the diamond is big enough to allow it, and if well treated will give a very long life indeed.

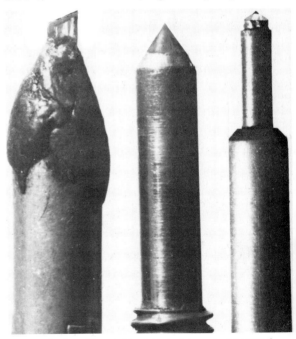

Diamond points. *From left to right*: An improvised mounted diamond chip for stippling; A large commercially prepared (brazed) diamond point; A diamond 'writer'

The Tungsten Carbide Point

More engravers now use tungsten carbide points than use diamond, for the very good reason that they are just as effective, more adaptable and much cheaper to use. Tungsten carbide is a very hard cutting steel which is used for a number of highly specialised engraving operations. It is manufactured as a powder which is subsequently cast and compressed to shape under very great pressure and heat. In general characteristics it is similar to the diamond – intensely hard but brittle – consequently the effectiveness of a tool must depend on the balance of hardness with strength for the work it has to do.

Typical tungsten carbide points. *From left to right*: A general purpose point; A worn out tungsten dental drill resharpened; A heavy duty point

Reliability and availability

The supply of points is rather restricted, which may be the reason why they are relatively expensive, but one or two manufacturers sell points of a general purpose quality which are very well suited to the engraver. The points are supplied as small sharpened rods 15×1.5mm ($\frac{5}{8} \times \frac{1}{16}$ in), which is a reasonable limit for 'feel', but they could be longer (even twice as long) which would give greater economy in use. The 'bite' of a heavier gauge rod might be preferable for some engravers, though this gauge is not readily available. No advantage can be seen in anything lighter than the 1.5mm ($\frac{1}{16}$ in) point, which is now a widely acceptable tool.

There is a lurking suspicion that some batches of points are more brittle than others, but it is difficult to be certain when so many other variables exist. Perhaps one cannot do better for quality of tungsten carbide than that used by the dental trade for drilling teeth; unfortunately, unless one has access to old worn drills, these tools are too expensive just simply to grind back to points.

Advantages

1 Points can be firmly fixed or changed at will, in a whole range of holders to suit the individual: in a hardwood dowel, pin vice, etching point or a clutch pencil holder with a strong grip. The first of these is best for most purposes for it is light and of a familiar, pointed, pencil shape. Separate points which may be interchanged in a pin vice are very easy to lose.

2 They can be shaped to any desired angle from $30°–90°$, though it is as well to follow the original angle of about $60°$ as first produced by the manufacturer.

3 Engraving can easily be watched as the work proceeds, and is much more under control when lines are being ruled.

4 A score of points, which will last a long time, will hardly add up to the cost of a diamond tool.

Disadvantages

1 Though very hard, the tungsten carbide point can easily fracture; the sharper the angle the more prone it is to do so.

2 Overlapping one firm line with another, such as might be attempted in cross-hatching, will certainly break off the point. With a difficult piece of work or a hard glass half a dozen points can fracture very rapidly, and unless the engraver has the means for resharpening this inconvenience can add up to misery.

3 Manufacturers will resharpen tools but at a cost in time and money.

Resharpening the point

It is a common engraving practice to grind or dress tungsten carbide tools with a sintered diamond wheel, and this is the only really professional way to reshape a point. No doubt the ingenious worker will search for cheaper alternatives such as revolving the point against a flat diamond file or even carborundum, but much time can be squandered in attempting to dodge the inevitability of providing oneself with a diamond wheel, or at least a flat diamond-surfaced burr or wheel disc, against which a damaged point may be resharpened in a twinkling.

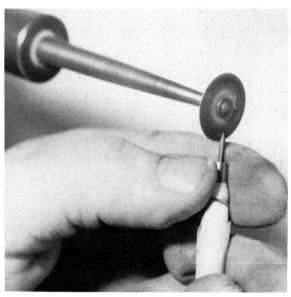

Sharpening a tungsten carbide point on a flat, diamond coated disc

LINEAR ENGRAVING

Using the Diamond Point

The ideal cut of the diamond is evenly incisive, breaking up the glass structure in one continuous frosty line, and when working at its best gives a characteristic sound, hopefully continuous, of a sharp point lightly dragged over fine glasspaper. In practice the diamond is more fickle than this whatever tool is used, and on some occasional changes of direction it will suddenly slide as though nothing had occurred. But this is almost invariably followed by a scarcely visible slit which, unless it is immediately re-engraved, may go further and deeper into the glass until, perhaps many days later, it breaks. Equally disconcerting are the very small fracture flakes which will appear within the line as it is being engraved, whether the glass be hard or soft.

It will be found that a diamond point works better in a vertical position, or as near vertical as the operator can hold his tool, but even when the optimum performance may be thought to have been found these faults will suddenly recur. Very little linear engraving can be found without them. There are so many variables – surface stresses may be one of them – that the diamond cannot be

The engraver at work

entirely blamed for this because some glass reacts to the cut of the diamond surprisingly well, but it does appear that each tool has a 'personality problem'.

All these difficulties which face a diamond cut line may be avoided by gradually building up the weight of the line from a series of short overlapping strokes. This is a perfectly good method for a great deal of work; indeed, the Heemskerk römer (drinking glass) illustrated was engraved in this manner, but in this particular instance the vitality stems from the design, not from the individuality of the single line which some artists find so attractive.

Using the Tungsten Carbide Point

Engraving fine lines with a tungsten carbide point presents the identical problems in angle of cut, quality of line and flaking as the diamond, but it is immeasurably better for delicate work, outlines, or small lettering, mainly on account of the wide choice of angles, and of expendable but repairable points.

STIPPLING

Choice of Tool

As regards stippling, angle for angle, there is not much difference between the diamond and tungsten carbide, but the sharper the tungsten carbide point, the deeper it will penetrate the glass, consequently giving a greater refractive and crisper/white effect.

'St Peter', diamond and tungsten carbide, by Jonathan Matcham, 1976

A civic coat of arms, combined line and stipple, by Peter Chaplin, 1980

A freely line engraved scene, about 1920. (*Courtesy H. Jones*)

The Stippling Process

The word 'stippling' implies the action. The point is tapped upon the surface of the glass, with greater or lesser strength and frequency, to produce the right tonal effect from a range between the black of the open glass to the white of a continuous broken surface. For a given area the closer the dots the whiter the effect, with a proviso that large dots must be more separated than fine ones to give equal tonal value.

It has been said that Dutch engravers produced their stipple 'by striking the diamond or steel point with a small hammer' but, as so frequently happens, the original writer of this statement, relying on hearsay, has misunderstood (he may even have been deliberately misled by some mischievous craftsman) the description of 'hammering'. It does not always imply the use of a hammer, and thus this myth has continued unchecked. All the same, it is possible to stipple and emphasise important areas by delicately tapping the diamond with a light billet of wood so that, although this repeated description of the process is most unlikely, such are the idiosyncrasies of separated craftsmen that some tenuous truth may be lurking in it.

Obviously the method will vary from one worker to another but whether the stippling is effected by a rapid tattoo from the wrist, or under more measured control, the 'pecks' should be given vertically to the glass otherwise small tadpole shapes might appear where the point slides fractionally before it bites into the surface. No matter how much care is taken to stipple evenly, it is surprising how often one hits the same spot or cluster of dots, and to do so too often will produce a tiny 'flake away' which will be seen as a larger and isolated white patch within the tone. With some effects this granulation may not matter, but if an uninterrupted stipple is wanted it is as well to stop before excessive granulation occurs, and patiently prick into the surface where gaps of open (black) glass can be seen.

Skilful control can only be obtained by practice, experience and the tackling of many difficult problems such as maintaining detail within the stipple, which is so marvellously controlled by some workers. The beginner will soon recognise where the greatest danger lurks – in taking too much open glass away around critical details – or where the use of edge masks, ruler, supporting linework and even polishing back may be leaned upon. But real success depends on artistic sensibility, which, in any uncertainty, is best comprehended by closely looking at the engravings by Laurence Whistler, whose fine work over the past 40 years has laid the foundation for a new generation of stipple engraving.

There are other ways of giving broken tone to glass: by a vibrating tool, sand blasting, a gently applied rotating dental point, even an eccentrically run burr or emery paper. Everything should be tried. Some workers rely heavily on the vibrator, which others may find too hard and insensitive a piece of equipment, but no doubt improved models will be developed which in vibrating frequency and controlled pressure will do everything the engraver might require of this method. However, it is not the means, but the artistic end which should be kept in

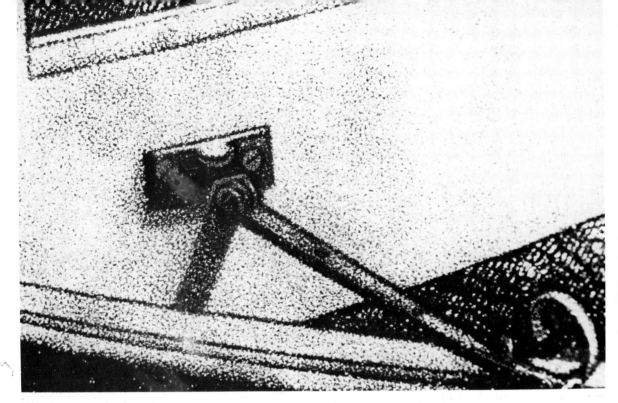

A much enlarged portion of 'A view from the Window', showing the detail which can be controlled within the stipple. By Jennifer Conway

mind, the textural interpretation of light and shade of figures, houses, trees or clouds, which add up to that luminous enchantment peculiar to stippled glass. Any mechanically-produced effect alien to the overall context or mood of the work, which the sensitive and patient hand can do better, should be carefully avoided.

Using the Shape of the Glass

There is always an urge to use the volume of a glass in order to reinforce the illusion of depth. If the picture stops short of the visible boundary of the sides of a glass it may have a confined, vignetted effect, but if it continues too far round one engraved side will overlap and confuse the other. These difficulties may in part be overcome by some clever framing of the image which suggests a continuous movement. If the picture allows a clear view through the glass, stipple some distant detail on the back, such as mountains or clouds, to add to the feeling of perspective. Naturally each glass, bowl or decanter will set a different design problem, for instance, a shallow bowl will much more readily support all-round lettering or a panoramic scene; and, of course, both surfaces of the glass may be utilised in order to suggest an extra depth to a design.

All this is one more reason why the diamond point engraver should return to Laurence Whistler's work, for not only does he always have something poetic to say, but his pictures are composed upon the glass with the greatest care and ingenuity. The inventiveness is hardly to be improved upon but, as there is no end to stylistic innovation, the way is still wide open for the diamond point.

Design Problems

Designs which depend on linework alone, for example, a foliate pattern or, more elaborately, a linear coat of arms, can be transferred directly from a simple line drawing. There may be some difficulty where lines need to be broken up so as to represent tone, but this can usually be dealt with on the glass as the work progresses. With designs which are more involved than this, where some form is to be represented by a range of stippled tones set against the open glass so as to suggest volume and perspective, the problem must be thought out differently: as a design of white upon black, more in line with modern wood engraving.

Indeed, the diamond point engraver cannot do better than to study the whole range of wood-engraving techniques, not only for the graphic invention but in order to comprehend the differing design characteristics of black on white and white on black. With the latter, which is mostly in the modern woodcut idiom, the structure of the picture is built up organically from the highlights to the darker detail and the black areas, almost determined by the tool itself, which encourages a much freer interpretation. After a short time it becomes natural to think and plan this way. However, not too much claim should be made for this method for, in the opposite direction, the vitality of a medieval line woodcut offers an equally valuable inspiration.

Transfering the Design

The simplest way of sketching out the design is by using white ink or gouache wash upon black paper. Black scraperboard is an alternative, but it is a rather limiting method, albeit suitable for some interpretations. The design may be an abbreviation of what will finally appear,

'The Encounter', stipple, by Laurence Whistler

leaving details to be developed on the glass as the mood takes the artist, or it may be fully worked out for copying.

Transference to the glass is readily effected by any of the methods already mentioned in chapter 4. It is possible to prick the design through the tracing to the glass with a point, but as the effect cannot be immediately seen the glass may be marked rather heavier than it should be. The safest way is to transfer the main details and outlines of important volumes (for example, tree trunks, boughs, profiles of leaves or movement of clouds), and gently delineate these with very fine stipple so as to allow some modification or change of emphasis as the work progresses – or, to put it another way, so as not to be irrevocable. It must be mentioned that even the slightest work on the surface will create irritating flying particles of glass. While this may be ignored by some workers as signifying no more than sweeping the garden path, it should be guarded against.

It is important to keep details (such as the separating black areas of branches against a white sky) rather bolder than it might first be thought desirable, for in refining the edges of the drawing the shapes can become thinner and thinner. Also, as the tonal range of stipple on glass is actually very short, some exaggeration of tonal contrast is very necessary to impart the right amount of vitality.

The New Movement

This survey of diamond point engraving should properly end where it began, with the Dutch masters whose glass can readily be seen in the museums and which can be an inspiration to engravers and artists alike. But there is at this moment in England a new movement of stipple engraving which has been stimulated, indeed it can be said activated, by Laurence Whistler, which follows and closely patterns the Dutch tradition. Whistler has already gained his niche in glass history, but those independent artists following him will, it is certain, form a competitive English school.

A beautifully engraved English glass by David Wolff 1791, one of the last and most prolific of Dutch stipple engravers. Although not the initiator of this form of engraving, his name will always be associated with this unique type of decoration. (*British Museum*)

'Tropical House at Kew'. Stipple by Peter David

'The Cat', diamond point. By Michael Hill

14 Flexible Drive Engraving

TYPES OF FLEXIBLE DRIVE EQUIPMENT

Most craft workers are familiar with flexible drive equipment of one kind or another now commonly in use for jewellery, dentistry or, at the furthest extreme, for heavy engineering abrading and polishing processes.

The principle is simple enough. It consists of a portable electric motor coupled to a flexible cable, linked in turn to a handpiece which houses the bearings and the chuck. It has the obvious advantage of allowing the tool to be brought to the work rather than the other way round.

Each drill or drive is designed for some particular or general purpose, but apart from heavy duty machines used for glass bevelling or drilling, it can be said that no drill has been specifically made for glass engraving, though some fairly adequately fulfil the need. Not all drills are flexible-cable driven; for example, the modern dental drill is turbine driven by compressed air giving spectacular speeds. Naturally, the more specialised the more expensive. Certainly, few engravers would wish to bear the cost of a particularly designed drill – even if it were possible to get half a dozen workers to agree on a specification.

Three categories of work may be considered: light, medium and heavy.

Light Duty

Light duty work consists of delicate engraving, outlining and filling in. Hand-held, battery-operated drills may be included under this heading and, though not robust, are very light and easy to use. But there are other light tools driven via transformers which can be either held in the hand or used with a very slender flexible drive, which put little or no strain on the hands compared with the larger models. Some glass engravers depend entirely on this type of tool.

Chucks vary from a simple expanding pin vice to collets of sufficient range to hold most dental burrs, but there is no guarantee that the collet-held drill will run more centrally than a good pin vice. Indeed, there is no certainty that even the heavier tools will better them for concentricity.

Medium Range

Medium range work involves engraving of a more continuous nature, using small or large burrs, and small abrasive wheels.

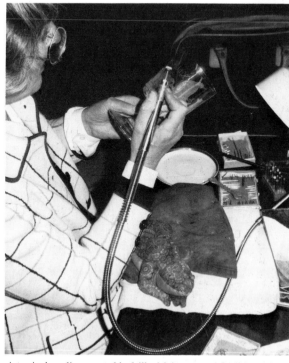

A typical medium portable drill with integrated flexible cable and handpiece. (The acute bend to the flexible cable should be avoided)

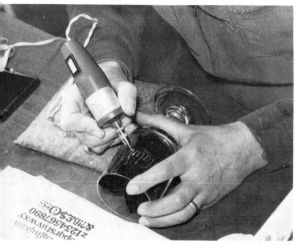

A light hand-held drill

Quite a number of flexible drive drills – the greater range – caters for this light to medium engraving. Usually the drive is integrated with the handpiece as one unit, with simple interchangeable collet chucks to take a number of shank sizes, which in all makes this a very good all-purpose tool. It tends, too, to be overworked for this reason.

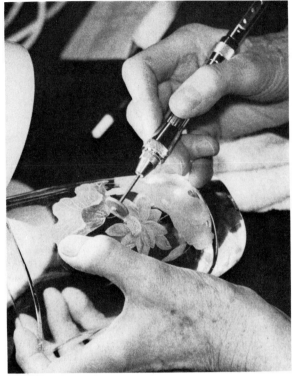

A high quality slip-joint handpiece, with an adjustable jaw chuck (0–2.35mm, $\frac{7}{64}$ in)

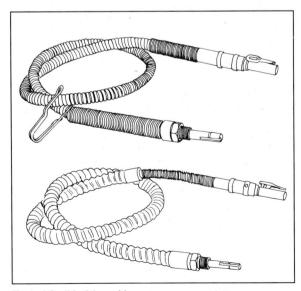

Typical flexible drive cables

Heavy Duty

Dental laboratory bench equipment, as distinct from commercial equipment, is used for continuous running under greater than ordinary pressure for rather vigorous cutting and polishing, e.g. panel glass. This equipment is altogether more robust in motor drive, cable and handpiece, and very suitable for work which may fall within the medium to heavy range.

But what is medium-heavy? One operator may handle a drill for a long time without trouble, while another, with equal workload, may carelessly pull it to pieces in half the time. Again deeper sculptural engraving will obviously put more strain on motor and bearings than say, lettering. Hence it is as well to anticipate the range of engraving to be tackled before thinking of investing, to examine every feature of the proposed equipment and to rate it for what it cannot do as well as what it may.

THE CONSTRUCTION OF THE DRILL

The Motor

In the main, standard portable motors are very reliable and good natured workhorses. The rated electrical consumption, stamped on the motor casing, indicates their power (750 watts equalling one horsepower) and will range from 75–100 watts ($\frac{1}{10} - \frac{1}{8}$ hp) for the average drives to 150–250 watts ($\frac{1}{5} - \frac{1}{3}$ hp) for the stronger. Maximum speeds vary between 10000 and 20000 rpm, which in all models can be variably controlled by a foot pedal much in the manner of a sewing machine.

In most cases the threshold speed is much too fast and the controls, whether variable or 'stepped', are quite inadequate at low speeds. Ideally, they should be continuously variable from a crawl to 8000 rpm. However, small, relatively inexpensive, by-pass speed controls may be inserted between the power outlet of the pedal and the motor, which give full control. Unfortunately the motor loses power in the process, but it is much better to have this facility. Electronic controls are made which enable motors to operate in full torque at slow speeds, but they are expensive, and even then the very slow speeds may be poorly controlled.

The Flexible Cable

Twisted steel cables are reliably engineered and safely coupled to the motor, but because of various methods of coupling it must be remembered that flexible drives of different manufacture may not be interchangeable with a motor of the same power and designed for the same purpose. It is a great irritation to have to abandon a perfectly good motor because of a badly designed drive or handpiece.

There are dozens of differently designed cables but those used in the glass or dental workshop are limited to 4 and 6 mm ($\frac{3}{16}$ and $\frac{1}{4}$ in) diameter, for medium or heavy duty.

The protective sleeves in which the cable runs vary from plastic to flexible stainless steel. Some are thicker or stiffer or heavier than others, but perhaps the flexible metal is more pliable than plastic, which can be surprisingly resistant. If there is any opportunity one must try them in the hand in the working position. The obvious aim is for the lightest and most flexible cable lead commensurate with strength.

The Handpiece

This is the most vulnerable element in the equipment and the most difficult to assess in advance. The extremity of the handpiece, which should be designed for comfort within the handhold, houses the bearings and the chuck. Both of these depend on accurate engineering for parallelity and concentricity; more simply, lack of movement of any kind which would give wobble or vibration to the end of the drill. There are two main types of handpiece: single-unit and slip-jointed.

Single-unit handpiece

The handpiece which is integrated with the cable as one unit perhaps forms the greater bulk of the drives used by glass engravers. A 4mm ($\frac{3}{16}$ in) cable is permanently fixed to a light handpiece housing an expanding chuck (pin vice type) or interchangeable collets which will usually accommodate drills of ·75, 1·5, 2 and 3mm ($\frac{1}{32}$, $\frac{1}{16}$, $\frac{3}{32}$ and $\frac{1}{8}$ in) diameter, the middle range having enough latitude to accept the two common burr sized shanks, 1·6mm and the more sturdy 2·35mm shank (mandrel) for small wheels. Burrs or small tools are held tight in this type of handpiece by screwing down the nosecap (by hand or spanner) while it is held firm against movement by inserting a small tommy bar right through the casing and core of the handpiece.

Bearings may consist of a phosphor-bronze sleeve or ball races. Some have a combination of both. Each is efficient, providing the machinery and quality of the housing are first rate. Theoretically, the ball race should be more reliable, but as the average drill is not designed to avoid the entry of grit, glass debris can cause rapid wear, particularly when the drill is uncared for or constantly in use, as it might be in a school. The evidence suggests that the ball race suffers more than the sleeve in this respect. However, with that inevitable balance of evils, the phosphor-bronze sleeve has the disadvantage that it heats up more rapidly.

Separate slip-jointed, straight handpiece

This is the tool mostly used by the dental mechanic, the foregoing perhaps being more adapted to general purpose jewellery work and engraving. Both 4 and 6mm ($\frac{3}{16}$ and $\frac{1}{4}$ in) cables are provided with an end spring catch into which a great variety of handpieces may be slip-gripped. This is the only standard fitting the engraver is likely to come upon. There is a bewildering range to choose from of

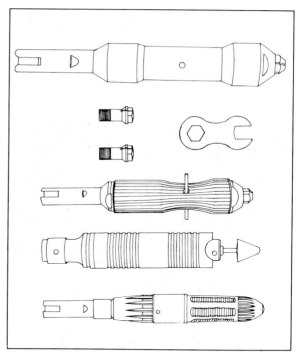

The top three are typical dental slip-joint handpieces, heavy duty with interchangeable collets. The fourth is a light duty one

all sizes, shapes and weights. All are well engineered, run in ball bearings and all are expensive.

Most light to medium handpieces are limited to one size of collet only, 2.35mm ($\frac{7}{64}$ in), some to two, 2.35 and 3mm ($\frac{7}{64}$ and $\frac{1}{8}$ in), and one or two – rarely and mainly heavy duty – will accommodate 1, 1.5, 2, 2.35, 3, 4, 5 and 6mm ($\frac{3}{64}$, $\frac{1}{16}$, $\frac{3}{32}$, $\frac{7}{64}$, $\frac{1}{8}$, $\frac{1}{32}$, $\frac{7}{32}$ and $\frac{1}{4}$ in). But none will take a 1.6mm ($\frac{1}{64}$ in). This is an extraordinary omission, since 1.6mm ($\frac{5}{64}$ in) is a standard dental burr size and, unfortunately, it is the one many engravers may depend upon. But there is a convenient alternative, the 'Goldsmith' slip-joint handpiece, with a variable chuck from 0–3mm ($\frac{1}{8}$ in), which is a good compromise. The 1.5mm ($\frac{1}{16}$ in) collet may have enough tolerance to take a 1.6mm ($\frac{5}{64}$ in) burr but this is not to be relied upon, besides being a poor answer to the problem.

Choice of handpiece

Therefore, in choosing one, there is much to consider: weight convenience in handling, range of collets, method of gripping the shank, complexity for repair. It would be wrong to influence the engraver one way or the other, beyond saying that the simpler the engineering the better,

A modern handpiece containing its own motor

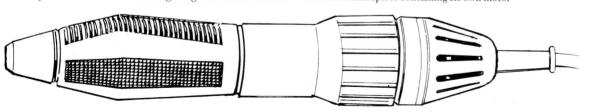

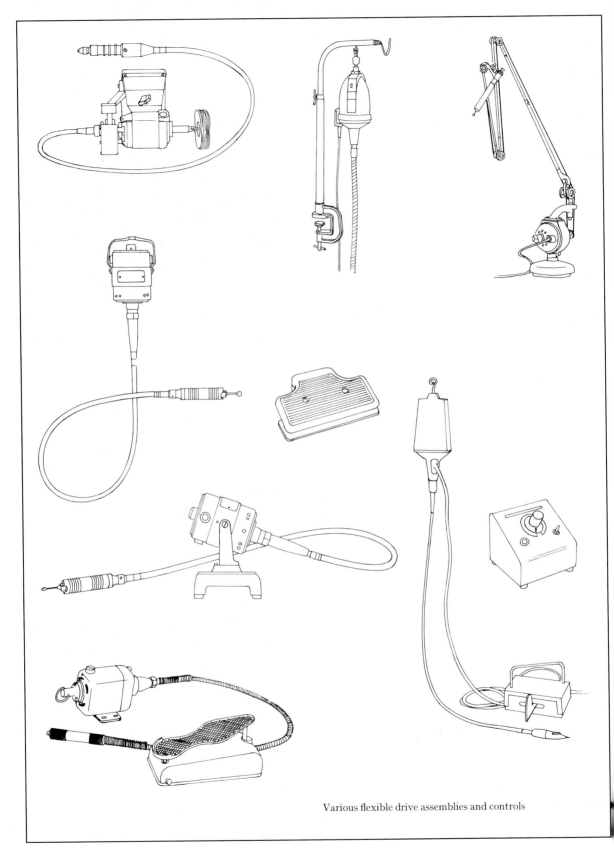

Various flexible drive assemblies and controls

and that if one is to pay a high price one should choose the handpiece which will take the greatest range of burr or wheel sizes compatible with lightness and strength.

These details by no means exhaust the discussion on flexible drive tools, any of which may prove valuable for some particular glass engraving purpose. No doubt some worker who has an old treadle-operated, cord-driven, dental machine would consider modern equipment quite unnecessary. On the nearest end of the scale, there are new handpieces of advanced design, linked only by a light electric lead, which have motor, chuck, cooling system and all moving parts in one slender component. The speed may be electronically pre-set or controlled by a foot pedal. Naturally, these are expensive and perhaps prone to overheating on continuous load.

Perhaps the nearest approach to a universal tool is one of those designed specifically for the dental mechanic as distinct from the dentist. Using sturdier motors of $\frac{1}{3}$ hp they have a dual purpose; a cord drive via a flexible arm from one side of the motor is employed for light work, and an orthodox flexible drive system from the other side of the motor is used for heavier work. Interchangeability of separate handpieces permits the use of a wide range of chuck sizes. However, such equipment is not very portable and requires a reversible switch on the foot control, for if the collet tightens in the direction of the drive it will tend to become loosened under work load.

One usually pays heavily for precision and efficiency beyond a certain sensible limit, so it is important to obtain as much first-hand advice as possible from practising craftsmen before choosing, confusing though that may turn out to be. Look askance at any fixed or inconvenient protuberance on a handpiece and critically examine the centring of a new drill in the chuck or collet at the slowest speed – any drill appears centred at high speed – and if there appears any vibration or eccentricity at the tip end, or play in the bearing, think further. Whether the equipment is best used suspended or held in some bench clamp is a matter of choice. Most assemblies, light or heavy, are designed for suspension, but the weight and swing of the free cable, or surge when the motor is switched on, is always a nuisance and may have to be held, for the right feel, by the most eccentric means.

THE ENGRAVING RANGE

Within the range of work envisaged, roughly from a wine glass to a large decanter, or flat glass up to about 600 × 600mm (24 × 24 in), the practical problems of engraving remain the same; it is only a matter of scale. Unlike wheel engraving, where the glass is offered to the wheel from a fixed position of arms and hands, the flexible drive opens up the widest variety of ways in which glass may be worked, and it is this adaptability, enabling one to use an improvised bench, dining table or even one's lap, which has made this form of engraving so attractive.

After some introductory experiments, which should soon indicate the limits of the tools, the ways and means become a matter of convenience and common sense which every flexible drive engraver seems to have ingeniously solved for himself.

An engraver at work. Note the improvised drip feed to minimise dust

Holding the Glass

It is assumed that the operator will know how best to seat himself comfortably at bench or table in a position that can be sustained without fatigue. The working height will depend on how the glass is held or cradled on the working surface relative to the comfort of the arms. It may be thought that a goblet will be more freely handled if dropped into a recess or, conversely, the forearm position built up in a cushion to obtain the right poise, but this will be rapidly determined by trial and error.

What may be a little more troublesome, particularly at a work bench, is how to deal with microscopic airborne glass dust thrown up by the engraving. Some engravers say they are unaffected by this dust hazard, neither wearing masks nor using water, but continued exposure cannot be good for the engraver's health and should be regarded as harmful. Much depends on the amount of glass being removed. With light outline engraving there is perhaps little to worry about. Beyond that – for example using dental burrs for filling-in lettering, or more robust engraving – it is better to keep the surface moistened or wet.

With the average type of work no particular provision beyond a small dish of water for moistening finger or sponge need be made. However, when engraving glass with the larger burrs or by small wheels the surface should be continuously wetted with a slow drip-feed from a conveniently suspended reservoir. This not only gives a better grinding action, which prolongs the life of the tool, but also enables the glass dust to be safely removed as a white slurry. But, as one usually progresses from small to larger work, this problem can be considered in the light of experience.

Some protection may be given by wearing a nose mask

of which there are several – gauze and paper – to choose from. However, there is no point in wearing a mask if, when the work is completed, the dust-loaded surfaces of wipers or benchtop are stirred up again. Even where water is used it is a good habit to wash away the drying dusty surface of a glass now and then.

Marking Out the Design

Most engraving designs consist of single elements which are simply transferred by the usual means already discussed, but there may be occasions where equal subdivisions are wanted. An engraver who becomes involved with such problems is usually very capable of solving them, but it may be useful to describe a simple way of overcoming any difficulty.

Horizontal subdivisions, for example parallels for lettering, are easy to mark out. The glass is simply turned round against a fixed marking point, which can be held steady to a block or a book of the right height.

Verticals are more troublesome. A series of concentric circles, up to 150–170mm (6–7 in) are drawn out by a compass on a firm flat card. All the circles are intersected by common radii, plotted by a protractor, so that the number of equal segments may be readily marked off and divided by 4, 5, 6, and so on according to the need.

By placing the glass, rim down, to fit one of the circles, the appropriate subdivision may be marked off at the rim. If the glass is now centred to a vertical plane surface against which a pencil may be flatly held, by sliding the pencil downwards against the profile of the glass from top to bottom, any number of verticals can be accurately positioned. (The professional answer to this problem, an indexing machine, is described in Chapter 11.)

TOOLS

Of the multitude of small precision tools available for use with flexible drive drills, those designed for the dental trade are the most useful to the glass engraver. Dental supplies have ranges of diamond burrs and wheels well beyond the average need, so that only a selected few will be discussed.

Diamond Burrs

A burr is a small steel tool, the working tip of which is embedded with sharp diamond particles which protrude from the surface. The working end is designed to drill and grind teeth, and the action is ideal for glass engraving. Considering the technology involved in the manufacture, burrs are very reasonably priced. They are conveniently standardised in two main sizes, 1.6×19mm ($\frac{5}{64} \times \frac{3}{4}$ in) and 2.35×44mm ($\frac{7}{64} \times 1\frac{3}{4}$ in).

Grades

Though there may be a slight difference in quality between one manufacturer and another of the same size and grade, if one starts out as a little coarse or granular, it will soon wear smoother. In any event, the quality of cut will depend on the hardness of the glass to be engraved. Burrs can be found in three grades, coarse, medium and fine – relative terms only – but the finest, a selective number, imparts an excellent quality of cut.

Profiles

The illustrated selection of profile shapes, each of which comes in various sizes, is considered the most useful for general engraving. The choice is entirely subjective. Some engravers may satisfy their requirements with a third of these while others would use all of them as supporting tools for larger or more sculptural work. The ball-ended burr is particularly useful since it will cut from any angle and in any direction with almost equal facility, and the engraver will soon acquire a number of new tools, and valuable half-worn ones, of this shape which range from 1–6mm ($\frac{3}{64} - \frac{1}{4}$ in) in diameter.

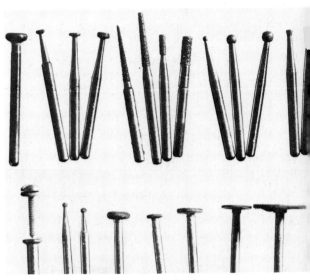

Diamond coated burrs; the most useful shapes

But it must be kept in mind that all tools of this type are *only surface coated* with diamond particles, so their useful life will depend on their treatment. Unless they are well lubricated with water and used with gentle pressure, they will rapidly wear smooth. As with all things, the individual must gain from experience, experimenting with each shape and grade in turn.

A selection of abrasive burrs and abrasive wheels: carborundum and corundum

Synthetic Abrasive Burrs

Enlarged versions of the diamond burrs, manufactured for heavier dental grinding, using synthetic abrasives, are equally valuable to the engraver. The various abrasives are evenly distributed in a ceramic binding which allows a reasonable consistency of cut from beginning to end. Clearly, grinding efficiency depends upon the quantity and quality of the abrasive, the grinding process, the ceramic binder, and the hardness of the material to be ground. Technically the problem is quite complicated, but with these smaller tools the choice is conveniently limited to three general qualities:

Carborundum: silicon carbide, green-grey colour, coarse, medium and fine.

Corundum: Aluminium oxide, pink-brown colour, medium and fine.

Corundum: very finely graded synthetic aluminium oxide white colour, very fine.

The bulk of these tools have standardised fixed shanks or mandrels, 2.35×44mm ($\frac{7}{64} \times 1\frac{3}{4}$ in). The terms 'coarse' and 'medium', 'fast' or 'fine' are relative only, since the abrasive ceramic mix may vary from one manufacturer, or batch, to another. It is not until we reach the larger wheels that the mix is standardised and coded for specific speeds and purposes. (See Chapter 8.)

Of the three types mentioned, the green carborundum which can handle both coarse and medium work, and fine white corundum tools, are the most effective. They can be used, in that order, to a near polishing condition. Medium corundum is prone to what might be called burning streaks. All need water lubrication.

Synthetic Abrasive Wheels

It is difficult to advise precisely on which wheels are best suited for bold flexible drive engraving, much depends on the magnitude of the task but, from practical experience, the following sizes will allow a wide range of intaglio and sculptural work:

10×2mm ($\frac{3}{8} \times \frac{3}{32}$ in)
10×3mm ($\frac{3}{8} \times \frac{1}{8}$ in)
20×2mm ($\frac{3}{4} \times \frac{3}{32}$ in)
20×3mm ($\frac{3}{4} \times \frac{1}{8}$ in)
25×4mm ($1 \times \frac{3}{16}$ in)

Sizes larger than these are hardly to be needed, but smaller ones would be useful. However, as wheels wear smaller, a varied range is soon assembled. Wheels near to these are available, as diamond-coated profiles, but they are coarse and grating in action. Carborundum and corundum wheels are far better. They are made in the same grades and have the same characteristics and consistency in wear as the abrasive burrs, and may be bought fixed to a shank or, more conveniently, as discs ready to be secured to separate, standard mandrels. Thus a mandrel may be used time and again or the wheel reversed when the profile becomes unevenly worn.

Profiles, of course, may be dressed to any shape with the appropriate dressing stick of coarse and fine car-borundum, but it may be done much more quickly by holding the wheel, at high speed, against a diamond-surfaced disc or to the flat, forward and unused side of one of the larger diamond burrs. Carborundum wheels should be left quite rough. Being finer and harder the corundum wheels may be seen to have a scratched surface when shaped by this means, but by following on with a fine carborundum stick the profile is soon brought to a good smooth condition.

All these tools can easily be sorted out from the dental manufacturers' catalogues, but it must be expected that the quality of the same grade and colour code will vary from one to the other. This could be exasperating but it does extend, if accidentally, the variety of abrasives.

Diamond Sintered Wheels

Small precision diamond grinding tools are now commonplace in industry. The cutting portion consists of accurately graded diamond grit distributed in a metal based (mostly phosphor-bronze) matrix. The mix of grit and metals is precision moulded under great pressure and temperature.

Two things occur in the engraving: any fracture of the grit will give equally sharp fragments and, at the same time, the softer bronze bond will slowly yield to wear, exposing fresh diamond grit. This, and the hardness of the diamond, accounts for its efficiency and long life – as well as for its high cost, and for this latter reason it is sensible to limit the choice to the following sizes:

3×1mm ($\frac{1}{8} \times \frac{3}{64}$ in)
6×2mm ($\frac{1}{4} \times \frac{3}{32}$ in)
10×3mm ($\frac{3}{8} \times \frac{1}{8}$ in)

Naturally, a larger range than this may be assembled of coarse, medium and fine (170, 250 and 400 grit respectively), but three wheels are costly enough, so that, for a start, one general purpose wheel, say 6×2mm ($\frac{1}{4} \times \frac{3}{32}$ in) (300–400 grit) should be tried, until experience can assess convenience against further investment.

Very small diamond wheels, particularly useful to the engraver, are now rather more difficult to obtain in Britain than they were, and few specialist engineering suppliers can be persuaded to make them. However, as the demand increases, no doubt the situation will change for the better. Wheels are now becoming available from the continent of Europe.

Some comparison between ordinary abrasive wheels and diamond wheels in action must be noted. Although 'consistency' in wear has been applied to abrasive tools they do on occasion wear smoother, perhaps due to the rapid surface exhaustion of the grit as against the bond, whereas the diamond tool is almost entirely consistent in its cut and effect, giving an unaltered texture, compatible with its grade and bonding, throughout its life.

Surprisingly, the ceramic bond abrasives can be much more roughly handled than their diamond counterpart. Ideally, the diamond wheels should be run at high speed with a plentiful supply of coolant, but with little friction; that is, not too much pressure. However, except for rather deep roughing out, this ideal condition can hardly apply for, with modelling – which forms the bulk of glass engraving with the wheel – the tool would become relatively unmanageable and quite half of the rated speed of the average drill – about **5000** rpm – would be needed.

Naturally, the speed depends on the size of the wheel, which may always be larger than first thought, since the engraved cut comes from a very small segment of the wheel. But whatever the choice, the tool should never be bullied or put under impatient pressure. Because of its structure the diamond cuts easily and fast. The action should be a confident but gently stroking movement. If for any reason the diamond were to run smooth, a light and short pass over with the lap stick will restore it.

Polishing Wheels

The problems of polishing by lead, wood, cork or felt wheels has already been dealt with in chapters 3 and 11. It must be appreciated that holding a glass by two hands and offering it to a firm fixed position gives a much greater control than using a flexible drive, where wheels of the same size would become unmanageable. Thus, for wheel control it is much more convenient to use abrasive impregnated rubber wheels, or some similar flexible material, which are manufactured for dental polishing. These are colour coded for the trade – coarse, medium and fine – but, in common with other small abrasive tools, they will vary from make to make. The firmer rubber bonds are of greater use than the softer, floppy kind.

Wheels of about **25** × 4mm (1 × $\frac{3}{16}$ in), medium and fine, will suffice for general purpose polishing, and as they rapidly wear smaller, convenient sizes are soon arrived at. Rubber wheels are more efficient (move more glass) wet than dry, but in the wet state rapidly wear down to a messy paste, making it difficult to follow the progress of the polishing. In quality of polish the dry wheel will give the better finish, but in this case dust will be created from the break up of the bond at the edge of the wheels. As this is heavy, and the time of operation short, there is not much inconvenience or hazard. On large areas, however, it could be a nuisance.

As with polishing by the felt wheel, the rubber wheel is applied fairly firmly in a circular, multi-directional manner, unless some particular emphasis is required. Speed is medium. When water is used and the polish is considered virtually complete, the speed is increased and the water allowed to dry up on the wheel, when a few light and intermittent bursts should add the final sheen.

Polishing which encroaches on the open glass will undoubtedly leave a bloom, which must be removed with a felt wheel – approximately **25** × 8mm (1 × $\frac{5}{16}$ in) – charged with cerium oxide and run at slow-medium speed. It is a simple and quick operation, provided the felt wheel is carefully kept free of grit. A few felt wheels will be found in the catalogues of dental tools, but the engraver should be on the look out for high quality felt which he may press into service.

CHOICE OF METHOD

A fair idea of the potential of this method of glass engraving should have been grasped from the foregoing outline. In the wide choice of designing it has to offer, from direct drawing with diamond burrs to intaglio or panel work with small wheels, there is, at the least, one area of particular skill which the artist, painter or calligrapher may immediately develop. Unlike wheel engraving, which depends on progressively controlled disciplines, the flexible drive may with a little application give an instant reward of creative pleasure. Thus, such work forms the bulk of engraved glass currently exhibited. Providing some aesthetic muscles have already been developed in drawing, modelling or etching, personalised skills will be built up so organically that there is little which can be said about methods that a few burrs and half a dozen experimental glasses will not instruct better. However a few comments on the choice and use of tools for average work are given.

Surface Engraving: Lettering and Two Dimensional Design

Using diamond burrs

Having examined the dental catalogue, the engraver is bound to buy a larger range of diamond burrs than is strictly necessary. Three basic shapes only are required: the ball end, the truncated cone and the rat tail. The ball is the most useful, so in the first instance it is better to invest in three or four different sizes of this shape than to diversify.

Surface outlining may be made with either the ball burr or the rounded end of a rat tail. Very fine lines can be cut with the sharp edge of a truncated cone, but it is not easy to control when turning a corner. The rat tail has an advantage in that when very blunted or worn smooth, the end can be ground back with a coarse carborundum wheel to give another sharp edge. Cutting a straight, determined line is very difficult, therefore it is better to build it up from a series of short strokes. The burr of course may be used to strengthen a drawn tungsten line, but as 'flaking' will occur along its edges some thickening must be allowed for.

For some work an old worn ball may be as valuable as a new one, for it can be used to smooth out the passage of a course cut. It may even be necessary to take away the sharpness of a coarse cutting burr by allowing the running tool to make gentle contact for a second or so with another burr, but this must be done with great caution. Matting or filling in between outlines is best done with a ball as large as can conveniently cover the area without risk of overrunning the edges. Some engravers may find the side of a fattish rat tail a better alternative, but it is far more inclined to be streaky.

Using abrasive burrs

Carborundun and corundum abrasive burrs obviously augment the diamond-coated burrs, but the ball ended tool is less useful for, after a spell of work, it soon wears out of shape. Once deformed it is virtually useless. The cone, of straight or curved sides, is a far more useful tool, which holds its shape much better in use. However, whatever is said here should not inhibit the engraver from experimenting with any other shape.

Textures which may be incorporated with a design, say, in the modelling of a flower or the surface of a building, will depend not only on the type and coarseness of the tools but how they may be combined, diamond point, burr and wheel together. Some particular effect may even be obtained from an unevenly worn, or eccentrically run, burr. Whether of coarse, uneven granulation, or a smooth white matt, the texture can be selectively polished back to give further nuances of tone and grain. There is no limit to the means; the end is a question of appropriateness and sensibility.

Intaglio Modelling Using Abrasive Wheels

All that needs to be said about the use of abrasive wheels for intaglio or relief engraving has been covered in the earlier chapters on wheel engraving. But there is some difference in that, as the tool is generally held in one hand

Cylindrical calligraphic vase presented to Heather Child, calligrapher. By David Peace, 1971. Height 30mm (12 in)

Goblet. 'Heart speaks to heart', using the whole glass in the seventeenth century Dutch manner. By Madeleine Dinkel

Engraved plate, 'Hallelujah', by Bryant Fedden

and the glass in the other, there is less control over the spinning wheel as it attacks the glass. Consequently, though the approach and the action of the wheel is the same as with copper wheel engraving, more patience is required in the stroking or brushing of the wheels to reach a similar intaglio form. At best it may be difficult to tell the difference between one method and the other, but the separate characteristics are usually detectable.

The greatest difficulty with the flexible drive is to maintain precise edges without granulation or miniature flakings, which is perhaps due to the unrelenting character of the hard bonded grit. The copper wheel is by nature more considerate to glass, for it offers a moving mass of oily abrasive grains at the point of contact which is less resistant and can be changed for a finer grade from moment to moment.

Engraved monogram, by Wyn Phillipson

'Geometric Interchange', by Jonathan Matcham. Diameter: 200mm (8 in)

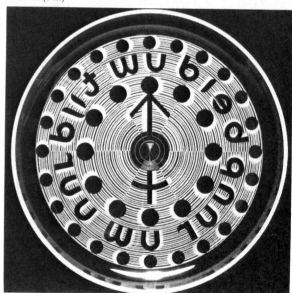

Floral design in relief, accentuated by selective sand blasting. By Elly Eliades Sti. Height: 180mm (7 in)

'Persephone'. Interference pattern based on a calligraphic stroke. By Jonathan Matcham

In the ultimate analysis, scale for scale, it can be said that the engraving is less clean and precise in fine detail – readily seen in quality heraldic engraving – than by the traditional wheel, but it may have a sympathetic control over calligraphy which can be a shortcoming of the wheel unless the engraver be very expert. However, the real benefit of the flexible drill is the total freedom it allows artists of all skills to impose very personal attitudes to decoration in vigour and invention. This in turn has stimulated the professional wheel engraver to more ambitious thinking.

A very decorative glass plate. Both sides have been engraved, which adds to the movement of the design. By Molly Haigh. Diameter: 460mm (18 in)

(*Above*) A highly symbolic plate. Diameter 280mm (11 in). Diamond point and stipple combined with drill. By Frans Smit

'Madrigal'. Combined lettering and intaglio, with a flautist on the opposite side of the glass. By Hilary Virgo. Height: 230mm (9 in)

Armorial glass, by Stephen Rickard

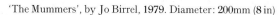
'The Mummers', by Jo Birrel, 1979. Diameter: 200mm (8 in)

Intaglio vase of higly philosophic and symbolist content
engraved by an independent German designer, Kristian Klepsch

'Wessex Nightfall' by Laurence Whistler. Stippling, as a miniatured technique, cannot always give the desired contrast when translated to a large vessel. In this example the slowly rotating burr is used with great effect, giving a broader tonal vigour than could otherwise be obtained

(*centre, opposite*) Rhododendrons on an engraved bowl by Ann Cotton

'The Castle of Elan Donan', by Len Connor. Height 9.5mm (3¾ in) (*below, opposite*)

MURAL AND PANEL GLASS ENGRAVING
Equipment

The limits imposed by the fixed wheel on flat glass have been discussed in chapter 12. With the flexible drive there is no such constraint. Naturally, as the scale increases problems will multiply. Wheels will become bigger and less manageable, the mechanics heavier and less portable, and the physical effort much more demanding, but there is really no end to the creative use of this tool.

The size of a design which can be handled by any equipment is dependent on the type of work. Quite large areas of surface engraved lettering, or linear patterns, may be worked by the average drill, but modelling of 2–3mm ($\frac{3}{32}$–$\frac{1}{8}$ in) in depth, which is quite deep, is work of a different order and will need much stronger tools. It ought to be easy to choose from a range of equipment which would enable the engraver to change from small to large work without fuss, but this is not so. Beyond a certain

limit a good deal of improvisation is required. What in fact will most likely happen is that one tool will be taken to the breakdown point before experience determines what next to try. To give some order to this wide ranging subject a generalisation must be made: it is assumed that the greater workload which is involved with modelling is being discussed in all cases.

The Drill

Starting with the general purpose drill with the built in handpiece, the expanding chuck or collets will usually accommodate the 2.35mm ($\frac{7}{64}$ in) and 3mm ($\frac{1}{8}$ in) dental tools for which a very large selection of carborundum and corundum wheels, abrasive burrs and rubber polishing discs are readily available. Therefore, providing the modelling is gently coaxed along by stroking the tool on the glass allowing the grit to do its work without brutal pressure, panels up to 600 × 600mm (24 × 24 in) may easily be managed. If the handpiece is protected from water, grit or overheating, it will give very good service. Separate slip-joints of 2.35mm ($\frac{7}{64}$ in) will not do better than this. But with panels of approximately 1 × 1m (40 × 40 in), which is over double the area, the strain will be greater, so that a sturdier handpiece with a 6mm ($\frac{1}{4}$ in) cable and driven by a stronger motor would be the more efficient alternative.

This area is about the limit for surface modelling or deep engraving from such tools, though there is no impediment to a large area being composed of small unit panels. Indeed, there might be a very good decorative

'The Three Graces', by John Hutton. 730 × 440mm (29 × 17 in)

expertly tailored to the full studio need. Cables of 10, 12 and 15mm ($\frac{3}{8}$, $\frac{1}{2}$ and $\frac{5}{8}$ in), may readily be obtained, and can be ordered to any length. Naturally, the longer and thicker the flexible drive, the heavier it will be to handle. Over-long cables may suffer from backlash, but at the manufacturers' recommendations this is unlikely to be troublesome. Straight handpieces designed for these drives will take collets up to 10mm ($\frac{3}{8}$ in) diameter, but a lighter piece to house 3, 6, and 8mm ($\frac{1}{8}$, $\frac{1}{4}$ and $\frac{5}{32}$ in) collets with its appropriate 10mm ($\frac{3}{8}$ in) cable, 2m (80 in) long may be all that the well-muscled engraver would wish to handle.

The Motor

The motors usually attached to such professional equipment are too powerful and much too fast for glass engraving. Even when they are infinitely variable, the bottom speed may be too fierce. Therefore it is better to take a standard $\frac{1}{2}$ or 1 hp, 1400 rpm motor, and link it up with a vee pulley system, to give the simplest and most useful speeds for panel work: half speed, 700 rpm; same speed, 1400 rpm; and double speed, 2800 rpm. The top speed, though much too fast, would be very useful for dressing the carborundum wheels. Of course, more steps would give greater flexibility.

It is essential to be able to move the equipment about the studio, but it is easy enough to bolt both motor and pulley assembly to a mobile wooden platform from which all the corners and sharp edges have been rounded away. Some practical help may be needed to fix up the pulleys and to make a simple belt change and safety cover, and to

The late John Hutton at work on a panel

reason for doing so. However, large single panels present different problems. For instance, a design which is acceptable on a small scale may tend to disappear or be much less significant on a large scale. Therefore the design approach must be altogether bolder and dramatic – perhaps extravagantly so if it is to excite any interest at a distance. Similarly, the engraving should take advantage of every light-catching edge or undulating modelling, employ every variety of matt or granulation which can give support to patterns, and use dark, strategic polishing within textures so as to give strong, glassy contrasts. And to do all this, equipment must be assembled which can withstand the continuous assault.

Each worker must find his own answer to this problem, which may be solved by a cable drive held in the nose of a variable-speed commercial hand drill, or something more

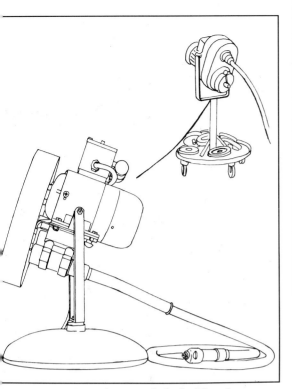

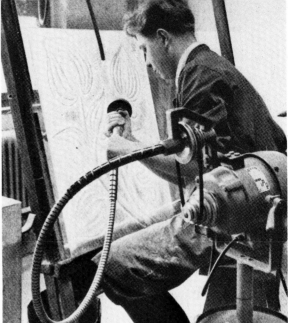

eavy duty grinding equipment and wheels. (Flextol)

student at work showing a stepped pulley being used.
heinbach School

rovide for the coupling from the end of the driving shaft
the flexible cable. But it is as well to steer away from the
evelopment design engineer' who may treat the artist as
captive customer on whom he can heap dubious costs for
finements and alterations to his own defective im-
racticable solutions.

At this juncture it must be mentioned that modern air-
riven engineering tools may be an alternative to the
quipment under discussion. Compressed air tools are
esigned for many purposes: filing, vibrating, hammering
nd a host of grinding operations. They have the very
reat advantage over the cable driven hand pieces in that
e power – compressed air – can be conveyed by a very
ght air line to any distance from the source, the
ompressor.

Handpieces are available which run at 10000 rpm and
ill house collets 3, 6 and 8mm ($\frac{1}{8}$, $\frac{1}{4}$ and $\frac{5}{16}$ in) to
ccommodate ordinary abrasive wheels up to the safe
aximum of 60mm ($2\frac{1}{2}$ in), but it is not known if slower,
ore manageable grinding speeds for panel engraving
lependent on a reduction of air pressure) can be obtained
ithout too serious a loss in torque.

Perhaps the biggest obstacle to the use of such tools is
e cost and size of the air compressor which, for the
uoted handpieces, would be 6.3 bar (90 psi), perhaps well
eyond the average studio capacity. However, as the
ompressor output would be sufficient for a medium sized
and-blasting cabinet, the feasibility of an integrated
ystem for the larger mural workshop should be worth
erious attention.

Abrasive Wheels

Abrasive wheels would rarely need to exceed 100mm (4
in); the most useful range falling between 40–90mm ($1\frac{1}{2}$ –
$3\frac{1}{2}$ in) diameter, and from 6–15mm ($\frac{1}{4}$ – $\frac{5}{8}$ in) wide. Centre
holes can vary, but 6mm ($\frac{1}{4}$ in) is a common mandrel size,
the fittings for which are widely stocked. 'Mounted
points', the engineering alternative to what has previously been described as dental abrasive burrs, have a
catalogue attraction, but apart from large balls they have
very limited or no use.

Obviously, diamond sintered wheels would be the best
answer for most of the donkey work, but the cost of a
complement of tools would tend to exceed the value of a
commission, and in any event may give too regular and
consistent a cut for the right effect. Since the glass would
undoubtedly be hard plate, relatively coarse carborundum (80–150 grit medium soft K bond) would
almost exclusively be used. Where line work or an area of
brilliant polishing is required corundum (220 grit N bond)
would have to be used but, for free pictorial modelling,
carborundum of one grit or another is all that is wanted.

The Glass

Generally speaking, there is no alternative to hard plate
glass for panel work. Softer, more transparent flat glass is
not ordinarily available other than as 'optical glass', a
term which embraces a great range of specialised
qualities.

The grade most likely to be obtained is white optical
spectacle glass, which, as it is produced in great quantity,
is cheaper than other optical flats. However it is quite
expensive and only feasible for small panel engraving.

Plate glass of any large dimension is dangerous to
handle. Where it needs to be manually lifted, the edges
should, at the outset, be protected with rough masking
tape so that when it is gripped between protective rags
there is no danger of slipping. Strong adaptable easels,
bench or mobile free standing, must be provided, against
which the glass can safely and securely lean. Once set in

position on the softwood or felt protective easel base, it should remain there until completed.

Much depends on the facilities, but the work should be in a position which renders it out of focus with background objects, that is, against a diffuse but variably lighted background. As the lighting conditions and the position of the engraving on the glass will change hourly, it is important to be able to move the easel from one vantage point to another. This is more important in the polishing than the matt stage, when the gradual development of polished blacks or dark tones will need to be scrutinised from every angle.

Some warning must be given against working on toughened glass. Toughened glass is ordinary plate glass which has been subsequently heat soaked (near to deformation) and then subjected to rapid, even, air cooling to both sides of the glass, with the result that the outsides remain under a different physical pressure or balance from the more slowly cooled interior. This gives a very tough glass which can withstand hammer blows.

However, strong as this equilibrium may be, once the surface is cut, the panel is liable to collapse. Certainly, if the edge is struck or damaged a dangerous break-up will occur. It has been claimed that surface engraving up to 1mm ($\frac{3}{64}$ in) is a safe limit, but experts say otherwise, so that there is every reason to avoid using it.

It is better for the glass specialist to solve this problem by toughening up the glass after the engraving has been completed. The question of whether deeply engraved or eroded glass of variable thickness has the same stability or equilibrium as toughened virgin plate is then left safely in the hands of the technologist.

Engraving Problems

The approach is roughly the same for small or large work. As the grinding proceeds, the working area should be constantly wetted, either intermittently with a sponge or by a slow downwash trickle of water over the area under attack. The action of the wheel is felt to be much more efficient when the debris is being washed away. Consequently, some large protective apron, waterproof up to the neck, will be a useful standby, even if some splash-guard for the wheel has been contrived to reduce the spray.

The unpleasant screaming noise of the wheel on the glass together with the shake and chatter, particularly when the wheels become eccentric, call for more than average endurance and strength – engraver's endurance and strength! For this reason then, artists with large commissions will seek the help of a sand blasting specialist to reduce the labour by breaking the surface of large areas, premodelling the deepest parts, or delineating edges to selected profiles. This is no more than a kind of underpainting on a canvas for, unless the design is a deliberate combination of sand blasting and engraving, little or no evidence of this initial work can be seen when the work is finished. The extent, and the manner by which it is done, is a matter of sensibility and forward planning. And, since the sandblasting process is irrevocable, it would be better if the artist were on site in order to avoid misunderstandings for, as the design may have been months in preparation (already under the skin of the

glass, so to speak), he will know exactly when to stop.

Polishing

The vitality of a work may entirely depend on polished accents and can be effected by any of the means already described. But another way has been found which preserves the textural quality of matts much better than with the orthodox polishing pastes, namely by the use of wet and dry abrasive paper. This we owe to John Hutton who experimented with every method and material to create the right effects to his famous glass.

Rubber wheels of, say, 25, 50 and 75mm (1, 2 and 3 in) diameter are prepared from door stops, or turned from hard shock-absorber rubber, the flat periphery of which acts as a resilient base for the abrasive paper. Strips of paper of exactly the correct width and length to cover the edge are prepared in advance, and the back coated with permanent tack adhesive. Thus, any grade of abrasive which can vary from 100 to 300 grit, may be attached and readily removed for another piece as it wears out.

The progress of the polishing is much more safely followed dry than wet. It is easy to make the same mistake as with wheel engraving of carrying the process too far, which results in an unpleasant greasy appearance. Abrasive paper of the same grit as a carborundum wheel will give a different, finer surface, and it has the advantage that, as the wheel passes over the engraved matt of texture, the combination of paper and rubber allows the abrasive to just catch the uneven surface to leave a polished 'structure', rather than plane the whole matt down to a level tone – as would happen with a wooden or very fine corundum wheel. More briefly, it actually emphasises the physical characteristics of the granulation.

There is a modern commercial alternative to this method. Pliable abrasive vanes, fixed into a central core act in the same way by brushing or flexibly slapping at the glass surface. They have the advantage of a long life and may be obtained in a variety of grades

All this means that, at one stage or another, a great quantity of dangerous airborne glass and abrasive dust is created. Whatever method of extraction may be devised, in order to be fully protected there is no option for the engraver but to wear an approved efficient mask. Such masks usually incorporate a single canister filter (replaceable) which is specifically designed to exclude the finer, most toxic, particle size below 10 microns. It fits snugly into the flesh around the nose and mouth so that with any intake of breath the air is safely drawn directly through the filter. Exhaled air is expelled under pressure through a one-way valve.

Anything less than this is asking for trouble. There are many designs of nuisance masks, perhaps quite adequate for intermittent dirty work, but there is a danger with these that air, along with some fine dust, may be drawn in from the edge of the mask where it imperfectly fits the face. Good separate goggles, too, are important.

The Approach to Design

This section has been limited to free modelling for the reasons that it has a very wide application, and that most artists associate engraved panel glass with the late John Hutton's magnificent murals. This has captured the imagination and set a pattern which most engravers would dearly wish to follow. But it should be understood that the wheels and tools are no more than brushes in the hand of a painter, and that the inspirational design skill is perhaps the greatest part of the creative task. John Hutton was a mural painter long before he applied his superb interpretative skills to glass. The painter is plainly to be seen behind both the Coventry Cathedral and the Shakespeare memorial glass. And, as he put it, 'I attach very great importance to the preliminary drawing; for instance, the screen at Coventry took ten years to complete, eight of which I spent on the drawing and two on the glass.'

In the first he approached the design with a decorative, almost medieval power, but with the memorial glass, the eye-level figures were conceived very differently – more sculpturally – to reflect the deep, brooding psychological conflicts within each shakespearean character. It is this extra insight and capacity which widens the gap between the artist and the graphic designer.

It would be difficult to follow the same path without ending up in woeful imitation. However, the sense of emancipation over what for many years had been very formal work has created a new environment which must stimulate further artistic invention.

And this is not the only goal. Linear work has hardly been touched upon. The fact that more orthodox disciplines and difficulties beset such work should not inhibit experimentation. Mural glass opens up immense possibilities. Once the architects feel the need or the demand exceeds the supply, it is certain that better machines will be found – as Mark Bowden did in 1840 with brilliant cutting – to improve the mechanics and reduce the physical exhaustion attendant on large panel work. And perhaps the new compressed air hand tools with their very light air lines may be a good start in this direction.

Naturally, some work can only be done *in situ*, in which event a suspended portable drill may need to be used from a scaffolding. However, in the main, the designs would consist of lettering or something much less exacting than modelling, though still exciting.

In conclusion, the appropriateness of an engraving may altogether depend on its location which, ideally, would be against a dark background with a strong open sky above. But it may be that the only position available is a blank wall at the top of a flight of stairs or a window against an open sky, when the engraving might be visible only for an hour or so a day when it reaches some early or late slanting light. Perhaps, in order to avoid misleading oneself – and the client – the best solution would be to have a sample panel, of about 600×600mm (24×24 in), ready to offer up in position in order to assess the effect either of lighting or the weight of the engraved design. There is nothing worse than that well-bred silence which can face the artist at the end of any commission.

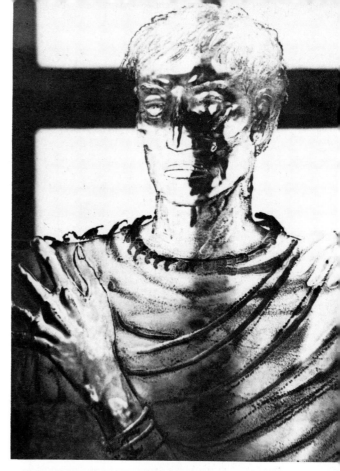

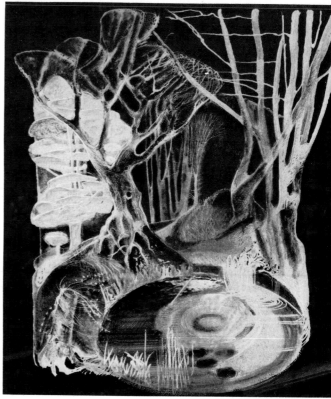

The completed panel, Hamlet, Royal Shakespeare Centre. One of a group. John Hutton

'Forest Pool', a fine example of the use of polishing within the matt engraving. Josephine Harris

15 Glass Etching

ETCHING ON GLASS

Working with Acid

This subject must be approached with great caution, mainly because of the highly toxic nature of Hyrofluoric acid, which is the mordant used for etching glass. The commercial use of hydrofluoric acid is hedged round by so many restrictions which the artist might find difficult to comply with, or might (more characteristically) be recklessly indifferent to, that etching cannot be recommended for the average improvised studio workshop. Indeed, it would be reprehensible not to sound a strong warning note about its use either privately or institutionally, even if the acid could be obtained.

The artist should not be misled by illustrations simulating the etching process, in which the acid appears

A Victorian pub window with 'white etched' designs in different tones embellished with brilliant cutting. This demonstrates the skilfull control of the etching process

to be handled without protection. Some solutions ar much more toxic than others, but all should be protecte against. The use of strong hydrofluoric acid to which th present day artist would undoubtedly be attracted for th purposes of deep etching or rotting in emulation o Maurice Marinot, the famous French glass worker, is quit dangerous. For this reason the council of Europe labellin, recommendations for this listed poison is given in th appendix.

Having said this, when one surveys the huge quantit, and variety of etched glass, linear, geometric, cameo panel glass, techniques reinforced by etching prod ced i Stourbridge from 1850 onwards, and later in America an France up to about 1930, it is a wonder how the skill could have survived had the danger been as great as it i said to be. The truth is, at that stage in industrial history that no risk was ever permitted to interfere with entrepreneurial objectives. As with other processes, nov defunct or modified, many workers survived to give the li to the dangers, others died younger than they needed to However, etching is a continuing decorative process and as such, it must be discussed as a process still open t development.

The Etching Process

The system of etching is very simple: a wax (or other resist, is applied to the whole glass surface. The desigr which is to be etched is laid bare by needle, scraper o scalpel. The glass is then immersed in hydrofluoric acid which eats away the exposed areas, giving depths and quality of finish (clear or matt) dependent upon the time of immersion, temperature, strength and type of acid and quality of glass, which for the average technician would b a matter of trial and error.

Design Considerations

Any method of decoration which involves the use o stencils is very limited and depends for its success on th ingenuity with which the cut stencil may be controlled t produce a number of effective shapes and, in the case o etched glass, a very restricted number of lines, tones and depths.

The design must take several factors into account:

1 How many stages or depths of etch will be required : For each progressive depth the resist will have to be partially removed or modified and the glass returned to the acid bath.

2 How many textures will be required? Is the design to be

formed of a single matt, or a variety of tones combined with open clear glass?

3 From which side of the etched glass should the design be viewed?

4 Is etching to be combined with other techniques such as brilliant cutting or sand blasting, which in most cases will have to be completed first?

This implies that before any design is contemplated a close familiarity of the process is necessary in order to understand the limitations or effectiveness of depth against depth, which may be difficult to see, and the control of tones which will be found to be a subtractive process (as it is with the polishing of white matt to darker tones). However, some examination of Victorian etched small glass, and Bank and pub windows and panels should give a good idea of what is involved.

THE RESIST

There are three main types of resist: wax, liquid and lead foil. Wax offers the simplest method while liquid resist allows more freedom of design. Lead foil is used particularly for flat glass, and requires the most preparation.

Wax Resist

The wax used is almost identical to that used for copper plate etching. The main constituents of the acid resist are beeswax and colophony resin (resin or rosin), combined in the proportion suitable for the purpose. Beeswax will suffice alone, but is soft and tacky. Additions of resin will gradually increase the hardness. Conversely, additions of tallow or lard will make it softer. There is no end to the treasured recipes for resists, which could incorporate Syrian asphaltum, Burgundy pitch, Venice turps, and the like, but beeswax and resin is the simplest and cheapest to make up.

There is no better way of applying the wax to a medium-sized glass than that used 100 years ago, that is, by dipping the *hot* glass into the melted wax and allowing it to drain away and harden. After some hours it should be tough enough to allow a scraper to cut through the coating without flaking, or leaving too many adhering bits of wax.

Liquid resist

Good quality bitumen solution should be used. It should come undiluted, as a thick, viscous mass which can be conveniently brought to the right consistency with petrol, xyllol, white spirit or turpentine, roughly in that order of solubility and speed of drying. Bitumen paint is a very convenient resist, but more prone to breakdown than wax. However, since a design may be painted directly on the glass, bitumen offers much more freedom to the operator than wax.

A long-haired sable brush should be used for fine detail, allowing the bitumen to flow from the end to form a consistent film. For blocking out, small 'squirrel' mops would be a cheaper alternative to sable. The biggest danger arises from uneven strokes from coarse bristles which may leave small transparent streaks or a stream of bubbles. If they are not eradicated they will weaken the film and leave it open to breakdown. A small quantity of methylated spirit mixed with the paint, though not compatible with white spirit or turpentine, will tend to disperse bubbles.

Bitumen is not an ideal medium, but with practice it can be worked quite readily with brush or ruling pen for quite intricate designs. This of course does not exclude other liquid resists such as solutions of resins or Japan size.

Lead Foil Resist

Thin lead foil free from pinholes gives much more prolonged protection against the acid than wax or bitumen. Special foil of about $0.075-0.125$mm $\frac{3}{1000}-\frac{5}{1000}$ in is manufactured for this purpose and supplied in rolls. It may be used for hollow-ware of flat glass – mostly the latter – which in general is so large or inconvenient to handle as to become the work of specialised establishments. However, as there must be a much greater future for decorated architectural glass of all kinds than architects appear to be alert to at the moment, it is important for the artist or engraver to appreciate the potential of this process and, if possible, experiment with the technique under the direction of some well-disciplined workshop studio.

1 Paint over one side of the cleaned glass panel completely with an even coat of bitumen.

2 Cut a sufficient area of undamaged foil to cover the glass, or at least the design, and prepare one side of it with a covering of beeswax/tallow.

3 Place the foil wax side downward in contact with the bitumen surfaced glass, and firmly and flatly burnish the foil into contact with it by rubbing over the foil with a small block of smooth wood or a firm pad. Continue doing this until the two surfaces are quite firmly attached to each other. Any area left bare on account of the size of the panel may be covered with odd pieces of spare foil in the same manner. allowing a safe overlap. It is important to have tested the wax/tallow backing in advance; it should have enough adherence to hold the foil in position, but not so great as to make any part of the cut stencil difficult to remove. Some workers avoid treating the back of the foil and apply it clean to the tacky bitumen surfaced glass.

4 Having, in the course of designing, determined the number of tones or depths which will be required and the order in which the foil will be removed for sequential etching, transfer the design to the resist and cut the stencil with a sharp knife.

The stencil may be cut directly through a tracing waxed down in position on the foil surface, or the foil may be prepared with a thin coat of white gouache upon which the design may be drawn, or transferred by means of a piece of graphite – backed tracing paper.

Cut round each element of the stencil – which is to take an etch of the same duration – with a stencil knife, just deep enough to allow the foil to be peeled away from the glass without tearing. Burnish every cut edge

Brian Gardener working on a panel. The plate glass has been covered with lead foil which has been whitened to accept the transferred design. The black parts are the areas where the stencil has been cut and removed to expose the bitumen adhesive base, which is subsequently cleaned away.

tight to the glass so that there is no possibility of the acid creeping underneath.

5 When the foil stencil has been completed, remove the exposed bitumen and old wax still left on the glass with a solvent. White spirit is efficient enough but it should not be left around to creep under the foil. Finally, when the glass is dry and free of any bitumen smears, degrease the whole plate with a soap solution, then swill it and dry it off in readiness for the etch.

THE ACID

Commercial hydrofluoric acid varies from 40% to 60% strength (the measure of active hydrogen fluoride dissolved in water) so that it is as well to consult the suppliers for the most suitable grade for glass and, equally important, how to store and handle it. All containers, bucket, funnels or trays should be made of thick, high density polythene, and the handler fully protected with rubber gloves, aprons and boots, with a full face mask in accordance with the code of practice. Actually the supplying chemists will gladly give all the information that is required for handling with safety, and may indeed be reluctant to supply the acid without satisfying themselves as to the working conditions.

Dilution

At full strength hydrofluoric acid is very fierce, giving off poisonous fumes. Obviously its activity is modified by dilution. For most work this will vary from two to four parts of water, depending on the original strength of the acid and the purpose for which it is required, which in the main falls between following categories:

1 Deep etching and rotting: 2 parts water, 1 part hydrofluoric acid.
2 Normal-controlled etching: 4 parts water, 1 part hydrofluoric acid.
3 Acid polishing: $1\frac{1}{2}$ parts water, 1 part sulphuric acid, part hydrofluoric acid.

The addition of sulphuric acid will, under the right conditions – at a temperature not less than 40°C (104°F and for very short immersion times – impart a highly polished finish to a finely ground or etched glass surface hence it was widely used commercially as an alternative to orthodox polishing. It is particularly valuable to the individual artist for the selective etching of matted or cased glass.

Note: when diluting the strength of the hydrofluoric acid it is most important gradually *to add the acid to the water*. If dilution is attempted the other way round a localised explosive boiling may take place and throw off dangerous splashes. (Any initial reactive fierceness in etching may be tempered by dissolving a small amount of glass in the acid.)

Timing

As a very rough guide, ordinary plate glass etched with acid diluted 1:3 will show a marked step in the surface in about half an hour, and a depth of 1.5mm ($\frac{1}{16}$ in) in one and three quarter hours. However, in workshop practice where unspent acid may be retrieved for further use topping up with neat acid will be necessary, in which event the quality and speed of etch will need to be checked by a test etching.

ETCHING

All the hard work has been involved in the preparation. Etching is the simplest part of the process, consisting of exposing the glass to the acid (in the case of small glass immersing it in the acid) for a predetermined length of time.

In order to use the most manageable amount of acid for etching flat plate, it has been the common practice for nearly 100 years to surround the design with a wax wall to act as a shallow tray to contain the acid. The plate glass is set up on blocks and levelled with wedges, with one side overlapping the bench in readiness for the drain-off.

The wax wall of about 20mm ($\frac{3}{4}$ in) high is manually pinched up in position from a soft mixture of beeswax and lard (or tallow) in the approximate proportion of 4:1 respectively, and can be prepared in the same way as soft ground for copper plate etching. By carefully and slowly melting the beeswax first, adding the tallow and then pouring the mixture into cold water, it may be retrieved and worked into a soft mass in the hands.

Enough acid should be poured onto the plate, in a smooth, continuous flow, to cover the design without risk of overspill. When the allotted time for the etch has elapsed, a break is made in the containing wall of wax at a convenient point on the side overlapping the bench for the acid to drain away via a funnel into a container. After swilling, the foil stencil may be removed and the surface

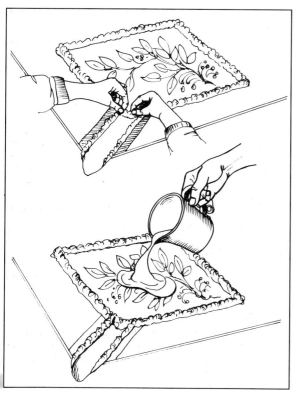

Preparing for etching. *Top*: Pinching up a wax wall on the plate glass. Note the small channel in readiness to drain away the acid. *Bottom*: Pouring the acid

washed clean of wax and bitumen with white spirit. Though elementary, the troublesomeness of the acid dictates that the whole operation should be approached in common sense order, having funnels, jugs, buckets and swill water at the ready. Any spillage should be diluted with plenty of water, neutralised with slaked lime and washed to drain. It goes without saying that all protective clothing must be kept washed and cleaned.

Embossing

All such etching using hydrofluoric acid alone will give a shiny transparent depression in the glass. Architectural glass was commonly etched in this manner with designs deep enough to permit the surface to be matted with emery flour to give a white contrast to the clear etched glass. It is described as 'embossing', a term which has lingered on for a century.

French Embossing (White Etching)

While hydrofluoric acid etches glass to a smooth, transparent condition almost identical to the original surface, the acidic salts of hydrofluoric acid, fluorides and bifluorides will, under the right conditions, attack glass to leave a white matt – obscure, as it is called. By exposing this dense white matt to hydrofluoric acid for varying lengths of time, the obscure is dissolved back, step by step, nearer to clear glass. Thus a series of well defined tones may be obtained. This process is distinguished from

the embossing described above by the more romantic term 'French embossing', and the solution of fluorides which are used as 'white acid'.

A white acid may be made by neutralising hydrofluoric acid with sodium carbonate, but it is now conveniently obtainable, ready to use, from specialist suppliers, probably formulated from sodium or postassium bifluoride. In its liquid working condition it is much less toxic than hydrofluoric acid, but should still not be handled carelessly, particularly when preparing white acid from a bifluoride powder which is poisonous to breathe in.

The following is a good working formula for white acid, in the adequate proportion of:

Ammonium bifluoride	2 kg ($4\frac{1}{2}$ lb)
Sugar	2 kg ($4\frac{1}{2}$ lb)
Barium sulphate	250 g ($\frac{1}{2}$ lb)
Demineralised water	2.25 l (4 pt)

(Barium sulphate and sugar are added to give a greater viscosity to the solution)

The process of white etching is a little different from embossing. The prepared plate is flooded with diluted hydrofluoric acid and allowed to drain away, to leave a clean and reactive surface. This is immediately followed with the white acid which, being of a creamy consistency, is allowed to flow slowly down the inclined plate from the top to the bottom. The plate is then levelled out to allow a fair mass of acid to settle over the design, where it is allowed to remain for about an hour. After this the thick residual deposit is washed and squeegeed away to expose, when dry, an even white obscure. Two or three etches of shorter duration may help to smooth out early signs of unevenness. Rapid drying out of the etching solution reduces its efficacy. The best working temperature is about 21°C (70°F). Protect all under edges.

If an area of the matt obscure is isolated and etched with hydrofluoric acid of embossing strength (1:3) it will be modified slightly, or acid polished to a grey, and if this is continued by stages, exposing the grey to further etching, two or three tones may be obtained. Only by experiment can the etching times be ascertained. As with other tonal controls, along with aquatint, times are approximately doubled to give equal increments of tone. A noticeable difference to the obscure should be obtinted in five or six minutes, and for further stages of grey the times would be roughly of the order of ten and twenty minutes. To give a good contrast to the juxtaposed tones, a sensible limit would be two stages of obscure reduction only, light and medium grey, which with the clear (black) glass and white obscure will give a few steps of tonal contrast.

The foregoing offers a digest of a process which, along with brilliant cutting, greatly contributed to the decorative vitality of Victorian England and America. It is still in practice, but only as a faint shadow of what it once was. Perhaps because of the rigidity or repetitiveness of design, or its plebeian association with the Victorian gin palaces, it may now be thought to have more archaeological than architectural importance. Nothing could be more wrong. Considering the acres of unrelieved glass

Enlarged detail of a tumbler, commercially etched and mass produced. The resist for this was transferred from an engraved block (relief) on which the open (etched) design was cut away. Stourbridge, about **1880**

with which we are surrounded, there must be the need and the necessity to nurture and develop these surviving skills. Fortunately a few specialist establishments still produce etched architectural glass, and perhaps because of their professional control over the working conditions certain commissions are best left with them, particularly if a good open relationship can be formed with the artist. But a few widely separated individual workers are using the process on cased or plain glass with great vitality, for items such as stained glass windows and screens.

Essential equipment for deep etching holloware

Before leaving this subject, attention must be drawn to the commercially etched hollow-ware glass which was produced in such large quantity and variety in Stourbridge and its American offshoot, between **1850** and **1930**. Every technique, manual and mechanical, was called upon, the use of templates for repetitive motifs, template etching in combination with obscure, etched cameo glass, and etching in combination with engraving and *intaglio*. Their sheer ingenuity and skill in the use of hydrofluoric acid at every level of design is perhaps underestimated and is worthy of objective study which, to the unprepared, may be quite chastening.

Deep Etching

The main drawback to deep etched or 'acid rotted' glass (the term given to the heavy erosion of glass to give textures of sculptural abstracts) is the toxicity. As stronger acid is needed to dissolve away an abnormal amount of glass, more fumes will be given off, both in the first instance and every time it is reinforced with strong acid against exhaustion – which may be frequent. The etching too, is not just the matter of an hour or so but for many hours or days, so the operator is exposed to the danger of pervasive hydrofluoric vapours for quite a time. This can be minimised by using the standard laboratory fume cupboard (or something similar) which is fitted with an exhaust fan to draw off poisonous fumes, and a door to shut away reactive operations. Obviously there is no point in expelling hydrofluoric vapours towards a wilting conservatory, and all such ventilation problems should be left to an expert.

With prolonged etching of this kind a considerable deposit is formed on the etched glass surface which, unless removed, may inhibit further activity. Or the deposit may fall away from certain areas or edges to the bottom of the tank, resulting in uneven erosion and possible breakdown of the resist. Unless some random acid effect is required for example, in the gradual breakdown of a gum arabic resist – periodic washing and repair or addition to the

Essential Equipment for Deep Etching Holloware

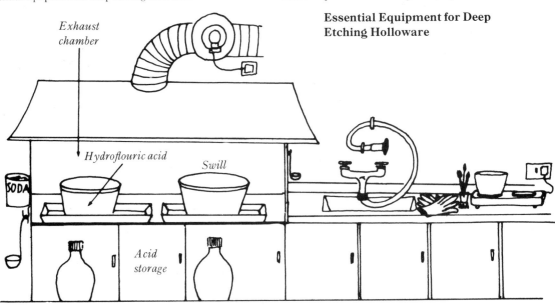

Exhaust chamber

Hydroflouric acid

Swill

SODA

Acid storage

(South Kensington Science Museum)

Three very interesting vases illustrating various stages of cameo work using etching as a part of the technique. *From left to right*: (1) A copy of the Portland Vase in an early stage of development: The base glass has been cased with opal glass (the limit can be seen on the neck) which has been subsequently matted with white acid. The (eventually) white figurines have been protected with bitumen preparatory to etching the background away. (2) A similar vase with the background removed and the base glass exposed. There is evidence of preliminary coarse wheel modelling on the silhouetted figures. (3) A typical Stourbridge cameo vase in its finished state showing the use of the dark base glass to give tonal modelling in the bold leaf design. (The tools in the foreground are hard tempered triangular scrapers such as John Northwood was said to have actually used in carving his reproduction of the Portland Vase and the Milton Vase between **1870** and **1880**. It is a tremendous tour de force, which raises many questions on the technique which up to this moment has not been repeated.)

Detail showing the deep but controlled etching of the surface from Maurice Marinot's work

Highly individualistic formed and sculpturally etched glass. Maurice Marinot, 1932. (*Victoria and Albert Museum*)

resist will be necessary. To state the obvious, it is a matter of experimenting with a difficult process which in the end may bring more failure than success.

The real aim is to have that aesthetic mastery over a dissolving shape or surface which augments the sculptural content rather than embarrassing it. This happens to be rather rare. There are some fine examples to be seen, but

A blue metallic lustred vase which has been etched (dipped briefly) to leave selected shapes of base glass, which visually overlap creating a variety of delicate tonal changes. Rheinbach, 1952

they are spread thinly and far among the galleries. Perhaps Maurice Marinot (1882–1960) is the finest exponent in this field. His elemental sculptured forms have an almost restless lava-like quality, somewhere within the glassy matrix itself, suspended between the liquid and the frozen form, which makes his creations real works of art. If hydrofluoric acid plays its part, it is a means to an end, not an end in itself.

MODERN ETCHED GLASS

In spite of the difficulties of etching and the limited resources of most independent artists, some excellent small panel work is being designed. However, as sand blasting can be used as a more convenient and relatively safer alternative to etching, there is an increasing tendency to rely on this method.

As far as modern etched hollow-ware is concerned, the decorative inventiveness of Gallé and Tiffany has gradually given way to the highly personalised sculptural art forms of Maurice Marinot or more recently to the beautifully controlled etched cased glass of Ann Wärff. And it is fairly certain that the present day student will wish to travel in the same direction. Such work is much closer to the furnace than other decorative forms, and for that reason the small studio glasshouses which have the ability to form and colour case glass, and perhaps to etch and recase or even to reheat and reform, will be the most hopeful starting point for the creative etcher.

16 Sand Blasting

THE DEVELOPMENT OF SAND BLASTING

Sand blasting is almost self explanatory. It is a method by which stencil cut designs are eroded or abraded into glass by air-blasted particles of sand or other abrasives. The stencil may be of any resistant material, thin enough to allow sharp edges but, at the same time, impervious to the eroding air-projected abrasive. The effect on the glass unprotected by the stencil is very rapid and irrevocable.

The action of wind-blown sand on stone, metal and glass has been known for centuries, but it was not until the latter part of the nineteenth century in that flurry of innovative energy such as attended glass etching and brilliant cutting, that machines were invented expressly for glass decoration. The first patent for a sand-blast machine was taken out by Benjamin Chew Tiligman in 1870, which appears to have anticipated every method: steam water jet, gravity, centrifugal force, and compressed air.

It is very difficult to know when sand blasting was first used on hollow-ware in an individualistic way, as an artform, as distinct from the repetitive 'etching' (a misnomer for blasting) of the commercial houses. It is certain that freely designed sand blasted glass was being produced in Bohemia in 1920 and, no doubt, had been experimented with long before that in isolated studios, schools, or glass establishments in Europe and America.

The technology of sand or shot blasting has closely followed the increasing commercial demand for surface abrasion of all kinds, metal, stone and ceramics, and for a wide variety of purposes. Glass decoration is just another of its uses and, as might be expected, the machines designed for this work are directed more towards commercial ends than to the individual studio. Perhaps it is the mechanical nature of this process and its adaptability to mass production techniques which has brought the method, artistically speaking, under suspicion. But some of the popular resistance must be due to the high cost of the blasting cabinets which, together with that of glass, is very inhibiting to the experimental artist. Perhaps the biggest impediment to the inquiring student is the lack of readily available examples which might excite him. The best sand blasted glass is to be found as individual pieces in museums and collections spread far afield, and never in sufficient numbers as to create an artistic environmental background.

There may be one other obstacle. Sculptural sand blasting apart, the main skill rests in the designing, the stencil cutting, and the sequential control of the mechanical blasting. Hence it differs from all other forms of glass decoration (except etching) where the bulk of the creative effort is in the manual engraving of the glass surface itself, from which most workers derive the greatest pleasure.

EQUIPMENT

The average sand blasting equipment consists of an enclosed cabinet provided with a hopper to contain the abrasive, a window through which to watch the work in progress, and two protective entry sleeves for the arms to hold the gun and glass. Compressed air to controlled pressures, from 88 to 4500atm (30 to 150 psi,) is fed to a blast gun which has a secondary linkage with the hopper containing the abrasives. These can be sand (although sand has now been abandoned), carborundum or corundum, or even glass beads of various grades from about 120 to 220. As the air is ejected from the nozzle of the gun, the carborundum (which is what is generally used

Open cabinet showing air gun and the separate air and abrasive supply hose

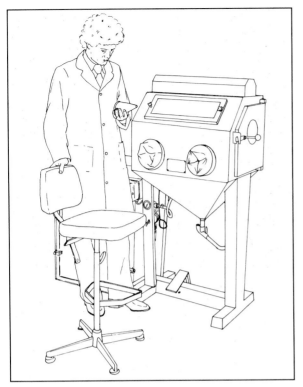

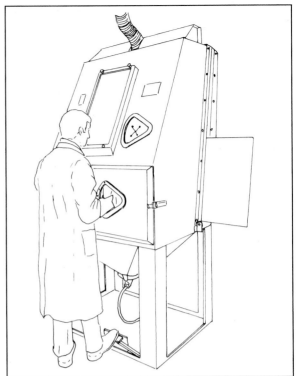

Left: A modern sand blasting cabinet for small work. *Right*: A modern cabinet designed to accommodate panel glass

for glass) is drawn up and expelled with the air in a fierce jet. The duration and intensity of the gun bursts, which can produce a matt surface in a second, is controlled by a foot pedal. The carborundum is recycled and the air extracted and filtered.

Cabinets vary considerably in size and function, so it is important to seek advice, or visit an art school where one is in operation, to understand fully what is required. Indeed, a glass school may be the best place for an introduction to the system. The minimum requirement both for efficiency and health protection is a cabinet such as described and illustrated. Improvised blasting without the protection from flying dust is asking for silicosis.

The machine shown in the illustration, which has been designed for glass work, is widely used by professionals, and it will do anything the engraver is likely to require for superficial or deep decorative blasting on quite large hollow-ware. It has also the valuable facility to take relatively large and variable sized panel glass through a slot in the back of the cabinet. This does not prevent the mechanically-minded worker from making a cabinet, but the problem should be well researched to avoid having too little or too much pressure.

THE RESIST

Choice of Resist

The qualities required for a stencil resist can be satisfied

by a range of materials.

1 It should have a firm but temporary adherence to the glass surface.
2 It must be impervious to the abrasives, which can be very searching.
3 It should be thin enough to give sharp edges to the finished design through the cut stencil.

Over the years every expediency has been called upon – blotting paper impregnated with glue, pigmented glue on its own, rubber and metal foil – but nearly all of these have now been abandoned for self-adhesive plastic sheeting of the Fablon type which is easy to apply, thin enough to be conveniently cut on the glass and flexible enough to be stretched or manipulated over a curved surface. However, there is for the impecunious student one cheap process which is worth mentioning, which involves a home-made resist using glue and glycerine.

Making a Glue Resist

1 Soak hard (carpenter's) glue overnight.
2 Bring it to a thin consistency in the usual way, by heating it in a water jacket, and adding water to the glue as required.
3 Add yellow ochre powder pigment to act as a filler until it reaches the condition of thick, viscous cream.
4 Add glycerine in the approximate proportion of one teaspoonful to the $\frac{1}{2}$ litre (one pint).

In its hot, liquid, painting condition, the resist should have the appearance of thick treacle, and when cold and set it should bave the physical quality of hard rubber. Trials must be made to discover the correct strength and resilience of the dried film (glycerine is the main factor), but once this has been determined the resist can be recycled and will last for a long time.

Applying the Glue Resist

1 Warm the glass before applying the hot resist.
2 Place the glass rim down on a round piece of cardboard to which it is allowed to adhere. (This will give protection to the inside against the subsequent blasting.
3 Allow the film to dry naturally (24–36 hours). The dried film should not be less than 2mm ($\frac{3}{32}$ in) thick for small glass or 3–4mm ($\frac{1}{8}-\frac{3}{16}$ in) for large, flat, panel glass.
4 Dust the surface with chalk in readiness for transfer of the design.

Although this method may appear a little archaic compared with modern photo or screen printed resists or even Fablon, the film so produced can be peeled back for sequential blasting and has the advantage that it can be applied to any intricate shape of glass. It is to be noticed that the average sand blasted design is set down on relatively straight-sided glass.

Self-Adhesive Plastic Resist

Thin white Fablon is now the most popular choice of resist, and its application is simply a matter of removing the protecting cover to the tacky backing and pressing it firmly down in the correct position. The plastic film has enough stretch in it to be made to conform to a mildly curved glass, but it is obviously easier to transfer the film to straight-sided glass, which is a feature of most commercially produced designs. With a little ingenuity more globular shaped glasses may be handled, but some provision for linear distortion must be allowed for in the design.

THE DESIGN

Designing for stencil work, whether it be sand blasting or etching, has the inbuilt disadvantage that the image must be converted into a limited number of areas of tone silhouettes which it is practicable to isolate with the stencil knife. Therefore, to be effective and free from rigidity, the design needs clever advance planning, for it cannot be built up as the process progresses. Two types of work are considered here: single stencil, one-stage blasting, for linework or lettering; and multi-stencil, sequential blasting for images made up of line and tone.

Single-Stage Stencil

The design, whether drawn or photo transferred, is simple enough: it is just the outline of the area which is to be blasted, and the result will be just as good as the stencil cutting. Naturally, any decorative flourish to lettering will be very difficult to control, but some astonishingly fine work can be stencil cut. It must be understood that fine lines must be an open part of the stencil, so a cut must be made both sides of the drawn line, the space between opened and the glass exposed, in order for the blast to reproduce the original single line. Thus, for the thin

Commercially produced one stage, photo stencil, coat of arms (The Worshipful Company of Glass Sellers). Ides

strokes of lettering or a corn stalk, for example, it must be within the capacity of the engraver to cut lines which are parallel and sharp.

Multi-Stage Stencil

Some small experience with glass will have made it clear that tonal values are determined by the quantity of light reflected from the eroded or stippled surface of the glass-open glass being the visual black. Thus the shorter the blast the greyer, and the longer the blast the whiter effect-up to maximum. Therefore any design must take into account the number of tonal components and the order in which they will be done; generally, the deeper dense white is developed first, followed by the light tones and greys. This artwork must be converted into a stencil through which selected areas may be blasted to give an approximate tonal impression of the original image. As the tonal range of matted glass is extremely short, some design ingenuity is very necessary if three (or at most four) steps of tone are to give any satisfaction.

Transfering the Design

1 Simplify the artwork, for example a photograph, to a four-step tonal image. This means conceiving the design as white on black, using the open glass (black) as a supporting feature.
2 Make an outline drawing of each separate tonal element which, when completed, will act as a contour map for the subsequent stencil cutting.

A commercially produced sandblasted goblet. A good example of clever designing and stencil cutting for multi-stage and vignetted blasting. Motif size width 70mm (2¾ in). Dent Glass

3 Transfer the line drawing to the resist. Whether the design is transferred to the resist material before or after its application to the glass depends upon the resist used. A resist which is painted onto the surface (such as pigmented glue) will obviously have the design transfered to it afterwards. A self-adhesive film however (such as thin white Fablon) may have the design drawn onto it first before it is fixed to the glass.

The brief instructions given here belie the complexity and professional skill which is now employed in designing for sand blasting. Every commercial aid is used: photographic enlargement and reduction, photo stencil transfer or direct screen-printed resists. However, unless the designer is very watchful of such technical aids, the result may appear rigidly unsympathetic, even slick. It is perhaps fortunate that the average studio engraver will neither have the means nor the need to do so.

Cutting the Stencil

There is nothing remarkable in cutting a Fablon stencil. All that is required is a very sharp scalpel and a little patience. The cutting is best done with one of those knives designed to take interchangeable blades, of which a wide variety are readily obtainable from artists' suppliers. The

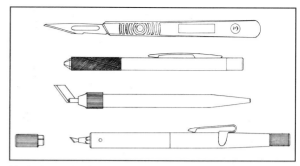

Typical stencil knives

blades should be abandoned as soon as the cutting point goes off. At first there will be a danger of damaging the glass surface by too heavy a pressure but, in time, the knife can be controlled so that the cut stops just short of this happening. When completed, the open areas can be peeled back without difficulty to leave precise profiles ready for the blasting cabinet.

Naturally the start can be made anywhere on the abbreviated image, closely following the contours, but it could be advantageous to complete each separate tonal element in the order in which they will be blasted. By doing so some of the problems of organising the tonal separation or contrast may be thought out in advance. With heavy blasting it is wise to stencil cut each separate tone, and blast, before proceeding with the next element, starting, of course with the deepest part.

SAND BLASTING

The Blasting Method

Whichever machine or improvised equipment is employed, the method of eroding the glass is the same.

1 Completely mask out all the open areas of glass which require protection from the blasting.

2 Peel away the cut stencil from those parts of the design which are to be the whitest and deepest, and blast for sufficient time to give the maximum whiteness.

3 Continue in the same way for the mid-light tone, and follow in sequence for the light and the dark greys.

Timing

There are so many variables in grit size, air pressure, distance, and hardness of the glass that only an approximate guide can be given for the time it takes to produce a tonal range. Deep blasting apart, the erosion is fast and furious, and over in a matter of seconds, so that it is easy to pass the point of no return. The following chart shows the pattern of action only, and on no account should it be taken for the actual blasting times.

1 minute: most vigorous detailed highlights.

15 seconds: next whitest tones.

5 seconds: light tones.

2 seconds: light greys.

1 second: lightest tone – near to open glass.

A happy and inventive sandblasted tumbler (combined with a little diamond point) of a continuous round-the-glass design; the work of a student of Hounslow polytechnic, Mrs Kate Dowding

A modern free blown, cut and sandblasted glass. By Stephen Procter

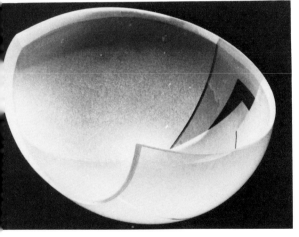

A very deeply sandblasted panel. By Patricia Kilpatrick, 1971

Shallow dish, showing an unusual use and the control of sand blasting. Possibly acid polished. By Ladislav Oliva, 1958

It can be seen that the exposure time is dramatically reduced as the tone moves from white to black, so that no single tone is much affected by the next and overlapping blast. Finally, although five tones may be clearly obtained if they are separated from each other on the glass, in juxtaposition they may be confused. It is well to limit the number of three plus, perhaps, a gently vignetted dark grey if a little movement is required.

Architectural Glass

The system which has been outlined for sand blasting designs on small glass is equally effective for large, flat glass. The only obstacles for the studio worker are the very large protective chambers and the elaborate equipment which must be employed. Therefore, unless one has access to a cabinet which has the facility to handle flat glass in reasonably sized unit panels, a large

Small panel, a model for a larger work. By Diana Radford, 1980

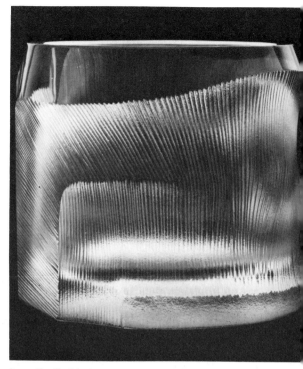

A small cylindrical vase. Fine lines have been incised into the simply sculpted form and then sandblasted and acid dipped, which gives it its unique texture. The rim has been finished with a broad, irregular facet and brilliantly polished to give a strong contrast to the ragged texture. By Ladislav Oliva, Prague

Amber glass, deeply chiselled and eroded by heavy sandblasting. Height 310mm (12 in). By Vladimir and Zdenck Kepka, 1973

commission should be left to a professional establishment.

Sculptural Blasting

Since a strong jet of coarse abrasive can blast a hole through plate glass in about a minute, the sculptural blasting of thick-walled vessels is an exciting alternative to superficial blasting. Such work of course has a completely different character. Deep eroded shapes – symmetric, asymmetric or abstract – are created by directional blasts which, with the intermittent use of stencils, give abrasive-swept craters and channels that dominate the original form of the glass. It is a very personal approach and, whether the result gives an unease or exhilaration to the observer, such work always has a creative sculptural content which is missing from much glass.

Generally speaking, the wheel engraver is isolated from sand blasting and perhaps would be hostile to it on principle, but the evidence of Victorian or modern Bohemian glass where two or more processes are brought together in powerful design combination should indicate to the experimental artist that the field is wide open for further development. However, because the young artist is always poor, this may not come about until more encouragement is given with the right leadership in disciplined glass schools.

17 *Corrections and Erasures*

Apart from accidental slips or surface damage it is not unknown for the best of engravers to make some stupid error of a word transposition or even a reversed letter.

Things may not be so dismal if there is some hope of removing the error but, at the most optimistic reckoning, resurfacing a glass will involve many hours of patient and expert labour. To this, of course, must be added the vexed problem of re-engraving, not only where the work has been removed, but also where it has been weakened in the process. Thus a small error necessitates a large remedy: the removal of a letter of 10mm ($\frac{3}{8}$ in) square would cause a grinding spread of about 50mm (2 in) square, more or less, according to the depth of the error.

ERASING AN ERROR

The method consists of four distinct stages: mechanical grinding with a wheel, manual grinding with a piece of glass, and preliminary and final polishing.

First Stage: Wheel Grinding

Wheel: 75 × 4mm (3 × $\frac{3}{16}$ in) copper.

Abrasive: 320 carborundum/oil paste.

Speed: slow.

The wheel may be a larger size than this, but it is the biggest likely to be called upon unless one is needed for a particularly large erasure. A rather more convenient alternative is to use a water fed corundum wheel, for which the specifications are as follows:

Wheel: 75 × 4mm (3 × $\frac{1}{4}$ in) corundum 220 M bond.

Lubrication: water.

Speed: medium slow (though rather faster than with the copper wheel).

The method is the same for both copper and synthetic wheels, but in this instance the corundum stone has been chosen for the reason that, although composed of a coarse grit in hard bond, the resulting ground matt is rather smoother and conveniently darker in tone than that of the copper wheel.

1 Gradually remove the glass from the unwanted lettering with the same travelling, circular movement as used when countersinking. Avoid doing too much to start with until the depth of the engraving has been assessed. Move the tool further and further out so that no early undue hollow is allowed to form. Continue methodically, regardless of the surrounding engraving, until the last vestige of the error has been removed and the surface brought as nearly as possible to the original curvature of the glass.

2 At this point the surface may appear deceptively flat to the eye, but a brief polish will rapidly reveal a great number of small undulations which can only be efficiently removed by manually grinding them away.

Illustrating the extent to which an erasure must extend if it is to be undetectable. The lettering has gone and the area half smoothed out, but the darker marks of the initial stone grinding are still visible

Second Stage: Hand Grinding

Grinding tool: a slip of flat plate glass approximately 75×20mm ($3 \times \frac{3}{4}$ in) with the edges and corners smoothed off.

Abrasive: 320 carborundum/water paste.

1 Charge the slip of glass with paste and work it evenly and flatly over the damaged area, extending the rubbing slightly beyond the boundary of the wheel-ground matt. Continue methodically until the darker wheel-ground matt has been completely replaced by the whiter water-ground matt. The glass tool should be allowed to ride over the curvature of the glass rather than be used as a file, which is too restrictive a movement. It has been found from experience that, if the finger is placed on the centre of the tool (providing the water abrasive paste is of a good consistency) it will move very freely about the area and naturally conform to the curvature. The benefit of the darker corundum matt can now be appreciated, for the overriding finer matt will expose undulations or imperfectly covered areas. Obviously, the grinding must continue until all evidence of the corundum wheel has been removed. The work cannot be hurried.

2 Wash the glass and slip grinder to remove all traces of the relatively coarse 320 mesh abrasive. Scrub the hands and nails thoroughly. Change to 600 grit water abrasive, which is fine enough to take a reasonable polish. A very hard soda glass will, perhaps, need 800 grit.

3 Repeat the hard grinding process. This secondary grinding is a rather longer job which must be conscientiously done, for it is difficult to know when the previous matt has been entirely replaced. Particular attention should be given to the rather stubborn outer edges, which means a further encroachment on the virgin surface but, fortunately, this should do no harm, to the surrounding engraving. Check the progress frequently.

Third Stage: Pumice Polishing

Wheels: poplar or firm cork $100 - 175 \times 25$mm ($4 - 7 \times 1$ in).

Abrasive: 320 pumice/water paste.

Speed: lower range, but not so fast as to overheat.

With the first experience, it is inevitable that some defects will be shown up by a preliminary polish. If they are slight, further polishing may remove them, but if this is taken too far the defects will reappear as an optical distortion which will render much of the previous work valueless.

1 Mark the limit of the matt on the inside of the glass with a chinagraph pencil as a guide to the extent of the polishing which, otherwise, may go further than is necessary.

2 Polishing has been described elsewhere, but it bears repetition. Firmly move the wheel at every angle to avoid directional polishing streaks. Apply the wheel in short, sharp bursts in order to keep the friction heat down, for the replenishment of cold abrasive on a localised hot spot could easily cause a fracture.

3 Examine the quality and progress of the Polishing by holding the cleaned glass up to a half light/half dark situation, when any residual grain will be exposed. Carefully watch the boundary which tends to hang behind and continue until the surface is quite free of granulation which, no matter how small, can always be detected.

Fourth Stage: Felt Polishing

Wheel: Felt $100 - 150 \times 20 - 25$mm ($4 \times \frac{3}{4}$ to 1 in).

Abrasive: cerium oxide/water.

Speed: slower than that for pumice.

At this point the task is almost complete. Apart from a slight bloom which has been left by the pumice, the glass should be free of blemishes or any visible optical distortions or, more accurately, it should be difficult to locate the areas of deletion. There remains the removal of the bloom.

1 Clean the work bench and the splash-guard of the wheel, clinically wash the hands and the glass, and change any previously used wipers for clean ones. All polishing wheels and cerium oxide paste should be kept well away from any other equipment or abrasives. The smallest particle of unwanted grit is a manace, and if any should become embedded on the felt wheel the edge will need trimming back.

2 Repeat the earlier polishing process: in every direction and in short bursts (3–4 seconds). The paste should not be dry but kept on the runny side. After some time wash the glass and examine the surface, when it is quite possible that remaining patches of bloom will be seen. If so, locate the defects, and re-polish until the whole area takes on the same sheen as the original surface.

When this stage has been reached it is possible to re-engrave the missing or weakened lettering or design. It follows from the foregoing that it is easier to make a mistake than correct it. But with all the care and resolutions in the world mistakes will still occur and, therefore, to have developed some expertise in this matter is an invaluable asset to any engraver. Small defects may perhaps be reduced by means of a sturdy flexible drive, but the grinding and polishing of the kind described is really a job for the lathe. Even then the engraver should be warned against putting too much strain on the lead bearings of a traditional lathe by the leverage from the large and sometimes heavy wheels necessary for this work. This does not apply with the sturdier modern machines which use phosphor-bronze bearings. To sum up, large errors on expensive glass should be left to experts, but for the general run-of-the-mill mistakes there is no reason why the wheel engraver should not solve his own problems. Obviously small scratches or shallow flemishes can be polished out with cork and felt wheels without recourse to grinding.

REPAIRING CHIPS

Rim Chips

Whether this is worth repairing or not depends on the size of the chip or how far the flake has travelled down the glass, for if too much glass is taken away the whole balance of the shape is likely to be destroyed. This applies equally to the foot of the glass. Such damage can be mechanically (horizontally) ground very quickly, but as most engravers are without this means the simple alternative is to grind it manually, rim downwards, on a large piece of flat glass, using the familiar sequence of abrasives. If the rim becomes too sharp and square edged it can be bevelled on the lathe with a fine stone before the final polishing.

Foot Chips

These are a little more troublesome because of the possibility of distortion. There is nothing worse than an oval foot, but with care and edge may be skimmed back and polished, after the top edge has been rounded off to its first natural shape. As a general principle, for every action use as large a wheel as possible.

Anything beyond these small types of damage is a case for the restorer or the dustbin.

REMOVING STAINS

Causes of Stains

The removal of internal stains and encrustations from decanters and similar vessels, which cannot be reached with the polisher, hardly comes within the purview of this book, but as the engraver will certainly be asked to solve this problem – or be trapped into it – a few warning notes are in order.

Imperfections may vary from superficial wine stains and lime deposits to outright physical damage for, contrary to popular belief, glass is not very resistant to chemical corrosion. Acid liquors will attack the alkali part of the glass structure and alkali solutions the silica part, while water, in a complex manner, will gradually affect both. The softer the glass the quicker it will occur. In the main, old and valuable decanters are more likely to contain these defects than new glass, simply because they have been around longer. This is is a very good reason why, beyond a safe limit, a stubborn decanter should be handed over to a reputable restorer rather than risk further damage in a reckless attack with brush and abrasives, the magnitude of which cannot be seen until the wet glass has fully dried out.

But such surface attack is not confined to very old glass. Decanters made in the last 30 years can be found to have suffered worse than Georgian glass, and much must depend on the composition of the glass and the conditions in which it has been kept. Some glass fresh from the distributors may at times contain a milky deposit, relatively easy but inconvenient to remove, perhaps due to inadequate rinsing after the grinding-in of the stoppers. Whatever the cause, the engraver should be on the alert for imperfections of this kind. Some can be tolerated but others, looking harmless and tractable enough (as for example the cloudy patches sometimes seen near goblet rims), have in fact been incurably fire/fused into the surface. Such faults must be detected immediately and the glass rejected.

Procedure for Removal

Determine the extent of any damage progressively.

1 Fill the container with soapy water or detergent and allow it to stand for 24 hours.
2 Brush out with a soft bristle brush (guarding against any exposed metal of the brush) to remove any loosened deposit.
3 Swill round and leave the stain soaking for some hours in vinegar (diluted acetic acid) or citric acid, which should remove any lime deposit. Citric acid has the added advantage of attacking brownish iron stains. (Diluted Hyrdochloric acid will readily dissolve lime deposits but it is best to avoid to it.)
4 Make a small mop of clean soft rag and with 400 Carborundum/oil paste gently massage the effected area. Oil paste is gentler and holds itself to the area much better than water. Nevertheless it is an abrasisve and if the mark does not respond quickly to this treatment it should be abandoned.

If cloudiness still exists, then it is a case for the expert – but not for a backstreet jobber. In conclusion, on no account use sand, household abrasives, strong alkalies or acids. And do not be tempted by hydrofluoric acid polishing. It is a technique best left to the experts.

A Note on Magnifying Aids

There is a wide variety of magnifiers available which range from a simple single lens to binoculars of advanced design. The engraver, who might be young or ancient, must seek his own answer to the problem. However, when purchasing a lens, the following considerations should be kept in mind.

Single lenses

The greater the degree of magnification the shorter the working distance between the surface and the lens, and the greater the linear distortion. And the wider the field of view (for the same focal length) the greater the distortion.

Simple double lenses

Magnifiers such as those used by metal engravers may consist of two component lenses. They give much better definition than the single lens, but may still distort or have a colour fringe at the edges. All such bench magnifiers, though acceptable in use on a flat plane, will obviously give trouble when engraving a curved surface.

Binoculars

Apart from surgeon's binoculars, perhaps the simplest solution is to use one of those universally accepted headband binoculars which, though excruciatingly ugly, fulfills the need for most engravers and can be obtained with a magnification from about 3 to 4.

BIBLIOGRAPHY

Beard, Geoffrey, *International Modern Glass*, Barrie & Jenkins, 1976

Boardman, John, *Engraved Gems*, Thames & Hudson, 1968

The British Museum, *Masterpiece of Glass*, Trustees of the British Museum, London, 1968 *The Golden Age of Venetian Glass*, London, 1968

Buckley, Wilfred, *Diamond Engraved Glass of the 16th. Century*, 1929 *Franz Greenwood and the Glasses He Engraved*, 1930 *Aert Schouman and the Glasses He Engraved*, 1930

Charleston, R.J., *Wheel-Engraving and Cutting: 'Some Early Equipment'*, Journal of Glass Studies, Corning Museum of Glass *I Engraving II Water Power and Cutting* 1965,

Charleston, R.J., *Ancient Glass Working Methods*, II Decoration (Abrasive techniques) Circle of Glass Collectors, 1962

Charleston, R.J., *Masterpieces of Glass*, Harry N. Abrans Inc., New York

Corning Museum, *Glass From the Corning Museum of Glass*, Corning Museum, New York, 1974

Duthie, A.L., *Decorative Glass Processes*, Architectural Press, London, 1908

Doppelfeld, Otto, *Das Diatretglas aus dem Gräberbezirk, des römischen Gutshofs von Koln, Braunsfeld*, Verlag Gebr., Mann, Berlin, 1961

English Counties Periodicals Ltd, *The West Window of Coventry Cathedral*, Leamington Spa

Gardner, Paul F. *The Glass of Frederik Carder*, Crown Publishers, New York, 1971

Gardner, Paul Vickers, *Glass*, The Smithsonian Institute, 1979

Gardner, Philippe, *Emile Galle*, Academy Editions, London, 1976

Gombrich, E.H., *Art and Illusion*, Phaidon Press, London, 1977

Guttery, D.R., *From Broad-Glass to Cut Crystal*, Leonard Hill, London, 1956

Harding D.B., *A History of Technology* Oxford, 1951 *Vol. 2. Glass and Glazes*

Heddle, G.M., *Manual on Etching and Engraving on Glass*, Alec Tiranti, London, 1961

Klesse, Brigitte, *500 Jahre Glaskunst*, Axe von Saldern, ABC Verlag, Zürich, 1980

Mariacher, Giovanni, *Glass, from Antiquity to the Renaissance*, Fratelli Fabbri Editori, Milan 1960, Hamlyn 1970

McGraw and Frost, *Glass in Architecture*, Architectural Press, London, 1936

Monro, Helen, *'The Art of Glass Engraving.'* A paper read to the Royal Society of Art, February 1960

Newman, Harold, *An Illustrated Dictionary of Glass*, Thames & Hudson, 1977

Norman, Barbara, *Engraving and Decorating Glass*, David & Charles, Newton Abbot, 1981

Northwood, John, *John Northwood II*, Mark and Moody Stourbridge, 1958

Pazaurek, G.E., *Gläser der Empire und Biedermeierzeit* Leipzig, 1923

Peace, David, *Engraved Glass (Lettering & Heraldry)* 1968

Polak, Ada, *Modern Glass*, Faber and Faber, 1962

Polak, Ada, *Glass: Its Makers and Its Public*, Weidenfeld & Nicolson, 1975

Pesatova, Zusana *Bohemian Engraved Glass*, Artia, Prague, 1968 and Paul Hamlyn

Savage, George, *Glass*, Weidenfeld & Nicolson, London, 1965

Schlosser, J., *Das Alte Glas*, Klinkhardt & Biermann, Brannschweig, 1956

Schmidt, Robert, *Das Glas*, Berlin, 1922

Steenberg, Elisa, *Swedish Glass*, New York, 1950

Sinkankas, John, *Gem Cutting, and Lapidary's Manual*, Van Nostrand, New York 1971

The Constable-Maxwell Collection of Ancient Glass, Sotheby ParkeBernet, London

Steuben Glass, *Steuben Glass 1947*, U.S.A. 1947

Thorpe, W.A., *English Glass*, A. & C. Black Ltd., London (1935) 1967

Thorpe, W.A., *A History of English and Irish Glass*, Holland Press London, (1929) 1969

Weiss, Gustav, *The Book of Glass*, Verlag Ullstein Gmblt. Berlin 1966, Barrie & Jenkins, 1971

Whistler, L., *Engraved Glass*, The Cupid Press, London, 1952

Whistler, L., *The Image on the Glass*, John Murray, 1975

Whistler, L., *Pictures on Glass*, The Cupid Press, London, 1972

Westropp, M.S. Dudley, *Irish Glass*, Revised Edition by Mary Boydell, Allen Figgis, Dublin, 1978

Wilkinson, R., *The Hallmarks of Antique Glass*, Richard Madley, London, 1968

Willson, R. Stennett, *Modern Glass*, Studio vista 1975

Vávra, J.R., *5000 Years of Glass Making, The History of Glass*, Artia, Prague, 1954 *Bohemian Glass*, Victoria & Albert Museum, London

SUPPLIERS

A list of suppliers runs the double risk of becoming rapidly out of date and in leaving out manufacturers who deserve to be included. Therefore the following could be considered as a rough guide only.

Wheel Engraving Lathes

Light and heavy and all auxilliary equipment:
Manufactured by Spatzier
Marketed by Kurt Merker Kelheim
Kelheim
Eisterstrasser 6
West Germany
There is no known American or British alternative to this

machine which is supplied direct from Kurt Merker.

Flexible Drive Drills

The dental trade tends to dominate the market for laboratory technician equipment. As the drills have a very wide application and the manufacturers are internationally connected, it is easy for the glass engraver to locate and select tools. However, there are some fine engraving small tools of the same kind – mechanical or compressed air driven – which should be investigated.

England

Panadent Ltd
15 Great Dover Street
London SE1 4YW
(U.K. distributers for W.H. Dentalwerk of Austria and Reco West Germany)

Kavo Dental Ltd
Industrial Estate
Raans Road
Amersham
Bucks HP6 6JL
(U.K. distributers for Kaltenbach & Voigt of West Germany)

J.S. Davis
Cordent House
34/36 Friern Park
London W12 9DG

Renda Motors
Bird in Hand Passage
Dartmouth Road
Forest Hill
London SE23

John Quale Manufacturing Co. Ltd
Derotor House
Worthing
W. Sussex BN14 8QN

Precision Petite
119 High Street
Teddington Walk
London

USA

Kavo America Corporation
Suite 320–2200 W Higgins Road
Hoffman Estates
Illinois 60195

Messrs. Pfingst & Company Inc. (W & H Dentalwerk)
P.O. Box 377
S. Plainfield
N.J. 07080

Foredom Electric Co.
Bethel
Connecticut 0991

Canada

Siemens Electric Limited (W & H Dentalwerk)
501 Oakdale Road
Downsview
Ontario M3N 1W7

Lux & Zwingenberger Ltd (Kaltenbach & Voigt)
609 King Street, West
Toronto
Ontario M5V 1M5

Pennwalt Jelenko (of Canada Ltd)
5266 General Road
Mississauga
Ontario L4W 1Z7

Australia

Rudolf Gunz & Co. (Kaltenbach & Voigt)
63–73 Ann Street
Darlinghurst, NSW 2010

Martin Halas Dental Co. Pty Ltd
209–211 Bourke Street, Sydney 2010

West Germany

Kaltenbach & Voigt GMBH & Co.
Postfach 320
D–7950 Biberach/Riss
Bismarckring 39

Reco Dental Laboreinrichtungen GmbH
Postfach 48–45
D–6200 Wiesbaden

Austria

W & H Dentalwerk Burmoos-Ges. M.B.H.
A–5111 Burmoos bei Salzburg

Sweden

Essemce Maskin & Vertigs A.B.
Lindas 5 361 02 Emmaboda 2

Small Power Tools

England

B.O. Morris Ltd
Briton Road
Coventry
CV2 4LG
(U.K. distributers for Foredon Electric Co., of Connecticut, USA)

Flextol Engineering Company Ltd
The Green
London W4

Pladd Production Aid Ltd
6 Milne Field
Hatch End
Pinner, Middlesex, HA5 4DP
(U.K. distributers for Aro Portable Air Tools of Ohio, USA)

USA

Industrial Air Tools
The Aro Corporation
Bryan
Ohio 43506, USA

Abrasive Wheels and Small Tools, Abrasive Points, Polishing Powders

England

The Carborundum Company Ltd
Bonded Abrasives Division
Trafford Park
Manchester M17 1HP

Universal Grinding Wheel Co.
Stafford ST 16 1EA

D.G.S. Grinding Wheels & Machines Ltd
92, Dovedale Road
Ettingshall Part Farm
Wolverhampton

USA

The Carborundum Company Ltd
Niagara Falls
New York USA

Universal Grinding Wheel Inc.
One Gibraltar Plaza
Prudention Business
Campus Horsham
Pennsylvania USA

Canada

The Carborundum Company Ltd
Niagara Falls
Ontario

Unicord Abrasives of Canada
192 Pearl Street East
Brockville
Ontario

Dental Diamond Coated Burrs and Abrasive Points and Wheels

The nearest dentist or dental distributor will give all the information on these universally standardized tools. The following list gives the country of origin only. Something equivalent will be obtained from the suppliers of the flexible drive equipment.

USA

R.R. Cutwell
Ransom & Randolf Division of Dentsply International
Toledo, Ohio 43691

West Germany

Meisinger
Hager and Mesinger
D4 Düsseldorf
Kronprinzenstrasse 5–11

East Germany

Drendel & Zweiding GmBH & Cokg.
Goerzallee 307
D 1000 Berlin 37

Switzerland

W. Hubschmid & Sohn 6900
Cassarate

Jota Dental & Schleifmittel AG
Postfach 56
CH 9464 Ruthie SG

Diamond Points and Diamond Grit

England

Shaw Abrasives (Diamond) Ltd
Waterloo Road
London NW2 7UN

Mary Whitehead Ltd
The Mount
Grayswool
Hazelmere
Surrey (U.K. distributors for Lunzer Lancer of America)

L.M Van Moppes & Sons Ltd
Basingstoke
Hampshire

USA

Lunzer Lancer
Lunzer Industrial Diamonds
48 West 48th Street
New York

Sand Blasting Equipment and Abrasives

England

Berlyne, Bailey & Co. Ltd
Fielding Street
Middleton
Manchester M24 3BS

Sommerfield Shotblast Division
Osro Limited
Trubro House
Mark Road
Hamel Hempstead
Herts HP2 7BX

Specialist magnifying aids

Keelers
Marylebone Lane
London W.1

PUBLIC COLLECTIONS OF GLASS

Great Britain

Bath	The Assembly Rooms
	Victoria Art Gallery
Bedford	Cecil Higgins Art Gallery
Birmingham	City Museum and Art Gallery
Cambridge	Fitzwilliam Museum
Cardiff	National Museum of Wales
Durham	The Bowes Museum
Dudley	Broadfield House Glass Museum

Edinburgh	Royal Scottish Museum
Glasgow	Art Gallery and Museum
Leicester	Leicester Museum
London	British Museum
	Museum of London
	Science Museum (Historic & Technical)
	Victoria and Albert Museum
Manchester	City Art Gallery
Oxford	Ashmolean Museum
St Helens	Pilkington Glass Museum
Sheffield	City Museum

The Travelling Collection of Cinzano (London)
The Wine Museum of Harveys in Bristol

Austria
| Vienna | Österreichisches Museum für Angewandte Kunst |
| | Messrs J. & L. Lobmeyr (works museum) |

Czechoslovakia
Liberec	North Bohemian Museum
Jablonec nad Nisou	Museum of Glass and Jewellery
Kamenický Šenov	Municipal Museum
	School of Glassmaking
Nový Bor	Museum of Glass
	School of Glassmaking
Prague	National Gallery, Collection of Applied Art
Zelezný Brod	Municipal Museum
	School of Glassmaking

West Germany
Coburg	Kunstsammlung der Veste Coburg
Düsseldorf	Kunstmuseum
Frankfurt/M	Museum für Kunsthandwerk
Hamburg	Museum für Kunst und Gewerbe
Karlsruhe	Badisches Landesmuseum
Kassel	Staatliche Kunstsammlungen
Köln (Cologne)	Kunstgewerbe-Museum
	Römisch-Germanisches Museum
München	Bayerisches Nationalmuseum
Nüremberg	Germanisches Nationalmuseum
Regensburg	Museum der stadt Regensburg
Rheinbach (Bonn)	Glasmuseum and Schools of Glass
Trier	Rheinisches Landesmuseum

East Germany
Arnstadt	Museum der Stadt Arnstadt
Berlin	Märkisches Museum
	Kunstgewerbe Museum Schloss Köpenick
Dresden	Staatliche Kunstsammlung Grünes Gewolbe
	Museum für Kunsthandwerk Schloss Pillnitz
Halle (Saale)	Staatliche Galerie Moritzburg
Leipzig	Museum des Kunsthandwerks Grassimuseum
Weimar	Kunstsammlung (Schloss)

Holland
Amsterdam	Rijkmuseum
Den Haag	Gemeente Museum
Rotterdam	Museum Boymans-van-Beuningen

Italy
Milan	Museo Civic Archeologico
Murano	Museo Vetrario
Venice	Treasury, St Mark's Cathedral

U.S.A.
| Corning N.Y. | Corning Museum of Glass |
| Toledo (Ohio) | Toledo Museum of Art |

U.S.S.R.
| Leningrad | Hermitage Museum |

BRITISH MANUFACTURERS OF FULL LEAD AND CRYSTAL GLASS

Caithness Glass Ltd, Caithness, Scotland
Cumbria Crystal Ltd, Ulverston, Cumbria
Dartington Glass Ltd, Torrington, North Devon
The Edinburgh Crystal Glass Co., Penicuik, Midlothian Scotland
Thos, Webb & Sons, Stourbridge
Nazeing Glass Works Ltd, Broxbourne, Herts
Royal Brierley Crystal, Brierley Hill
Stuart & Sons Ltd, Stourbridge
Tudor Crystal (Stourbridge) Ltd, Stourbridge
Webb Corbett Ltd, Stourbridge
Wedgwood Glass, Stoke-on-Trent

IMPORTED HIGH QUALITY CRYSTAL GLASS

Belgium	Val St Lambert
France	Baccarat
	Daum
Holland	Leerdom
Norway	Hadelands
Sweden	Orrefors
	Kosta
	Stromberg

BRITISH STANDARD SPECIFICATION 3828:1973 (COMPLYING WITH E.E.C. DIRECTIVES) FOR CRYSTAL GLASS

The above specification is very technical and designates four categories of glass. In Britain three only need to be considered:

1 Full lead crystal 30%: Glass containing not less than 30% lead oxide.

2 Lead crystal 24%: Glass containing not less than 24% lead oxide.

3 Cristallin: Glass containing Zinc, Barium, Lead or Potassium oxides which alone or together is not less than 10%.

These are category requirements. English Glass may be found containing more than 30% lead oxide or between 10% and 24%. Crystallin, it appears, may have as much as 10% or none at all.

BRITISH STANDARD SPECIFICATION ON ABRASIVES

Grit size designations

There is an increasing tendency for grit (grain) sizes to be expressed in regular micron increments rather than the number of spaces per linear inch which at the moment is the widely accepted wire mesh standard. It is a more sensible system but may be confusing to those workers, including the authors, who are conditioned to the present structure.

The following table gives the approximate micron sizes relative to the range of grit most familiar to the engraver:

Mesh No.	Aperture size in Microns
80	191
100	150
120	125
150	105
180	87
220	68
240	63
280	54
320	43
400	30
600	20

A micron is a unit of measurement equal to a millionth of a metre or a thousandth of a milimetre. The mesh limit is about 350 apertures per linear inch; sizes smaller than this are separated by other means. Fine diamond, sub-sieve, powders are designated in micron sizes (for example 30/60, 20/40).

GRINDING AND POLISHING ABRASIVES

Modern High quality abrasives

The number which precedes the main grinding materials gives the relative hardness on the Mohs scale which takes talc as the softest material as 1 and Diamond, the hardest substance, as 10. It is not quantitative and therefore rather unsatisfactory. A small difference of half a point, say between quartz and tungsten, or carborundum and the diamond, is much more significant than is implied. However it is the only scale for minerals and is universally used.

10	Diamond.	Natural and synthetic crystalline carbon. Although known to the Greeks, singularly little has been recorded of its use as a tool until the sixteenth century.
$9\frac{1}{2}$	Carborundum.	Synthetic crystalline silicon carbide (U.S.A. 1891)
9	Corundum.	Pure Aluminium oxide (Alumina)

Traditional abrasives

9	Emery	Naturally occuring impure variety of crystalline corundum combined with iron oxides and silica. Found in Turkey and Greece (Naxos) and probably used from Biblical times.
$7\frac{1}{2}$	Garnets	Complex metallic aluminium silicates, said to have been used for 'jade carving' (the equivalent of high relief glass engraving) in China as early as the Tang Dynasty AD 618–906. It has a harder crystalline structure than quartz.
7	Quartz	Silicon doixide, commonly sand. Along with sandstone it was probably used for grinding purposes from the Neolithic times. Still useful as debris sludge for grinding and polishing.
	Pumice	Volcanic ash. An aluminium silicate, probably derived from the volcanic breakdown of feldspar.
	Tripoli	An unusual siliceous earth, amorphous and friable, which has the unusual capacity to breakdown further as more pressure is applied.
	Rouge	Impalpable iron oxide, made by decomposing iron sulphate.
	Magnesium Oxide	A fairly recent fine grinding and polishing medium.
	Cerium Oxide	A relatively recent super-fine polishing precipitate.

THE USE OF HYDROFLUORIC ACID AND FLUORIDES (SOLUBLE)

These are classed as highly toxic, producing kidney and liver damage and osteosclerosis, and inhalation of fumes can result in lung damage – only after some years in the case of the flourides. In addition, the acid produces severe and painful skill burns with ulceration. As these burns do not manifest themselves immediately, there is a danger that the skin may not be washed until chronic harm has been done.

The fluorides can produce contact dermatitis.

Council of Europe labelling recommendations (1971)

Serious risk of poisoning by inhalation or swallowing, or skin contact.

Causes severe skin burns.

When using do not eat or smoke.

Use only with adequate ventilation.

Keep away from foodstuffs and beverages.

Wash immediately after handling.

Wear face mask, rubber gloves, aprons, boots.

If feeling unwell, show the doctor the label.

In case of contact with skin or eyes, wash with plenty of water.

INDEX